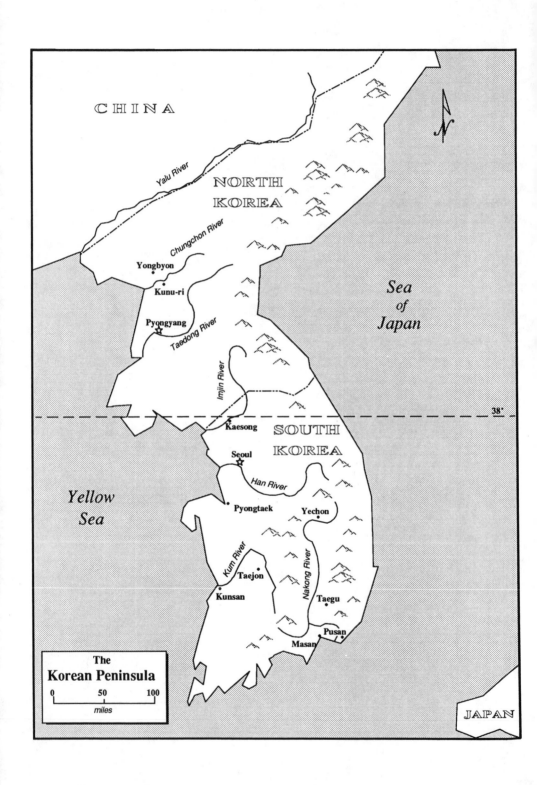

CHINA

NORTH KOREA

Yalu River

Chungchon River

Yongbyon

Kunu-ri

Pyongyang

Taedong River

Imjin River

Sea
of
Japan

38°

Kaesong

SOUTH KOREA

Seoul

Han River

Yellow
Sea

Pyongtaek

Yechon

Kum River

Nakong River

Taejon

Kunsan

Taegu

Pusan

Masan

The
Korean Peninsula

0   50   100

miles

JAPAN

N

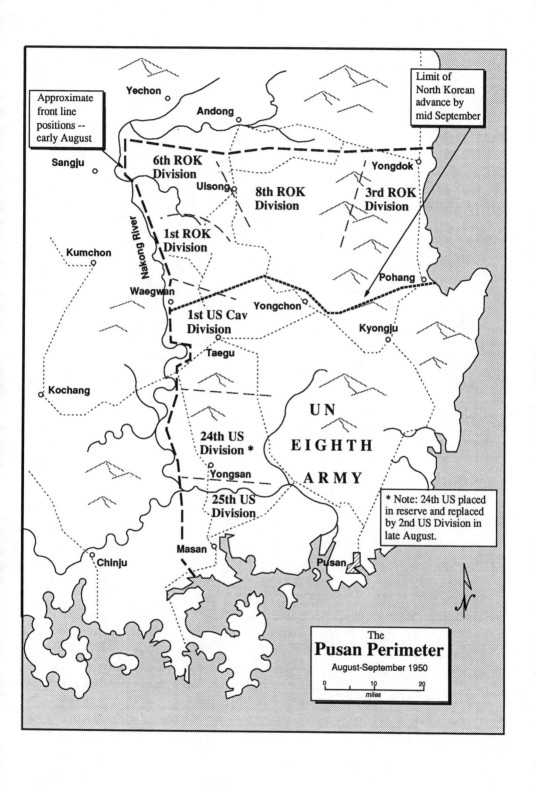

FIREFIGHT AT YECHON

Courage and Racism in the Korean War

Lt. Col. Charles M. Bussey, USA (Ret.)

UNIVERSITY OF NEBRASKA PRESS
LINCOLN AND LONDON

First Bison Books printing: 2002

Library of Congress Cataloging-in-Publication Data
Bussey, Charles M.
Firefight at Yechon: courage and racism in the Korean war / Lt. Col. Charles M.
Bussey.
p. cm.
Originally published: Washington: Brassey's, 1991. With new afterword.
ISBN 0-8032-6201-9 (pbk.: alk. paper)
1. Bussey, Charles M.   2. Korean War, 1950–1953—Personal narratives, African
American.   3. African American soldiers—Biography.   4. Korean War, 1950–
1953—Participation, African American.   5. United States. Army Air Forces—
History.   6. United States—Race relations.   I. Title.
DS921.6.B87   2002
951.904′23—dc21   2001056860

This book is dedicated to those gallant young men of the 24th Regimental Combat Team, including the 77th Engineer Combat Company, who fought a formidable and determined enemy for the American and United Nations cause in Korea in 1950–1953. Although denied their basic rights of equal opportunity and human dignity, they nevertheless put their lives on the line for their nation. Although the Infantry men were poorly led, poorly trained, and unprepared for the reality of that war, they fought hard and, despite their detractors, fought well.

Here I stand.
I can do no otherwise.
So help me God.   Amen.

—MARTIN LUTHER

God and the soldier we adore
In time of danger, not before
The danger past and all things righted
God is forgotten and the soldier slighted.

—ANONYMOUS

Contents

Acknowledgments

I acknowledge gratefully the assistance of Col. John R. Brinkerhoff, U.S. Army Retired. His patience and understanding contributed greatly to the publication of this book.

Much also is owed to David K. Carlisle, whose exceptional memory for times, dates, and circumstances made it possible for me to bring the noble efforts and sacrifices of the soldiers of the 24th Regimental Combat Team to the attention of the American people.

Col. John A. Cash, U.S. Army, reviewed the manuscript and made many helpful suggestions on facts, dates, and terminology to improve the quality of this work.

Finally, my thanks to Mary Auther and my son, Edmund Bussey, for their patience and indulgence.

Preface

I am the man who led your son in battle. I led him in his transition from Sunday school student to a bloodletter on the "killing floor" in Korea. I made your son a soldier. I am the type of man who defeated the Canaanites. I felled Jericho. I was the victor at Thermopylae and the hero at Valley Forge. You are free because I believed in your freedom. Without me, or men like me, you could be enslaved or worse.

Further, I returned your son a far better man than when he came to me. I sent him back to you when trouble was past, a man without rancor and without venom but with the spleen required to keep you and himself free. I gave him discipline where you failed him. I gave him vision beyond your knowledge of that perception. Above all, I gave him confidence in himself and in his fellow man. With me he learned of men and of God. I returned him to you a man—better than his fathers and better than his sons.

Much has been said and written of soldiers in all times. No group has contributed more to the development of mankind, and no group has been more reviled.

It is not my intent to make you admire me or men like me, but I want you to know close up the life and times of fighting men. I want you to understand their lives, their deaths, their strengths, their weaknesses, and, yes, their prayers, for prayers are big with fighting men. When the chips are down and the cards are poor, most men draw sustenance from their religious faiths. At times there is nothing else. We believe out of stark necessity. When danger is past, however, we too often forget. We too are frail.

This book is not a full autobiography with complete details on my personal life. The focus is on my experiences as an officer in the United States Army in the Korean War. My service during the Korean War has stirred forty years of controversy in the U.S. Army, the Department of Defense, and the Congress of the United States.

After my firefight at Yechon the colonel told me that I should receive the Medal of Honor, but because I was "a Negro," he could not let that happen. Other controversy has raged over the role and performance of black soldiers in Korea. The white press emphasized stories about Negroes bugging out. In those early days in Korea, the black 24th Infantry Regiment performed better than the regiments of the white 24th Infantry Division and just as well as the other regiments that came later to Korea. The only real successes during the first months of Korea were a few scattered engagements, including the small first firefight at Yechon. Many of the other engagements were terminated with U.S. forces scattered and retreating at battalion, regiment, and even division level.

The U.S. Army's official history of the first part of the Korean War, *South to the Naktong, North to the Yalu*, by Roy E. Appleman, strikes me as unfair and not representing what I saw personally. His book suggests that the Negro soldiers and their units were no good. The official history cites twenty-four instances of poor behavior by the 24th Infantry Regiment that I served in. Mr. Appleman was never in the combat zone, and some of the interviews upon which his account is based took place as much as five years afterward. Mr. Appleman interviewed only one black officer and no black enlisted men. He never talked to me. In his reports of the behavior of Negro troops, he quotes only their white officers. In some cases, these officers may have provided self-serving accounts seeking to blame the troops for their own leadership failures. In the official history, the instances of bad performance by Negro troops appear to be emphasized more than similar behavior by white troops. The difference may be nothing more than another manifestation of the antiblack racism that was prevalent in American society and in the American Army from 1776 through all wars prior to Vietnam in the late 1960s.

Unfortunately, until recently, I felt that the few histories written about the Korean War have been tainted by the Army's "official history" by Mr. Appleman. A more balanced picture is presented in recent books by Clay Blair and by Bernard C. Nalty.

Dave Carlisle (one of my officers) and I, and some other black veterans of Korean combat, have sought for many years to overturn the Army's official version and obtain justice, but the U.S. Army has ignored the new evidence and has stuck to its original story. We have been successful to the extent that the Army finally has agreed to have a commission of historians and other experts review the record and reevaluate just how black soldiers compared with their white comrades in a time of desperate measures and overall poor performance by the U.S. Army in Korea.

The quest of black Korean War veterans for truth has been questioned by some who see no point in our crusade for justice. They say that it was so long ago that it doesn't matter now. Why rake up old coals when so much progress has been made in the Army and in society toward racial integration? Finally, was it really so bad?

The answer is that it really was bad, and it is important for Americans to understand. Many blacks growing up today have no idea of what it was like to live in a racist society and be part of a racist Army. They need to understand how it was, if for no other reason than to understand how much progress has been made. And it is unfair to deny those who fought their dignity. Suppose it was your son or brother who fought and perhaps died out there, and his performance was denigrated unfairly because of his race? Would you want the truth to be told? After over forty years, many other Korean War veterans—both black and white—and I are still filled with rage at the failure to paint a full and accurate picture of black men's failures *and successes* in the Korean War.

I have been asked many times by many people to tell about my eight months in Korea, and that is my primary task in this book. I have included enough information about my early life and about my military career before I went to Korea for you to understand how I, a black man, came to be the way I was in that particular time and place. In the final chapter, I have presented some of my story after I left Korea to give you some idea of how I was affected by that killing field.

What follows is my account of a very small part of the last war in which I participated. This is my account of my own experiences. I can be criticized for being candid, but I will not be criticized for lack of veracity. I tell it the way it was. I am relating what I saw and what I heard with my own eyes and ears. We are all captives of our own individual experiences, and none of us can know what really happened everywhere. I was there. The historians were not. Some will be embarrassed, but I have no feelings for them. In retrospect, some of my judgments of certain individuals may be harsh, but they are not unjust in the context of the time of that terrible war.

Out of these pages shrieks the obvious: war is not an adequate substitute for diplomacy, love, tolerance, or other human alternatives. But this is primarily the story of American fighting men— a story of courage and racism in the Korean War. Now you can judge for yourself.

FIREFIGHT AT YECHON

The Road to Korea

1921–1942,
Bakersfield and Los Angeles, California

The road to Korea started in Bakersfield, California, where I was born in 1921. Like all of us, I am the product of my upbringing and experience. My youth as a black in a bigoted town taught me some hard lessons—survival, resolution, reason. I took some beatings there—physical beatings, emotional beatings, psychological beatings. But the town also taught me to recover fast, prepare myself, plan, and try again. It didn't allow me to quit or to recognize that I'd been beaten. It taught me to birth a baby and to shoe a mule. In a way, growing up as I did helped prepare me for being a company commander in combat.

Perhaps Bakersfield was a microcosm of the world and life as a whole, because in all the world over, which I've traveled since leaving Bakersfield, I've found in other towns the same baseness, greed, bigotry, avarice, cowardice, and ignorance afflicting an extremely large segment of the local society. If not white versus black, it was Christian versus Jew, Catholic versus Protestant, haves versus have-nots. It is always ugly, always pernicious, and always destructive. A pity on a planet of such plenty.

I had the benefit of being integrated all of my life. I was able to measure myself against Asians, Mexicans, and kids of Middle Eastern and European extraction. Early in life I learned that I

1

was more proficient than some of my contemporaries and less proficient than others. It became obvious to me that academic and physical acumen was in no way related to race, although there were always influences that implied that the whites were somehow superior. However, in my experience, if there were any differences, the advantages went to the Asian and Jewish kids. Their advantages appeared to be a result of the additional schooling they received at church or temple plus a lot of motivation at home.

Home was a place of sanctuary for me, and in my town one needed sanctuary. People there were automatically the enemies of their fellow men. It was perhaps natural that I became a soldier, because I spent my entire youth fighting—fighting for ill-defined causes usually as a result of ridicule or abuse aimed at me because I was black. Blackness alone, to a large segment of the white population of Bakersfield, was sufficient motivation for vituperation, abuse, and derision—a fuse for expressions of enmity and comtempt.

I had to learn to survive with bigots, racists, and normal human beings who by inference, innuendo, and blatant remarks let me know where I stood with them. Strong parents taught me how to deal with this adversity. I heard all of the lies, the jokes, the put-downs, the denigrating statements, and to a degree I was affected negatively by it all until Jesse Owens and Joe Louis became champions. I realized that I was not a champion at anything, but I realized that being black did not diminish me in any way. In all, I thought I was a damned good person. And with that attitude, I was.

One of the greatest influences in my life was my mother. I called her Momma. Her nickname was "Charlottie," but that name was reserved for adults. We had many altercations because I was born a male chauvinist; but Momma knew how to deal with me. She was a strict disciplinarian. There were only a few rules in Momma's house, but they were carved in stone—inviolable. My older and smarter siblings were seldom punished, but I had built-in troubles, and my acts of mischief kept me in deep difficulty quite often.

Momma had a theory that young Negro males needed specific guidance, which involved both self-respect and respect for people and the property of others. That was a plateful, but she also felt that strict discipline had to be imposed on young Negro males so that they developed a strong sense of self-discipline to carry them through the abuse they would suffer at the hands of law enforcement officers and court officials. It was not that young Negroes were different in any particular way from young white males, but the major element of society was more tolerant of the foibles of their own kind than they were of those of Negroes. She based her theory on the statistics that showed an inordinate number of Negroes in jails and penitentiaries.

Momma was bound and determined to educate her sons in a manner that produced free men, no matter how much effort was required. Fortunately, she was reinforced in her efforts by the "Titan," my dad—all five feet and seven inches of him. Dad was the authority for what I considered capital punishment for serious breaches of discipline. He intimidated me. Between the two of them, I was forced into discipline, good citizenship, and patriotism. I loved them for their principles and for their persistence.

The discipline in my parents' home prepared me perfectly for the regimen of military service. Reward and punishment was the mode of life. It fit me. I hungered for an opportunity to prove myself, and opportunity came, first as a fighter pilot and then as an engineer officer.

I always wanted to be a soldier, as far back as I can remember. One of the reasons for my desire to be a soldier was because my father had served in the Army in World War I. Another reason, perhaps, was the stories I heard from Old Man Caldwell when I was just a kid of about five or six.

Old Man Caldwell, 1926, Bakersfield, California

Old Man Caldwell would come by the house from time to time for a visit. He lived on Cottonwood Road, not far from our house in Bakersfield. Momma slapped me once for referring to him as

"Old Man Caldwell," but in my mind, that was his name. It fit him. He was rickety and fragile, slow and feeble. No derision. He had been a slave and later a Union soldier and an Indian fighter. I liked him, and he liked me. He had served as a sergeant in the 9th and 10th Cavalry regiments, along with my grandad and with Dad Thompson. They had all chased Pancho Villa, and they had brought Geronimo back from Mexico to the reservation. They'd all been together on San Juan Hill with Teddy Roosevelt. Sometimes he'd show me the three arrowheads he carried in a pouch around his neck. They had been removed from his chest and thigh.

Once he let me feel an arrowhead that was still lodged in his neck. He claimed it only bothered him in damp weather. The missile in his neck was in the bone in a way that made its safe removal impossible. That arrowhead, in my mind, was equivalent to the Congressional Medal of Honor.

Mom said Sergeant Caldwell was eighty-five years of age. She'd known him when he and her father were Horse Soldiers at Fort Riley, Kansas, and Fort Huachuca, Arizona, when she was a young girl. She admired him immensely. The old, retired soldier drove around in a buggy drawn by an ancient horse called "Shad." In my infant mind, Sergeant Caldwell and Shad looked alike, both ancient, rickety, and arthritic. He was like a grandfather to me. I loved him dearly.

It was difficult for me to see this aged man as a young vital soldier, but he told me stories of ancient conflicts, and he told his tales with a vigor and credibility that left no doubt in my mind of his veracity. As a young man, he had fought at Gettysburg, Shiloh, and in the Wilderness. After that he fought Indians, Mexicans, and briefly, Spaniards. My imagination would go out of control. I vowed to become a soldier. Momma was categorically opposed to that so I didn't mention it to her, but I knew. Even at six, I was dedicated.

Momma resented my hearing these tales, because she knew I was impressionable, and she knew the nature of soldiers' lives. She wanted something better for me.

One day the Sergeant came by and called me out to his high-seated wagon at the curb. He wore an old tattered Army greatcoat, even though it was hot in the early summer. I remember well that our lilacs were in bloom. He had me climb up on the seat beside him, and he gave me the leather pouch of arrowheads that he wore on the string around his neck, "Just because I want you to have them."

He said he was going away soon. He asked me to go to "Africky" when I was "growed up": "Just put your feet on the ground there, anywhere on the continent and give one long thought to me. Just one thought, and it'll be all right. My life's aim was to git back home, but I didn't make it. I wasn't borned there, but it is home. Oh, how much I wanted to go back."

"Where you goin', Sergeant Caldwell?"

"Heaven, I hopes, son."

When I got to Africa, long, long afterward, I gave that thought to him and Shad, and it was all right. I owed him that for his profound inspiration and the loan of the three arrowheads, which had once lain within his bones. I threw them far out into the Niger delta, and I knew that Sergeant Caldwell was "home, home, home!" In a way, so was I, but I was more American than he was. My identity with Africa was not so strong, but there was something kindred there, and I've always appreciated the Sergeant's impact upon me. His was a rare dignity.

Citizens Military Training Camp, 1938, Los Angeles, California

I grew up in Bakersfield and went to Bakersfield High School. My life was not unpleasant, but I did know the prejudice of that time and place. While in high school, I got a break that set my course for a military career. This was the opportunity to attend the Citizens Military Training Camp (CMTC), perhaps the best thing to ever happen in my life.

It was true that before CMTC, I had always attended integrated schools. I was always exposed to the best available education, but that also meant that I was subject to tons of abuse, mostly from teachers but followed up by students, always anxious to emulate their adult leaders and to impress their peers. Many of the teachers deliberately downgraded my work and gave me little or no personal attention or instruction. I found myself excluded from the developmental aspects of education, such as chess club, athletic teams, and debating teams. I also noticed that when dating age came that all of my white "friends" abandoned me socially. My folks supported me through the long series of denigrating experiences. I survived it all, but "integration" was an abrasive experience for me. It was worth it, however, for the quality of academics to which I was exposed. The alternatives were infinitely poorer.

The result of having been exposed to both blatant and subtle discrimination, interspersed with obvious neglect, is a questioning of one's social values. One's self-worth is eventually debased. That is the price for being born a member of a minority group. I was becoming doubtful of my social value. The feeling of being second class was becoming a reality. Little by little my fabric had begun to erode. I worried a lot about it. I was getting less support than I needed. There was only one black professional person in my town, and he was inconspicuous. The pimps, gamblers, hustlers, day laborers, janitors, and porters of my acquaintance were not adequate to shore up my flagging confidence in myself and in my people. Life had become ugly and unfulfilling.

Then I found out about CMTC from an unobtrusive notice on a bulletin board in the school administration building. I was emotionally involved with everything military, and I pursued the program application for the summer camp, which required a favorable endorsement from the professor of Military Science and Tactics. When I went before the professor with my application, he had no objection to my attending the camp, even though I was not enrolled in Reserve Officers' Training Corps (ROTC) classes. The endorsement to my application was as follows: "Recommend approval for attendance at an appropriate camp for Negroes, in accordance with military policy."

In due time I was advised officially of my acceptance to a camp that accepted "colored people." Transportation and per diem while in travel status were provided. I left home to go to camp for the first time in 1938, the most exciting and enlightening thirty days of my life.

This was the finest time of my youth. It was a continuous adventure. CMTC was a system for developing Army officers, and it was a good system. Unlike ROTC, which in California was for whites only, CMTC was open to blacks. I was at camp with other Negro teenagers. That in itself was good for me because I was exposed for the first time to high-quality young black men who had matured in the progressive urban centers of California. These were young men of the highest quality I had ever known.

The encampment was at Fort McArthur, California, and most of the cadets were from the Los Angeles area. They were sons of doctors, lawyers, and businessmen, as well as porters, janitors, teachers, policemen, and gardeners—a wide spectrum of Negro involvement. More important were the cadets themselves. They were everything young men could be: students, musicians, orators, actors, marksmen, and athletes of all kinds. They were potentially everything that the American environment could develop. They were vigorous of mind and body. They had no doubts about who they were or what they were or what they would or could do with their lives. They had not been subjected to the life of a small town, and in their integrated schools they made up at least half the enrollment. Nothing had dwarfed their minds. They inspired me. They caused my self-esteem to rise, to tower, to soar. It has never flagged since.

The cadets were grouped by size for barracks assignments and organized into squads, platoons, and companies. The training was strenuous. Many hours were spent daily on close-order and extended-order drills, marksmanship, area police, kitchen police, guard duty, and military instruction. Instruction was provided by a cadre of white officers and black enlisted men from the 25th Infantry Regiment, stationed at Fort Huachuca, Arizona. Training was pitched somewhere between cadet life at West Point and basic training at Fort Benning, Georgia. After duty hours, a lot of time was spent on athletic competition. Competition was a constant theme of life at the camp.

One of the most important competitive events was scheduled for Open House when parents, friends, and girls came to visit the camp. A minor track meet was held, three innings of softball, a retreat parade, and finally, a drill-down. The drill-down was a close-order drill competition from an open-ranks formation. In response to commands from the battalion commander, cadets performed the appropriate maneuvers. When mistakes were made in position, timing, or performance, the perpetrator was disqualified and dismissed. The last man remaining on the field was the winner.

All cadets participated in the drill-down. It was judged by the cadre from the 25th Regiment. About 350 cadets were on the parade ground that day for the drill-down to see who was the best man-at-arms.

The competition began, and as cadets made mistakes in their responses to the commands, they were told to leave the field. At the command, "H'ordal—h'ahms," twenty cadets bit the dust. The commands and the mistakes continued. The event took a lot of time because most cadets were highly proficient, but gradually— very slowly—the ranks were thinned. My dad was directly in front of me in the audience. He held up four fingers, which I assumed meant that there were four cadets remaining on the field. I was unable to look around, so dad was keeping score for me. I was determined to win that competition.

Finally, there were only three cadets left on the parade ground: Cadet James Carlisle, Cadet Norman Houston, and me. I felt that I would, and could, win. Moments later Norm Houston was eliminated. Jim Carlisle and I deftly slapped those rifles. It was glorious! I knew my dad was happy. We two remaining cadets performed for what seemed to us an eternity. "Right shoulda— h'ahms. Left shouldah—h'ahms. H'ordah—h'ahms. Left face." On and on.

Our hearts were running like trip hammers. The competition was becoming boring; it had gone on too long.

"H'at ease." I relaxed and moved my left foot about ten inches to the left; my competitor simply slumped slightly in place. Either was acceptable by the book, but I was thumbed out.

Jim Carlisle won the drill-down. Dad was more disappointed than I was. I was not harmed, and the winner was a worthy adversary. Besides, to be number two in that environment was a towering success to me.

I did better with the boxing. I was a welterweight then, and after the sorry showing that I'd had in an amateur tournament earlier, I had taken some lessons and become pretty good. I had developed some good punches—as amateurs go. As luck and determination would have it, I won my division and got the golden glove. I also won the top marksmanship award.

The cadets in my barracks put on a play and insisted that I play a part. I did. I enjoyed it. I learned the lines and did a passable job. I also made the company debating team. I excelled in all aspects of the military curriculum. I found myself for the first time a first-class citizen in a first-class society.

It became obvious to me while at CMTC that I was going to be a soldier, an officer, a flier, a builder. So it became. My upbringing in the mean, prejudiced town of Bakersfield prepared me to function in the mean, prejudiced Army. Despite the bigotry, the Army was home. I was dedicated to it. Dedicated more to what it could and should be than to what it was. I was prepared to live for my country, fight for my country, and if necessary, to die for it. I knew that the changes I could make would be infinitely small, but I was resolved to make those changes. I knew that I would be good—damned good. There was no longer anything second class about me. I would give it my best, in exchange sometimes for a miserly return.

I went home from camp that first year a far better person than when I had arrived, and I planned to return the following year. While at camp the second year, in the summer of 1939, there were ominous rumblings of war on the part of Herr Hitler, and the world quaked before "The Moustache."

The second year's encampment was even better than the first, and my ambition to become a soldier grew. I received a lot of encouragement in my desire for a military career from members of the enlisted cadre from Fort Huachuca, Arizona, but I also got some discouragement from Private Hawkins, who was one of the cadre at the camp.

Private Hawkins, 1939, Fort MacArthur, California

Private Hawkins was a veteran of World War I, who was approaching thirty years of service. On his sleeve he wore one stripe up and several rockers below—a first and sixth. That meant he was only one step up in military rank but got extra pay for his technical proficiency. He cornered me one morning and told me there were some things about the Army that I should know, and that if I was interested, he'd fill me in. He said he wasn't trying to discourage me, but that there were aspects of military service, which weren't readily discernible at summer camp, that I should be aware of.

Hawkins explained that hard difference between commissioned and enlisted ranks. He stressed the towering reluctance of the Army to commission Negro officers—no matter how capable and how well educated. On the other hand, he related the jealousy and antipathy of Negro enlisted men toward other men of their race who were well educated or had advanced in rank.

He talked about Fort Huachuca, which sat alongside the Mexican border. It was not a fit place for white soldiers, and only a few had ever been stationed there. Fort Huachuca was in a treeless ocean of sagebrush and cactus. The closest large city was Tucson, about ninety miles away. Huachuca was a poor place for women or families. The officers assigned to the post were a miserable and appropriately disgruntled group; they were there due mostly to poor politics or misbehavior. The post had been built at its present site during the Indian Wars, shortly after the Civil War, because it was a good location from which to fight Indians or pursue them into Mexico. White soldiers didn't like either mission in the 129°F summertime temperatures. A hellhole at best! There was a contingent of Negro soldiers at Fort Benning, Georgia, and some cavalry at Fort Riley, Kansas, and maybe a few Negroes at some other posts, but most went to Huachuca. Such was the nature of the Jim Crow Army.

According to Hawkins, it was hard for a Negro to advance or even get into the Army. There was a ceiling on Negro enlistments; so for a Negro to enlist, there had to be a retirement, a death, a desertion, or a failure to reenlist somewhere in a Negro unit. All of those conditions were nebulous and uncertain. The only possibility was to go to Fort Benning or Fort Huachuca and make friends with a senior noncommissioned officer, preferably a first sergeant. If the proper relationship could be established, the first sergeant would obtain permission for the prospective soldier to become a "striker." A striker was a flunky who worked in exchange for meals. He performed tasks considered unpleasant by the troops, duties such as kitchen police (KP), shoe shining, and car polishing—sometimes for a small wage. In those days, KP was an important element of Army life and consisted of all the menial but essential tasks associated with food preparation: cleaning tables, floors, and windows in the mess (dining) hall; preparing food for cooking; washing trays, pots, and pans; and peeling potatoes. Available enlistments were filled on a seniority basis from the ranks of the strikers. It was a lousy system. It was at this point that my enthusiasm flagged.

Hawkins asked me some questions. "Was your dad a soldier?"

I responded, "Yes, sir."

"I don't rate a 'sir,' " he stated. "What unit was he in?"

"My dad was in the infantry—815th Regiment. They fought in France."

"No, they didn't fight in France. They did grave registration and burial details for white soldiers."

I was shocked. Hawkins continued, "Only a few Negro soldiers were allowed to fight. They were poorly trained and mostly given menial tasks. The 92d and 93d divisions—Negro troop units with mostly white officers—saw some action, but they were just a pitiful hodgepodge, not really well trained or equipped. It wasn't intended for them to do well, or for them to do anything other than serve in port battalions as stevedores or in grave registration. Under no circumstances were Negroes allowed to outperform white soldiers, and the most effective way to accomplish that was to eliminate any areas of comparison.

"That happened during the Civil War too, in the 54th Massachusetts Infantry. Some of the black enlisted men in that Union regiment had been ex-slaves who had hatred stored up. They vented their anger on the battlefield against soldiers of the Confederacy. White folks, even Northerners, couldn't stand that, and since that time there's been a conscientious effort to keep those few Negroes who are in the service isolated and in a position to do no harm to white folks.

"Oh, there were a few Negro fighting men in France. The U.S. Army loaned them to the French, who used them well, were very happy with their performance, and decorated them highly as units and as individuals. All this was much to the displeasure of the U.S. Army, which played down the effectiveness of their cast-off Negro troops."

I was stunned but replied, "Well, I believe you, but I'll join anyway, maybe after college. I don't want to waste any time being a striker. I'll go for a commission. I'm sure the service will be more rewarding that way."

When I returned home from CMTC that second year, I was a different, new person—confident, strong, resolute. It was obvious to me that I should find a better place to live than Bakersfield; I knew life offered infinitely more elsewhere. The day after I graduated from Bakersfield High School in 1939, I left that town never to return. I moved to Los Angeles and studied engineering at Los Angeles City College for two years. At that point, I decided to join the Army. As fate would have it, I became a fighter pilot.

Fighter Pilot

1942–1945,
Tuskegee, Alabama, to Italy

In September 1941, when I became twenty years of age, I volunteered for the Army. Because of my CMTC record and my good standing in school, I was accepted for aviation cadet training in the U.S. Army Air Corps. I was assigned to Tuskegee Army Flying School for my flight instruction, and I took the train from Los Angeles for my first military experience.

I had never traveled first class before, so I didn't understand the terms set forth on my travel voucher. It was easy enough to understand, however, that although several white youths and I were going to various military bases in the South, the Jim Crow laws precluded my sharing a drawing room with them east of El Paso, Texas. The pullman porter explained to me the bigotry, the hatred, and the duplicity that I would meet in the southern states of the United States. The porter was embarrassed by the explanation of the country's great weakness. His lecture was paternalistic and judicious.

The same Jim Crow laws also forced me to sit behind a curtain during meals, either to deny me the opportunity to see the white folk eat or to deny them the opportunity to watch me. I wondered about that, because my table manners were better than those demonstrated by most of the diners.

All of my life I had heard of Jim Crow segregation, and I had experienced some of it firsthand. I had also been exposed to decency from white people, and most of the time I had been treated with respect and human kindness as I earned it in my community. But my experience had not prepared me for the reality that was the South. Even the red, clay soil looked poor. What passed for cotton was dwarfed, stunted stalks no more than twelve to fifteen inches in height, with three to five light, lifeless bolls of hungry-looking growth. The livestock were bony and ill fed. The people appeared to be in the same condition.

Except for select parts of the villages and towns where well-painted homes rested in the shady comfort of the middle class, the people lived in shotgun houses turned a dismal grey from the effects of weather on pine planks. Hovels dotted the barren landscape. The only abundance in that environment was children. There were children of every size, color, and description waving at the train from every shady spot near the tracks. Children, somehow surviving the misery of summer in the Deep South. The hot, hyper-humid, sticky atmosphere was stygian.

It was barely possible to survive within that black monster of a train, huffing and belching, whistling as it coursed, viciously clicking on the endless rails. It vomited coal smoke and spewed cinders into the many cracks around its doors and poorly fitted windows. A noxious and grimy condition existed in the interior of the train. There was no form of air conditioning, so the passengers perspired and fanned themselves over the impossible miles to their destinations. Even in this situation, meticulous efforts were undertaken to keep Negroes and white people segregated, separated.

Well, that train moved night and day until it arrived and disgorged me at a place called Chehaw, Alabama. Tuskegee Army Flying School was located in the wilderness nearby, the site selected by Dr. Frederick D. Patterson, black president of Tuskegee Institute. Negroes had brought enough political pressure to bear on the Democratic administration in Washington, D.C., to convince the government to train and utilize Negroes in the war effort against Nazi Germany and feudal Japan. It was a matter of grave concern to American Negroes, because the mentality that denied military participation to Negroes was the same mentality that sired and maintained racial segregation in other areas of American society.

Whether drafted or enlisted, most Negroes in the U.S. Army during World War I and World War II saw duty mainly in labor or port battalions. Many were theoretically infantry, but, as Private Hawkins had told me, they were given only noncombat tasks, such as grave registration and burial. Negroes buried men who considered Negroes not good enough to fight alongside them. It was a demeaning, second-class status from which the Negro leadership begged and demanded to be released.

Tuskegee Army Flying School was the palliative given to the Negro citizenry. It was a segregated training facility hidden deep in the Alabama woods. The location of the Flying School gave an economic boost to the state in the form of rental housing from the institute and board for the aviation cadets during the preflight phase of flight training. The Negro portion of the city and its commerce also benefited materially from the patronage and cash expenditures of the Cadet Corps and the support troops. The citizens and commercial establishments of the white portion of Tuskegee were hostile. So were the citizens of the surrounding countryside. Assaults and abuse of Negroes were rampant off the military base. In all, it was a miserable place for American servicemen to live and train to fight the enemies of the nation.

Life on the air base differed significantly from the hostility and meanness of the city, county, and region. The Army practiced the segregation policy of the War Department and the local environs, but without the brutality. The white officers involved with the command and operation of the air base were "good ol' boy" types who wheedled and mewled the Negro soldiers, while maintaining the strictest segregation. A good example of segregation was in the operation of the base cafeteria, a single-story building of approximately five thousand square feet. The building was divided lengthwise by a five-foot wall. One-half of the building and services was devoted to the white population of thirty to forty personnel. The other side of the building, identical in size, was available to the four hundred to five hundred Negroes, whose line extended halfway around the block for lunch. That was a disgrace before God Almighty.

The selection policy for aviation cadets, established by the War Department for the Army, was the same for Negro and white youths. However, the course-completion rate for white cadets was 50 to 60 percent, while the completion rate for Negroes was under 25 percent. This disparity was caused by a lack of commitment to produce a Negro fighting force of any real significance and by allowing the "good ol' boys" to waste the taxpayers' dollars by performing their training duties poorly. Some of the instructors were fine men, but there was always an abundance of those whose mission was of a destructive nature. There were many instructors who were abusive, inefficient, and of poor quality as men, flyers, or officers. As a consequence, the training and combat readiness at Tuskegee was only a fraction of what it should and could have been.

Congress should authorize a medal for every Negro who was required to serve in the Jim Crow South. The duty was hazardous, demeaning, and beneath human dignity. Ironically, no white person has ever admitted to participation or knowledge of this abuse, even those who perpetrated the inhuman abuse.

The only redeeming aspect of the entire Tuskegee experience was the beautiful girls who were in Tuskegee and other Alabama towns in abundance. They made the harsh life a little more acceptable.

I completed pilot training at Tuskegee Air Base as a member of Class 43-E, and on 28 May 1943, I won my pilot's wings and was commissioned a second lieutenant in the U.S. Army Air Corps. Momma and over nine hundred other Negro mothers came to Tuskegee to watch their sons graduate and receive those silver wings. Momma was proud that day, not only of her son, but of the progress that had been made in the Negro's journey up from slavery, up from the cottonfields. Momma conceded that my being an Army officer was not a bad thing, and she gave me her blessing. I was on my way.

Selfridge Air Field, 1943, Mount Clemens, Michigan

Most of my class was assigned to the 332d Fighter Group and sent to Selfridge Air Field, Mount Clemens, Michigan, for unit flight training. Our training at Selfridge Field suffered from the same neglect we had encountered at Tuskegee. The few instructors assigned to Selfridge were theoretically combat veterans from the Pacific theater. In reality they were lousy pilots who seldom flew and, after their initial ignominious defeats in mock combat with us in our P-40s, never went aloft when the trainees were in the air. It was an embarrassing situation in which the students were superior to their teachers.

One of the most significant efforts of the training commanders and staff was directed at keeping Negro officers out of the Officers Clubs at Selfridge Field, Michigan; Godman Field, Kentucky; Walterboro Field, South Carolina; and other air fields where Negro troops were stationed. At Selfridge, segregation and malicious enmity toward blacks were the primary preoccupation of the airfield commander, Col. Robert Selway. Colonel Selway was a tired old man who rarely, if ever, engaged in flying. It was obvious to us that his concern was not with developing fighter pilots or effective flying organizations, but with "keepin' those nigra offisahs outa the Club." This effort at segregation was also evident at Oscada, Michigan, where aerial gunnery training was conducted.

Selfridge Air Field had only one club, a beautiful facility that could accommodate many more officers than those assigned to the airfield. Colonel Selway and the staff were unable to control the situation because the Negro press was continually exposing the situation and embarrassing the Army and the administration in Washington, D.C.

Colonel Selway was supported in his segregation policies by Maj. Gen. Frank O'Driscoll Hunter, commanding general of the U.S. First Air Force. General Hunter was a tall man whose countenance was that of a miner or sharecropper, but whose demeanor and speech would have embarrassed either group. General Hunter's major accomplishment in the war was his harassment of Negro pilots. He caused Negro units to be moved around, at great expense, from one Jim Crow duty station to another. These were duty stations where he could deny the black officers what are now called civil rights. General Hunter flew into his Jim Crow stations and berated the black fliers in the most demeaning terms because they insisted upon utilizing the Officers Clubs. He made their lives miserable with his racial diatribes, to which no response was possible on pain of trial by court martial.

The general was the voice of the U.S. president, the U.S. Congress, and their constituents. These were the same people who incarcerated Japanese citizens on the West Coast of the United States. We blacks could be consoled, perhaps, by the fact that we were free, although we were second-class citizens.

Tuskegee and the other airfields that we endured were ugly experiences. No thanks to those who made it so, but we benefited from the ill treatment and duplicity of those whose arrogance we overcame. We stayed and excelled and won the struggle against their bigotry. We grew monumentally under their yokes, and we thrived in the face of their manufactured adversity.

Looking back, Tuskegee and its aftermath was, despite all the many negatives, a fantastic experience for the Negro of the 1940s. Mr. Roosevelt's experiment, his palliative to the worrisome Negro press and politicians, bloomed in many ways and spawned a brand new type of man. It produced many a Negro who had demonstrated his potential and his technical prowess. The American Negro became aware of himself, his enormous and powerful skills, and his soul. Nearly one thousand pilots, navigators, and bombardiers were trained in Tuskegee. Many were highly competent bomber crews, and many were fighter pilots possessing the most demanding military skills of that time.

After we completed our transition training at Selfridge Air Field, the 332d Fighter Group moved to Camp Patrick Henry, Virginia, early in 1944 to stage for sea transportation to the Mediterranean theater of operations, although we did not know it at the time. While at Camp Patrick Henry, I struck a small blow for freedom and almost got into a lot of trouble for doing it.

All of us were both glad and sad to be leaving Selfridge Air Field. It was sad for those who were leaving their wives and loved ones, but it was good to get away from the hard Jim Crow regime.

2 January 1944, Camp Patrick Henry, Virginia

I knew that we were at Camp Patrick Henry because a tobacco-spitting conductor came stomping through the railroad cars our squadron occupied advising no one in particular, "Camp Patrick Henry." Camp Patrick Henry was at Norfolk, Virginia, a major port of embarkation where thousands of troops boarded ships on the way to distant wars. The 332d Fighter Group was staging through there on its way to join the war. We had no idea where, but we knew it would be combat.

It was a gigantic place. All I could see was miles of rows of barracks. The train crept along at a snail's pace, and I noticed a sign, "Colored Only." A block farther down the street was another sign, "White Troops Only."

Eventually, we detrained. From the train window I had counted twenty-three signs stating "Colored Only" or "White Troops Only." I knew at that moment that I had to do something. If I could risk my life in the service of my country, I could afford to risk it in my own service. For sixteen months in the Army, I had been subjected to the bigotry and discrimination of the military Jim Crow policies. I was about to be sent overseas to fight to defend the freedom of the very people who denied me freedom. I vowed to strike a blow for my own freedom. I'd had enough.

We carried out our personal baggage, and a detail carried our heavier baggage. The Bachelor Officers' Quarters (BOQs) were directly behind the Orderly Room. Directly across the street from the Orderly Room was a theater with a capacity of four hundred seats and a sign saying, "White Troops Only."

After I was all squared away in the barracks, I decided to walk around a bit. Winter in Virginia was something less than pleasant. There had been some snow, which had largely melted, and there were scraps of trash still frozen to the ground. A cold wind lurked around every corner. It was a bleak and forbidding place. My walk took me up to the first cross street, where I found a large post exchange and, characteristically, the "White Troops Only" sign. The white post exchange was only half a block from our barracks, while the black post exchange was seven blocks away.

I began to steam, quietly. I was getting damned tired of the constant racial insults that I was being subjected to. I talked with Larry Wilkins about the Jim Crow system we were involved in at Camp Patrick Henry. I'd known Larry since high school, and he was long on guts. We both agreed that discriminating against the nation's fighting men was bigotry at its worst. We agreed and sympathized with each other, but we hadn't formulated a plan to shake up the system. The trick was to protest in a manner that wouldn't bring on a court martial or cause physical violence.

Time moved grudgingly, but eventually Sunday came, and I was still smoldering. A church service was conducted, but I was not in the mood to listen to a mewling preacher promising me milk and honey by-and-by. I was concerned with the problems of the moment, and I knew that the chaplain was not going to deal with those problems. I just stomped about the squadron area and watched the issue of weapons and ammunition incident to our departure for combat. Spratmore said that once the ordnance issue is made, departure takes place within forty-eight hours. Spratmore was the god of barracks rumor, and his word was usually correct. He was often referred to irreverently as "Sprat," but he enjoyed a significant level of regard for knowing what was happening.

The ordnance issue went smoothly, along with the detailed safety instructions, even though we had undergone extensive training previously. Eventually noon came and, with it, the opportunity for Sunday dinner. But my smoldering insides had precluded my breakfast from digesting properly, so lunch was impossible. I retired to my bunk.

I was consumed by the outrage of Camp Patrick Henry added to the towering insult that was Tuskegee and the racism of Selfridge Air Field. I was powerless to ignore it or console myself. I knew about the penalties—the floggings and the lynchings for those who resisted the revered traditions and folkways of Jim Crow. Many Negroes had been murdered for their resistance, and I really don't want to go that route. I felt compelled to do something about it. But what?

Larry Wilkins came by and sat on the foot of my bunk. He asked, "Are you still steaming about the discrimination?"

"Yeah, I guess I am."

"Sort of a waste of time, isn't it?"

"Yeah, I guess so."

"Is that why you missed turkey for lunch?"

"Yeah, I've had heartburn from breakfast."

"Got any new ideas?"

"Umm, think I'll pull that sign down off the theater, and then go to the window, and demand a ticket."

"What if they won't sell you one?"

"Then I'll just walk in."

"Military police?"

"Hell, I don't know. I just know that I'm desperate to protest this Jim Crow business."

"Well, I'm with you. I understand. Can you handle the sign by yourself?"

"I'm sure I can. I'm just going to rip it off the building and throw it in the ditch, then walk up to the window and demand a ticket. Damn the consequences!"

"OK. I'll get some Negro enlisted men to back you up. I don't want some military policeman caving your head in. You obviously don't give a damn, but what do you think the Old Man will do?"

I responded, "There ain't a helluva lot he can do. It isn't serious enough for a court martial. But I'm sure there's something the Army can do to make me more miserable, and they'll just have to do it. I must strike a blow for freedom."

"I know what you mean, but it may have a helluva price. I'm in on it, as you know. The movie starts at 1400 hours. I'll check with the troops. Be back soon." And Larry was on his way to the enlisted barracks.

I felt better after Larry left, because no matter how stupid it was, I at least had a plan of action.

As I walked out of the barracks about ten minutes before show time, I noticed a lot of our Negro troops forming up by the enlisted barracks area. I hadn't mentioned my plan to any officers other than Larry because I felt his support was enough.

Over to the theater I went. I looked back over my shoulder.

Our men were coming, but it really didn't matter; I was committed anyway.

There were at least one hundred white soldiers in line, with a few of their officers at the head of the line. As I passed along toward the ticket window, I noticed a hush as the casual chatter stopped. At the window I crossed the line and proceeded along the face of the building. When I reached the offending sign, I placed my foot about three-and-one-half feet up on the building, hooked my hands behind the sign, and ripped it off the building. I was somewhat surprised that the sign came off, but it did. I carried it over to the storm drain along the street and threw it in.

Larry and I joined the rear of the officer line. My enlisted backup force joined the enlisted line. We were anticipating trouble, but it didn't come. I bought two tickets, and Larry and I entered the theater. Our troops entered the line, bought tickets, and entered the theater, and that should have been the end of the story.

Humphrey Bogart played with his cigarette, and words came out of his mouth. That should have been enough for entertainment. But we had anticipated physical conflict, and all of the emotions engendered by the racial abuse of the previous months welled up in me. I didn't enjoy the movie.

Racial expletives could be heard coming from the white members of the audience during the latter part of the movie. It appeared that the situation in the movie theater was going to get out of hand and become violent. I didn't know what to do about stopping the violence that was on the way; hatred had set the scene for trouble.

However, when the fictional "forever afters" were over, the theater lights came on, and in the hard revealing lights the potential for violence evaporated. In their anger and frustration, four of our men ripped out a row of seats, but the audience departed by all available exits, and the danger of a fight was gone.

Larry and I were silent during the short walk to our quarters, but once inside, he asked, "Well, what do you think?"

I replied, "I pulled that sign down, but there are probably four or five hundred more like it on this camp, and I can't do much about them. The Man has been doing his thing for a couple hundred years, and I don't think there's really anything we can do to change things."

"You're right," he replied, "but it was good striking even that small blow."

Then out of the night came gunfire. Two, ten, fifty, one hundred shots came out of our barracks area. I heard pistol shots, rifle shots, semiautomatic fire, and small-arms fire of all types. It was chilling. A heavy volume of fire. A small war.

Larry said, "There's real trouble. It made sense to issue weapons today, but it was damned dumb to issue ammo. We could've anticipated this after this afternoon. Did you feel the tension in that theater? If the lights hadn't come on when they did, this trouble would have broken out then, and we'd have had some killing.

"What we are hearing now is just noise, a lot of noise, but just noise. They just want to get the Man's attention. Right now, it's only our men, but it'll probably catch on in the other Negro units. We're gonna have a long night."

Larry was right. The shots were only being fired into the air, but even so there was great danger, because bullets do come down, and with great velocity. I knew that the random firing I was hearing was a chain reaction from my small demonstration in front of the theater.

I heard sirens wind up in the distance. They were heading in our direction. A military police vehicle appeared and slowed down, but when the police heard the level of fire, the vehicle sped up again and left the area. The military police (MPs) probably considered that their stateside duty didn't include participating in a small war. While the military police cruised well outside our area, the random shooting continued into the night.

About 0200, the squadron commander came into my bunk area and called me. I certainly had not been asleep. He directed me to go down to the enlisted area and stop the firing.

I said, "Hell, Skipper, there's nothing I can do about the firing down there."

The squadron commander said, "You damned sure better try. Spratmore says you started that foolishness yesterday afternoon over at the theater. If anything serious comes out of this mess, it won't be difficult to tie you into it. Go down there, get some of your Los Angeles friends, and get that noise stopped."

By that time I was nearly dressed and convinced that I was in some serious trouble. I didn't know if I could contribute to peace, but I was dedicated to trying. While I was still within earshot, the squadron commander added, "Make it fast. The post commander's arming infantry troops to come down and take over this part of the camp. That could provoke some killing. You are now my provost marshal. Get at it. You are in trouble, hoss."

I adjusted my tin hat and ventured down into that no-man's-land. I looked for Tech. Sgt. Joe Johnson, an old friend from Los Angeles. I told him that the situation was too far out of hand, and that some infantry was on the way. We had to get that firing stopped immediately. Without hesitation, he said, "OK, let's go from barracks to barracks. You do the talking, I'll back you up. Most of the guys want to quit now anyhow. After the movie yesterday, they had ammo and guns, and since it was difficult to identify any one individual, they could just bang away. They wanted to let the 'Man' know they were unhappy with Jim Crow, especially since we're going overseas so soon."

We walked into the first barracks. In the semidarkness I yelled, "All right, men! Stop the firing!" To my complete surprise, it stopped immediately.

We did the same thing in the next barracks, and someone wanted to know, "Who says so?" With far less bravery than I felt, I bellowed, "This is Lieutenant Bussey of the 302d Fighter Squadron, Temporary Provost Marshal, and I'm telling you that it is time, right now, to stop this firing. You have made your point. I'm proud of you, but let's knock it off now."

Someone in the semidarkness said, "Yes, sir." And the trouble was over in that barracks. Sergeant Johnson and I continued until it was all quiet and nearly daybreak.

When I returned to my quarters, the "Skipper" was waiting for me without a smile. He said, "I expect Colonel Davis will be wanting to see you in the morning. It'll behoove you to be on your best behavior with a minimum of 'lip.' He's really got you by the short hairs. It probably depends on how much pressure he gets from the post commander, but if you can show some humility about this Jim Crow business and how it's been eating you all these months you've been in the service, he may hear you—or he may not. Remember, he's Negro too, and he took all the bigotry and hatred up at West Point. He may not hear you, but you've got little else going for you. We're leaving tomorrow, and that's another thing in your favor. If they try to court martial you, it means leaving a lot of witnesses behind. Awkward. I'll let you know."

It was a long wait. I took some precautions. I called my brother, Ed, and listened to his excoriation of my conduct. Without telling me, brother Ed then called our Uncle John, who was a politician; and Uncle John called the governor, who did whatever governors do. Brother Ed prepared wires to each of the leading Negro newspapers: the *Chicago Defender;* the *Pittsburgh Courier;* the *Baltimore Afro American;* and several others, but it didn't become necessary to involve them.

Around noon, the squadron commander called me in and took me apart. He berated me professionally and concluded our meeting with a query about my intentions. I was ready for that, because I was anxious for Col. Benjamin O. Davis, the group commander, to get that information before I had to meet him. I was intimidated by the group commander. Hell, his reputation had me downright scared. As a lieutenant colonel, Davis had commanded the 99th Pursuit Squadron, the first black flying unit. In April 1943 the 99th, stationed in North Africa, had flown combat missions against the Italian island of Pantelleria between Sicily and Tunisia, and later against Sicily and mainland Italy. In September 1943 the 99th moved to a base on mainland Italy and engaged in dive bombing and strafing German positions and personnel. Since the output of Tuskegee far exceeded the requirement for replacements in the 99th Pursuit Squadron, additional black flying units were formed. Then-Lieutenant Colonel Davis had been sent back to the United States in 1943 to form the 332d Fighter Group and bring it to the Mediterranean theater of operations. While in the States on this mission, he was promoted to full colonel.

Finally the colonel sent for me. I began to sweat. Then he kept me waiting for about twenty minutes. Finally, a master sergeant advised me that the colonel would see me.

I sort of stumbled into the room and stood before his desk. I tossed up a salute, which he ignored for what seemed to be a long, long time. I would have liked to pull my salute down, but I dared not. When he finally returned the salute, I jerked mine down and started to say, "Second Lt. Charles Bussey reporting as ordered."

But before I could complete it all, he said, "I know who you are, but I wish I didn't." And the chewing went on from there. He rebuked me for ages. He declared that I was not fit to be an Army officer, and I almost believed him. I was thoroughly intimidated. His chewing was more thorough and professional than my father's, but my dad had never become a colonel, and had never perfected his techniques. Through it all I stared right back at the colonel—eyeball-to-eyeball—but down inside I felt as weak as tapwater.

I did notice, however, that the colonel wasn't threatening me with punitive action, which was a standard element in the chewing of a miscreant. Finally, it was over. He concluded with the remark, "As long as you and I are in the same Army, you will never be promoted. I am going to run you through my Underwood typewriter. Your scars will never heal. You will not recover."

He excused me. I saluted him, and he returned it snappily. I was glad to get out of his office.

I was going back to the barracks, making up a lot of half truths about my encounter for public consumption, when I noticed a large fatigue detail with a stake-and-platform truck taking down those offensive signs. I walked directly across the street and into the post exchange, where I bought all the cigarettes and goodies that I needed for a long ocean trip.

I had the opportunity to tell those half truths back in the barracks, and I also knew the whole truth—that I had struck a blow for freedom.

1944, 332d Fighter Group, Italy

The next day, 4 January 1944, we moved to the port and found out we were going to the Mediterranean theater of operations. We were stationed initially at Taranto, Italy; then we moved to Salerno, to Naples, and finally to Termoli on the Adriatic Sea.

The 332d Fighter Group was part of the Fifteenth Air Force (Strategic). The Air Force had B-17 and B-24 bombers and P-38, P-47, and P-51 fighters. Our fighter group had trained on P-40s in the States, and we were equipped with P-39s for the first few months in the Mediterranean. Then we got P-51 Mustangs and used these fine aircraft until the end of the war. The 332d Fighter Group included the 100th, 301st, and 302d Fighter squadrons. Later, the 99th Pursuit (Fighter) Squadron also joined our group.

The pilots of the 332d Fighter Group had the finest combat record of World War II. Strategic fighter units are not rated by the number of enemy airplanes shot down; they are rated by the number of bombers that are saved under their protection. Under the hard, disciplined, but enlightened leadership of Col. Benjamin O. Davis, the 332d Fighter Group flew 250 missions covering American bombers and never lost a bomber to enemy fighters. They also bombed and strafed enemy positions. No other group can claim a performance record to equal that of Davis's group. Colonel Davis had the training and temperament to command such a select and diverse group effectively and to retain his desired direction. Only Ben Davis could have done it. The pride and confidence engendered by that towering success contributed singularly to the aggrandizement of Negroes. It removed the last white justification for continuing the ignominious vestiges of Jim Crow by keeping blacks out of combat duty.

Benjamin O. Davis was one of the most outstanding men of his time. He became a general officer and retired from the U.S. Air Force wearing the three stars of a lieutenant general. He seized the rare opportunity to thwart all those naysayers. In essence, he forced the integration of Negro airmen into the highly successful and progressive U.S. Air Force. No one recommended him for the Nobel Peace Prize, but the success of the 332d Fighter Group was the harbinger of freedom for his people. Through his leadership, a positive and highly visible demonstration of Negro technical abilities and patriotism was submitted for all the world to observe. Under that scrutiny, the conventional wisdom faltered, later to be assaulted and defeated under the leadership of Dr. Martin Luther King, Jr.

April 1944, A View from the Cockpit

It was a fantastically beautiful morning with visibility of more than one hundred miles. No haze. No smoke. Just good clean air. The 332d Fighter Group was aloft on a combat mission. We were cruising at twenty-five thousand feet in our fighters. Our P-51 Mustangs were well suited for escorting heavy bombers, and we were on the way to a rendezvous with elements of a heavy bomber wing.

The target was Schweinfurt, Germany, and its critical ball-bearing plants. Our job was to fly "top cover" for the bombers, that is, protect them from enemy fighter planes. We were to rendezvous at thirty thousand feet sixty miles from the target, escort the bombers over the target, and then back to the northern shore of the Adriatic Sea. Intelligence had reported nineteen hundred antiaircraft guns at Schweinfurt, and I believed it. We had been there before, and we knew about the tremendous loss of aircraft over the ball-bearing factories. From the quantity of flak in the skies above, below, and into the bombers, I believe that all nineteen hundred guns were being fired with tremendous accuracy.

The flak guns were intended for and aimed at the bombers. The shell fuses were cut for the altitude at which the bombers were flying. We fighters were always well above the bombers and were rarely affected by the fire the enemy put up. The flak was always below us. That allowed us to concentrate on looking for enemy fighters threatening our bombers below.

Top cover was really one of the less hazardous missions, when one considers the casualty rates on strafing missions and dive-bombing runs. Plus, there was the distinct possibility of making kills during encounters with enemy fighters attacking bomber formations. Every fighter pilot looked forward to racking up aerial victories over enemy aircraft, particularly enemy fighters.

At that time, the enemy had very few fighters to send aloft. The Allies had destroyed the Ploesti oil fields, stifled the oil-barge traffic on the Danube River, and effectively accomplished the destruction of rail-vehicle traffic on the way to Germany. The Nazis were denied much of their oil supply.

We'd had some field days shooting up barges on the river and railroad rolling stock between Ploesti and all points in the Fatherland. We had sorely curtailed the availability of fuel for aircraft. Additionally, hundreds and hundreds of bombers had been destroyed on the ground as a result of bombing and strafing by Allied planes. We'd been out to the Ploesti oil fields many times, and we witnessed the pasting of the gathering system, the refinery, and the entire area roundabout.

I was leading Blue Flight and feeling pretty good about it all. We were flying in a four-ship tactical formation heading north over the Udine Valley. My history courses reminded me that the area below us had been fought over many times previously. I was enjoying the fabulous summer weather, but I was not lethargic. The business we were in was far too serious for anything other than extreme alertness.

Venice had disappeared under my nose, and Verona had passed under my left wing, in front of Lake Garda. Switzerland always looked beautiful, enclosed by the Alps. We overflew Innsbruck and Augsburg.

We were easing up behind a bomber wing—a stranger. The bombers we were responsible for were still miles ahead, and our commander was advising of the approaching rendezvous. The closer bomber formation was many miles long in the morning sky. The bombers seemed to hang in the blue like droves of gnats. We were two thousand feet above the bombers and all seemed to be going well.

Suddenly out of the radio came the stark warning from Lt. Larry Wilkins, "Bombers under attack at one o'clock low." Larry had the best eyes in the group. He saw it all, from the ground up to fifty thousand feet.

Our squadron, "Doorknob," was the rearmost squadron in the

group that day, so the Old Man called, "Doorknob Blue and Yellow Flights, get 'em."

I signaled Blue Flight to drop their wing tanks, and we were on the way to fight. It was weird. I'd neither seen nor heard of the tactic the German fighters were using. There were six ME-109s in a continuous loop right up through the bomber formation, and every time a Messerschmitt reached a vertical flight attitude, he shot up a bomber, which exploded in a mass of fire and rubble. The German plane then climbed right up through the formation, over on his back, nosed down in a dive, and did a repeat of the aerobatics. The ME-109s were line-astern in the continuous and deadly loop. I was fascinated by it all. I had never seen nor heard of this maneuver, but it was being accomplished right before my eyes.

It was time for action. I set my timing with the progress of the planes in the loop, taking advantage of our greater altitude and consequently greater speed. I joined the loop behind one of the ME-109s, became vertical directly behind him, and blew him out of the sky before he fired at the bomber over his nose. His debris showered me as I passed dangerously up through the bomber formation. The same maneuver was occurring behind me. I was unable to get a second victory because we were observed by the other ME-109s, who split for home. It had all happened so rapidly and so instinctively that I hadn't even breathed during the brief encounter.

I rolled over in an Immelmann and climbed up to see what was going on. My wingman was not with me, but I could hardly expect him to stick with me in that killing sky. It was too crowded, and it would have been more appropriate for him to shoot down the German plane that had been on my tail when I joined the German formation. I pulled up abruptly into the sun, hopefully to thwart a rear attack on my ship. A turn at thirty-five thousand feet indicated that I was alone, so I dropped my nose and headed for the barn.

It was a glorious morning. I made frequent and numerous turns to be sure it stayed that way, with no surprises from enemy fighters.

A lone pilot is appropriately apprehensive when flying over

enemy-held territory. It's not bad at high altitude because I could out-dive attacking enemy fighters. I had descended to twenty-five thousand feet heading southward, and I was feeling pretty good about myself. I was turning, searching the skies, while heading for home. I could feel a long trickle of cold sweat starting at my shoulder blades and running down my spine. I made it a routine: always turning, looking down, looking to the rear, another turn toward the south, looking up, looking down, looking around.

Way out in front I noticed a speck in the sky, much lower than I. I closed on the speck and identified it as an aircraft heading my way. I still couldn't tell what type it was, but I knew only a German aircraft would be flying north. I switched gas tanks and set my flap stop at 20° as the aircraft approached me. When the aircraft ran close under me, I saw that it was a Focke Wulf 190. I rolled my P-51 Mustang over into a split "S" to come out immediately behind the Focke Wulf without overrunning him. All the while I was praying that some other "son of the Fatherland" wasn't aligning his sights on me.

My initial altitude advantage also gave me a speed advantage. I closed in on the Focke Wulf rapidly—too rapidly. I didn't look at my instruments, for the Focke Wulf had my total attention. I tried to align my sights, but I was gaining too fast on the target. I slapped down my flaps and slowed abruptly. I got a good burst of fire into the Focke Wulf and then sucked up my flaps and speeded up.

A panel flew off the Focke Wulf, and the pilot—obviously a novice—panicked. A veteran would have hung the Focke Wulf on his prop and climbed away from the Mustang, or perhaps made a very shallow climbing turn to get into the sun. But this pilot did a steep diving run away from home and away from life. I was on him like a duck on a June bug, adrenaline was pumping like a geyser, and there were pains in my spinal column. I cut off the German's turn and got another burst into him. The German pilot was inexperienced and dropped his nose still further. I closed on him slightly. There was no escape for the German ship.

My fighter was bore-sighted so the bullets from all 6 machine guns converged at a point 300 yards ahead of the aircraft. The guns fired at a rate of 650 bullets per minute. A lot of lead passed through the aiming point in even a short period of time. Every tenth bullet was a tracer, which allowed me to see where my firing stream was concentrating.

I began firing again at long range, five hundred to six hundred yards behind the Focke Wulf, and the pilot began making frantic turns. At each turn, I cut a little off the distance between us by turning inside, tighter than the arc flown by my prey.

I had no idea of my throttle setting. Everything was forward, way forward. I was "locked on." The Focke Wulf and its pilot were an impersonal entity—just an airplane, a target. My brain pulsed. The excitement was intense and indescribable. Killing became a drive, and my mind closed out all else.

I fired another burst. The pilot had not learned his lessons well. He began to dive again. This was the wrong thing to do. American planes were faster in dives, and German planes were faster in climbs. So when in trouble, the smart German pilot climbed. This was particularly effective at about thirty-five thousand feet, and the American planes ran out of power while the Germans could still climb effectively and rapidly. But this poor pilot chose to dive, and that was his downfall and his demise.

I bore down on him. Another burst and small pieces flew off the Focke Wulf. He turned again, and I fired again. We were down fairly low by now, and the Focke Wulf still had his nose down. Eventually we were down in a valley with peaks higher than we were. As dangerous as it was, I couldn't let him go. We were flying only slightly above a dry streambed, which rose at a slight angle. The Focke Wulf was turning with the streambed making it impossible for me to get any more shots into him. The peaks became higher above us, and I was at maximum power. I wanted to quit. Then I got another firing opportunity. I fired a burst but without effect. Suddenly the Focke Wulf hit the sand, cartwheeled, exploded, and burned. I pulled my Mustang up through the Focke Wulf pilot's funeral pyre.

I nursed my ship up out of the valley amid the spires of rock. I was scared. The engine was running roughly, and the ship was extremely close to stalling. I was praying.

Then I was clear. As I throttled back, I looked into the cockpit for the first time in what seemed to be a long time. I noticed that I was pulling seventy-three inches of manifold pressure and three thousand revolutions per minute. This exceeded take-off power, and I had been applying it for a considerable period.

As I climbed and turned southward, I saw the burning Focke Wulf. I didn't know whether I was in Switzerland, Austria, or Italy, but I was glad to be heading home. I was turning, looking, reaching for home; then I saw Trieste way off on my left. I began to feel better, but there was still a lot of pain in my spine near the kidney. I was gratified to see the bright blue of the Adriatic Sea. Then I gave a small prayer of thanks:

> Oh Lord, God in Heaven,
> I am grateful for Thy protection,
> For providing me with safety
> And success in the face of my enemies.
> Thanks, O God, for my preservation.
>
> Please, Heavenly Father,
> Accept the soul of the vanquished.
> Keep him in Thy bosom.
> Forgive the sins and weaknesses
> Of my enemy and me.
>
> And Dear God, I ask protection
> For my loved ones at home.
> Shower them with Thy blessings.
> For all Thy bounty, I thank thee.
> Father, teach me to be strong
> And resourceful in Thy service,
> And in service to my fellow man.
> If I have sinned this day,
> Lord forgive me.
> Amen.

When I passed Ancona and was heading south, I relaxed a little. I was inordinately proud of myself. This was a long way from home.

I thought for a moment about Momma. She'd be extremely proud of me, but there had certainly been many times when she hadn't been, and I reminisced about my times and tribulations with her. I recalled her numerous visits to my elementary school, where my mischief caused my teachers gross consternation. I thought briefly of the neighborhood pranks in which I participated. As I neared the home field, my mind ran wild and memories came into my mind like popcorn on a hot griddle. It was Momma and me. We had some times and some confrontations; there were a few draws, but I lost most of the time. In retrospect they were good times, and I was glad for the self-discipline that came out of it all. Mostly I reflected on her visit upon my graduation from flight school, the receipt of my commission, and the acceptance of those beautiful silver wings. She was proud of me that day.

I was just another guy, not stifled by lethargy, nor consumed by hyper-initiative. Particularly on this day, I knew that I was a damned good man. I was happy and proud and blessed to be a member of the most select group in the world—the fighter pilots. We were special.

I completed seventy combat missions with the 332d Fighter Group. I destroyed two enemy aircraft and damaged two more. In April 1945, I was reassigned to the States to be a flight instructor at Tuskegee Army Air Field. I was there when the war ended.

Between the Wars

1946–1948,
Los Angeles, California

WAR ENDS! JAPAN SURRENDERS!!!!

The newspapers had a field day, and the hoopla began. It was 14 July 1945—shouting, boozing, weeping, wailing, and praying amid a conscientious effort to erase the ugliness of the preceding four years of war. There was laughter, relaxation, and booze. It was time to restart, to rebuild. It was a time to be whomever, whatever, wherever we really were without the strain, worry, and apprehension that wars impose on human mentality. It was a time to live. It was a time to go back home.

Like millions of other young men, I got out of the Army as fast as I could and went home. I mustered out on 1 February 1946. I returned to reality, to college, to a poor level of employment. The brass buttons, shoulder bars, and silver wings of a fighter pilot became instant nothingness. I made the futile attempt to pick up where I'd left off, but the world I'd known before no longer existed.

My first marriage had been a typical wartime romance, to a young girl I grew up with in Bakersfield. We married in 1943 as I was on my way to the war. Our marriage lasted only eighteen months and we were divorced shortly after I got back from Italy in 1945. I had no children and no regrets from that wartime episode.

I met my second wife, Thelma, in 1945, and we were married in 1946. Thelma was a lovely, highly talented woman. She was a fine pianist and vocalist—a rare combination. I loved her dearly. We had four children together. Our son, Charles, arrived in 1946, and our daughter, Fay, in 1949. After I returned from Korea, we had two more children—Patricia in 1955 and Edmund in 1958.

Thelma had a master's degree in education, and she loved teaching the sixth grade. I had no problem with her teaching, except that I wanted her at home until our youngest child started school. I wanted my children to have manners exactly the same as my own generation's. She acquiesced on that point.

When strong men marry strong women, there is always potential for a clash of personalities. Sometimes the clash is verbal, loud, and expressive. Frequently, one of the parties yields, and a real difference is avoided, quietly. It is essential that the rough corners be rubbed off with a minimum of abrasion. In any case the accommodation requires close participation by the married couple. Military men are by nature and by profession hardnosed, and when the wife has some of the same characteristics, long periods of separation widen the chasm of misunderstanding. Prolonged separation certainly contributes to the failure of many service marriages.

I had the hard-nosed attitude all right, and I was something of a chauvinist, but I had a good marriage to a fine woman, who should have been married to a school teacher or a postman who arrived home at 5:15 P.M. daily without the reek of booze on his breath. We had one very basic problem. My wife could not be happily married to a flier. Aerial flights and happy hour were synonymous in those days. Liquor she could tolerate, but she was deathly afraid of flying. That was a basic problem. I was a flier before I met her. Flying was my life. The truth is I had no idea of her phobia about flying until much later. We had never discussed it. She kept that from me. She knew how I felt about it, and she knew that a declaration of her feelings would have created a problem between us. It was just a question of time, however, before this problem would surface.

The GI Bill was a great blessing in that period of my life. Like tens of thousands of other ex-GIs, who could never have afforded it otherwise, I went back to college—five nights a week at the University of Southern California. Employment opportunities were poor, but with the $105 per month from the GI Bill, I managed to support my wife and myself. I finished up at San Francisco State University and was awarded a bachelor of arts degree in political science in 1949.

Earning that bachelor's degree was one of my life's most worthwhile accomplishments. I fought the books at night school until I earned my degree. The degree was good, not only for the education, but because it gave me greatly increased confidence in myself, in my intellect, in my reasoning power, and in the dictates of my conscience. I would have been a cripple without that degree and the study that led to it. I'm about as smart or stupid as the next guy, but I believe "an ant can eat a bale of hay."

The job market was very limited for ex-fighter pilots. The National Guard offered an opportunity to make some money, and in 1946 I joined the California National Guard. The guard armory was nearby—another blessing. The unit at the armory was an Engineer Combat Group, so like many guardsmen, I transferred from the Air Corps (which was still part of the Army at this time) and became an engineer officer. I enjoyed the involvement, and my guard experience kept me in good stead later.

Civilian life was full of frustration for me. The service had been filled with young men of integrity, but integrity was a quality totally lacking in the civilian populace. Military relationships were strong and meaningful. One could rely explicitly on the character and strengths of one's military associates in all matters. Not so with my civilian associates. I didn't enjoy civilian life.

I would have loved to have been a farmer, perhaps raising grapes or poultry, but there was no possibility of that. I didn't have the money, and I really didn't try to find it. My wife would hear no part of farming. As I matured, I realized that my occupation had to be of my own choosing and that my wife and children had to go with my choice, or not at all, particularly if my choice provided them with all their needs and a substantial quantity of their desires.

My little world had changed drastically during the four years that I'd been gone. Many of those changes were not progressive. I found that having a bachelor's degree and appropriate credentials did not provide an opportunity for me as a Negro male to teach school. The teaching field had opened up somewhat during the war for Negro women, but the men were left out of it.

I was thoroughly disgusted. One would have thought that almost five years of honorable wartime military service would at least afford a qualified veteran a fighting chance. I felt perhaps it would have provided something that resembled equality. It wasn't there.

In desperation, I tried to make a living in many ways, including joining the local police force. I was number one in my class at the police academy, but then I was taken out of the class to work vice in the black ghetto just taking shape. I was assigned to "busting" prostitutes and bookies. I was not good at it. I felt that if a "John" was deprived enough to lay a prostitute or to bet his money with a bookie incident to a horse race at a remote track, that was his privilege. By golly, he should lose his money. But in my mind, booking horses and selling bodies were something less than crimes, especially when I was ordered to make arrests only when the perpetrators had not paid off. I was so lacking in sophistication that I was unable to handle myself in the circumstances of my work.

One night I arrested my next-door neighbor on charges of assault with intent to do grievous bodily injury upon his wife. I made the arrest at the demand of his wife, who had been seriously and brutally battered. I delivered the arrested neighbor to the police station in my car. Before I could complete the voluminous forms incident to the arrest, the wife had bailed her loving husband out and returned home. I had made an enemy of my neighbor. I resented the outcome of that affair, because more than most things in life, I had a towering need to attend to my own business and leave everyone else's business strictly alone. A police officer, however, must be alert to everything within his sight. I was not happy being a policeman.

Eventually, I came to the realization that civilian life was not worthy of my efforts or concerns, and I applied for a return to military service. There were, however, a few obstacles. The National Military Establishment had been formed. In 1947, the Air Force became autonomous, and I was in the Army National Guard. Irrespective of the problems of entering the service through the Army and then transferring to the Air Force—an eighteen-month process—I opted for it. Even going back into the Brown Shoe Jim Crow Army was preferable to what I'd seen on the streets.

I went back on active duty in the Army in August 1948 and was assigned as a platoon leader in the 74th Engineer Battalion at Fort Campbell, Kentucky. I had become an engineer officer, which was acceptable, but I really wanted to be a fighter pilot again. I started the long process of transferring from the Army to the Air Force, but it was all in vain.

The orders transferring me to the Air Force didn't reach me until eighteen months later in Korea in late December 1950, when the 25th Infantry Division was dug in on the south bank of the Imjin River awaiting a Chinese attack. We were building culverts along the main supply route. The assistant division commander, a general, had my orders with him, and he stopped to talk for a few minutes.

He said, "Well, Hot Shot, I've got some good news and some bad news. Which would you like first?"

"The good news, sir."

"The good news is that your transfer to the Air Force is authorized—by these orders." He showed them to me.

Then came the bad news, "But we can't let you go at this time. We don't have a replacement for you. I know you understand. I could make a joke about it, but this isn't a funny time."

"No, sir."

The Army of Occupation

January 1950–10 July 1950,
Gifu, Japan

After a year and a half at Fort Campbell, I was reassigned on 1 January 1950 to the U.S. Army of Occupation in Japan. This was inevitable. After the end of World War II and the surrender of Japan, the U.S. Army occupied the Japanese islands. Almost one-third of the U.S. Army's fighting forces were stationed in the Pacific theater. The 7th, 24th, and 25th Infantry divisions, and the 1st Cavalry Division (actually infantry) were in Japan. The 29th Regimental Combat Team was in Hawaii. All of the divisions were filled with new replacements and were in a poor state of combat readiness. For economic reasons, and with only one exception, all of the regiments had only two of their three infantry battalions, and the artillery battalions also were short one of their firing batteries.

The 25th Infantry Division, with which I would serve in Korea, included the 24th, 27th, and 35th Infantry regiments. The division, located on Honshu in the middle of the Japanese islands, was spread out over several smaller posts, and spent its time on occupation duties, with little regard for readiness for war. It was typical of Army organizations in Japan at the time.

Military duty in Japan as part of the U.S. Army of Occupation was comfortable and leisurely. Good living was the order of the

41

day. Occupation meant occupying the best of Japanese commercial, residential, and recreational facilities, holding a glass in one hand and a Japanese girlfriend, or *moosimae,* in the other, and seeing how much food and drink one could indulge in and how much hell one could raise. Single soldiers concentrated on the good life with lovely Japanese girls, and married soldiers concentrated on opulent living with families, if they were present, and female servants, who were omnipresent. The only fighting that U.S. soldiers engaged in was negotiating a price for a single night's favor, for professional services on a month-by-month basis, or for Noritake china and Mikimoto pearls.

Eighth Army and the Supreme Headquarters gloried under the clouds cast by two atomic blasts. A future war was impossible; an immediate war, unthinkable. Training was conducted accordingly. It was slipshod and routine—not a serious or focused professional activity. The senior officers were there essentially to get their tickets punched for promotion to higher rank or pass the time until retirement. Their troops, many of whom were hangers-on from World War II, felt that the American people, and certainly their former enemies, owed them a good living. Japanese occupation duty was precisely what they were entitled to—a good deal.

The long-established military "pecking order," temporarily relaxed during World War II when men such as Audie Murphy showed what a real soldier could do, was reestablished rigidly. It was the Regular Army up top: West Pointers by permanent rank or class first; and other Regulars next, from The Citadel, VMI, Texas A&M, or honor graduates of ROTC. The reservists, no matter how well qualified or capable, were at the bottom. There was a strong, very strong, propensity for protecting Regular officers regardless of professional weaknesses or personal failings, even at the expense of "the good of the service."

A large number of lower-ranking enlisted men were products of the 1948 draft. They loved their fat, tomcatting life and reenlisted in overwhelming numbers. Any U.S. private could afford to share his bed and board with a native lady. The Sears Roebuck Catalog provided mail-order attractions necessary for a happy relationship otherwise denied to original raw goods suppliers:

silk stockings, silk underwear and lingerie, silk blouses. If living was easy, cohabitation was smoother.

Perfunctory training meant an occasional spell of maneuvering at the Gotemba Training Area beneath the majesty of Mount Fujiyama. Training was not designed (nor apparently intended) to maintain or even to create a "fighting" Army. Night fighting, cold-weather operations, and counterguerilla tactics were not only not emphasized, they were not even considered.

The Army of Occupation was in bad shape. The general physical condition of the troops was poor, morale was low, and the general level of intelligence was reduced. Many who stayed in the service during peacetime, or who had been drafted in 1948, did not have high IQ scores. Serious drug problems had begun to be manifested but were not always discovered by those who themselves were becoming addicted. Heroin and alcohol ran rampant through veins just as venereal diseases ran rampant through the ranks.

The black market was a significant factor economically. Cigarettes, sugar, coffee, and even tea were among the items that, being scarce, commanded exceedingly high prices. Money itself was valuable beyond its actual denomination. Military scrip was very much in demand, and real greenbacks sold at extraordinary premiums. Many, many soldiers routinely (but illegally) supplemented their pay through transactions, which they hardly bothered to hide, on the money market. What most of them considered the prevailing rate resulted ultimately in a higher price than America could ever afford to pay—a gradual weakening of the moral fiber of the Army.

The all-pervading attitude was: occupation may not last forever; get yours whenever and however you can.

Racial segregation continued to flourish in the Army. Sure, President Truman—a World War I–vintage artillery battery ex-commanding officer (CO)—had issued an executive order in 1948 that banned segregation. But the president's order was not followed, and he could not see all the way from Washington, D.C., what continued to take place in the Far East.

Of the four black regiments that had been established immediately following the Civil War, only one remained: the 24th Infantry Regiment. Stationed in Japan as part of the 25th Infantry Division, the 24th was the only regiment in Japan with its full complement of three battalions. In the 25th Infantry Division, the 159th Field Artillery Battalion and the 77th Engineer Combat Company were also segregated black units. There were also some segregated engineer construction battalions on Okinawa and Japan, including the one to which I was assigned initially. In these segregated units, the enlisted personnel were black, and almost all of the officers were white. The few black officers were company grade—lieutenants and a few captains. The regimental commander and staff, all of the battalion commanders, and most of the company commanders were white.

It was still a Jim Crow Army. Segregation was practiced routinely and administered religiously. Black infantrymen and black soldiers of any branch were treated discourteously in military life and mistreated brutally in military courts. Negro soldiers existed to serve under white officers. Their lot was to be subservient while serving whites of whatever rank, grade, or status and to be constantly derided before those who, being yellow, were after all only off-white. The Japanese were accustomed to feeling racially superior to the Koreans and other Asian people. Now they were being conditioned by the Caucasian majority to mistreat, cheat, and even to hate the Negro and other minorities. Insofar as possible male Negro soldiers were discouraged from having intimate relationships with Japanese females.

Bigotry toward blacks was a manifestation of the same mindless mentality of white racial superiority that had already contributed to a shameful disaster on the Asiatic mainland when the Chinese Communists had defeated the American-supported government. It was rapidly creating serious problems later to be manifested on at least two major island nations—Japan and the Philippines. Most Americans considered all Asians—Japanese, Chinese, Koreans, Filipinos, and the rest—to be "gooks" and openly referred to them as "gooks." The Asians were not respected as people and polities. Certainly they were disregarded as military powers. They had, after all, all been defeated in our time. Only the Russians enjoyed a measure of respect among American military leaders who, mistakenly, continued to regard the Soviet Union as a monolithic Caucasian nation.

Certainly it was an Army not ready at all for what was about to happen.

The General and Me, 1 May 1950, Gotemba, Japan

I was serving in the 538th Engineer Service Battalion, comprising black troops and mostly white, mostly prejudiced officers. I was not assigned to an established position; I just defended enlisted men at the numerous and frequent courts martial on charges of drunk and disorderly, disrespect, absent without leave (AWOL), desertion, larceny, and conduct unbecoming. I was no lawyer. I was an engineer officer—a fighting man. Out of place. Out of time.

Frustrated, I discussed the matter with the battalion commander. He advised me, "Ah run this battalion in accawdance with the policy of the Depahtment of the Ahmy and rules of the American people. You don't like it? Take a jeep. Go down to Eighth Army Headquarters. Tell the G-1 to move ya. Ah didn't want you or no other nigra offisahs heah in the fust place."

"Yes, sir." I saluted and left his office.

I drove the eighteen miles to Eighth Army Headquarters and asked to see the G-1—the personnel officer. Not some personnel flunky, but the big gun himself. I was received by the G-1, a full colonel, with great concern and respect.

The story I told the G-1 was no secret. He had heard it before, and for sure he had heard the white side of the story. In any case, he heard me out and picked a sheet of paper from the stack in his in-box.

"Read this, Bussey," he said as he extended the paper to me. He reached for the telephone with his other hand, dialed, and said, "Send me the file on 1st Lt. Charles M. Bussey immediately."

The G-1 took a long look at me and said, "General Wilson is assistant division commander of the 25th Infantry Division. He's at Gotemba, at the base of Mount Fuji. The maneuver area there is his special preserve, and his job is training. He has the separate engineer company there to maintain the maneuver area. Right now it's commanded by a competent infantry officer, but the General needs a strong, very strong, engineer to command the company. I think you are the man.

"I caution you, the General is tough, smart, fair, mean, and dedicated. In order to survive with him, you must be the same. And, lest I forget, he has a Bailey Bridge, which he somehow had sent up from the Philippines. He's obsessed with having it erected across an arroyo in the training area. Do you know the Bailey Bridge?"

I lied, positively. "Yes, sir. I've spent many training hours on Baileys."

Actually, I'd never seen a Bailey Bridge, except in pictures. But I knew that I'd seen a copy of the *Bailey Bridge Manual* in the battalion library—*TM 5–277*, or maybe it was a field manual (FM). Either way, it was going to be my road map.

The G-1 said, "This is not a key to integration of Negroes in the service. If it were in my power, I'd end segregation within the hour. As you well know, having been a fighter pilot in Ben Davis's Group—incidentally, we were classmates at the academy—he has capitalized on the record of his fighter group during the Big War. He made the Air Force take note of the record and has influenced integration of the personnel of his composite wing into the total Air Force. Maybe you'll never have the opportunity Ben Davis had, but you can help establish the credibility of Negro officers, which frankly is not strong at the moment for many reasons, none of which are the fault of the Negro officers. Go with it, Bussey, and good luck! Look me up in six months."

I stood tall, saluted, and said, "Thanks a million, sir."

"You're entirely welcome, Bussey. I hope I'm doing you a favor."

Well, I waited around downstairs for copies of my reassignment orders. I clutched them in my hand all the way back to my miserable battalion. The reporting date was one day hence, so I dropped a copy at the adjutant's office, went to the library, then to my quarters, packed, signed out, and left that lousy situation. No goodbyes. No regrets.

The next day, 1 May 1950, I reported to the Maneuver Area Headquarters. Brig. Gen. Vennard Wilson came out of his office to meet me. He offered me a seat alongside an ornate coffee table and seated himself opposite me. He began, "The G-1 up at Army told me he was sending you down. He spoke highly of you; hope you can live up to your billing. I want you to know that you are on trial! I'll watch you closely. It will take a tall man to do what I want here. Not just a good man, but a damned good man. I hope you're it. Do you know the Bailey Bridge?"

"Yes, sir," I answered, "I've worked all the standard configurations and some nonstandard erections as well. Nights, days, all weather."

"Good, Bussey. This is Monday. I want that bridge in place at 1300 hours on Thursday. I want a ribbon-cutting ceremony at that time. Come. I'll show you the bridge site.

"Miss Morton, have the jeep brought around. Notify my aide."

We talked while we waited for the jeep about troops, weather, barbed wire, mines, and the overfull sewage tanks in the barracks latrines. The general introduced me to his aide. We saddled up and hightailed toward the bridge site. On the far side of the arroyo there was a road about fifty feet from the bank running parallel to the arroyo.

The general wanted a bridge that was possible, but hard. Connecting the bridge to the road would be difficult because the road was so close to the bridge abutment on the bank. It would require a tight turn. But I knew I could handle it, and I told him so.

He came back to me. "The division engineer says it can't be done. What makes you think you can do it?"

I responded, "Trust me, General."

"I'm testing you, Lieutenant."

I smiled a little, always looking him in the eye. He was an intimidator, but I had his number, and I knew that once I passed his test, I'd be nine feet tall. I had some advantages over the textbook engineers. I had imagination. I believed that an ant could eat a bale of hay. I knew that David slew Goliath with a small, round stone. I had plenty of stones.

I completed my sketch and my notes, and we saddled up for Maneuver Area Headquarters. Surprisingly, General Wilson invited me into his office again, and after he sat, I did also.

He asked, "Are you as good as you infer?"

"Yes, sir."

"Well, a lieutenant was commanding your company at one time. He attended a briefing. I asked him some engineer questions, but he didn't know any answers, so I chewed his butt. He came apart at the seams. Had to get the medics for him. He's still in the hospital. What will you do if I chew you up into small chunks?"

"The General will never have a requirement for chewing me. I'll always have the answers and always the performance."

"Damn. I hope you're that good."

He excused me, and I went to work. I called a meeting of the commissioned officers and the senior noncommissioned officers. I let them all know that I was a "can-do" guy, and that was the way it was going to be. I addressed my two platoon leaders and gave my orders: "Lieutenant Peoples, contact the town mayor. Tell him I want the sewage removed from the latrines within twenty-four hours. No cash transaction. No politics. Get a receipt for the estimated gallonage.

"Lieutenant Benefield, I want to meet you and the Field First Sergeant at the pile of rusting Bailey Bridge members in thirty minutes." That gave me time to change into field gear. I continued, "First Sergeant, we'll have a retreat formation at 1700 hours. I will address the troops.

"That is all for now."

Lieutenant Benefield, Master Sergeant Walton, and I met at the bridge storage site and discussed the erection of the bridge. I could talk a helluva show, because I'd studied the manual for two days. I sounded like an expert. I knew the weights of the members, and team compositions, and other particulars.

The problem with the bridge was that it had been placed over a gorge in the Philippines, and due to a misalignment of the abutments, the bridge had warped under heavy traffic. It was twisted out of shape. That's why the division engineer said it couldn't be erected. Now was the time to eat that "bale of hay."

We went out to the bridge site and surveyed it from both banks. We had a problem. The span called for single-double trusses to carry the loads the general prescribed, that is, enough capacity to carry his tanks. That part wasn't difficult, but what to do about that awkward warpage? Over that span, the south end of the bridge would be forty inches too high when the north end was tied down.

Simple! Before erection we would dig twenty feet down and about thirty feet in from the abutment. We'd install a deadman (heavy metal object) as an anchor, tie some cables to it, fill the holes above the deadman, and winch the cable tight enough to pull the south end of the bridge down to level spans. There was a possibility that the bridge might rise out of level on the other bank, kitty-corner from the original deadman, so we'd install another deadman on the other bank to take care of that.

There was plenty of heavy equipment available, so work began immediately on the abutments and the excavations for the deadmen. We also began widening the existing road away from the arroyo, so that vehicles could turn in either direction coming on or off the bridge.

I met the troops and gave a pep talk about how good they were going to be. I think I impressed them with my sincerity. I'd watched many commanders, and I tried to assimilate their best habits. I had the feeling that there was much to do as rapidly as possible. I wanted the company to be combat ready. I had a foreboding that my survival and theirs (the troops') were completely intertwined.

I personally supervised all aspects of the bridge erection. It went like clockwork. We sweated all day Tuesday and all day Wednesday. At 1600 hours on Wednesday, I called General Wilson. "Sir, your bridge is complete. We can accept traffic as of 1600 today."

No sound for a moment. Then, "I'll be right there."

General Wilson arrived at the scene and dismounted from his jeep to inspect the near-shore abutment; then he walked across the bridge with pride showing in every step. The general was extremely happy with his bridge. He looked at the cables holding down the warped members. He took a long, long look at me and matter-of-factly stated, "Test completed. You're on my team. Keep it up."

I didn't know it until much later, but he called the division engineer, Lt. Col. Wyeth Rivers, and ordered him up to the ribbon-cutting ceremony the following day. I'd made a ton of points with General Wilson, but I'd showed up the division engineer, who was also the engineer battalion commander, and who was unimaginative and inept. I made an enemy who would make it rough for me as time went by. Colonel Rivers, the moment he saw that bridge, had a hard-on for me at least 3 feet long.

But I was a hero for the moment. I gave all the credit to my troops at the ceremony. In all, I was a winner.

General Wilson and I had many encounters after that. When we moved to Korea, he frequently stopped by at chow time because, according to him, I had the best mess in the division, and he'd tried them all. He had stomach trouble, but our food pleased him a lot. I could do no wrong in his sight. I respected him, and he respected me. It was simple. We were both performance oriented.

Also in Korea, he bypassed the intermediate headquarters and promoted me to captain on my thirtieth day in country, my first day of eligibility. General Wilson personally brought the orders to me, along with a set of double bars he scrounged from some rear-echelon captain in his headquarters.

77th Engineer Combat Company, 26 May 1950, Gifu, Japan

There are times in one's life when specific desires are overwhelming—driving. And so it was with me in Japan in 1950. I had to be a company commander. Not the commander of a service company or a foot-slogging infantry company—I wanted to be the boss of a combat engineer outfit. It fit my personality. It fit my person. The work was the most stimulating of any in an infantry division. The men had many, many skills. They were builders, sappers, and bridgers. They were builders of roads, structures, barriers, and minefields. They were experts at demolitions and water supply. And when necessary, they were first-class fighting men. They were better than infantry soldiers, and they loved to prove it. At some place and time I had been told not to wish too hard for anything because I might acquire it, and so it happened.

It was a time of life when I had the maturity and the physical, mental, and emotional strength necessary to command a company of combat engineers. When the opportunity came for me to assume command of the 77th Engineer Combat Company (ECC), I reveled in it. I worked at it from sixteen to twenty hours a day. Fortunately, it was when I was overseas in Japan, and fortunately, my family had not joined me. I was free to work all the hours I needed or wanted, and I did. There was no better job for a workaholic. There was a strong training requirement. There were literally tons of specialized tools, equipment, and weapons to maintain, including heavy vehicles, air compressors, gauges, test equipment, water purification sets, and on and on. But the biggest demand on my time and attention came from the men. The men had problems of all kinds, and those who didn't have problems usually generated some.

The 77th Engineer Combat Company was a separate all-black company assigned to the 25th Infantry Division to provide black engineer support for the black 24th Infantry Regiment. It was not a part of the white 65th Engineer Battalion, which provided engineer support for the rest of the division. The 77th Engineer Combat Company had an authorized strength of 5 officers and 153 enlisted men, but most of the time it had well over 200 troops. This was because almost all black combat engineers in the Pacific theater were assigned to the 77th.

The 77th Engineer Combat Company was subdivided into three combat platoons and a headquarters platoon. The headquarters platoon took care of administration, maintenance, and supply, and provided additional equipment to back up the combat platoons. The combat platoons normally worked in support of the three battalions of the 24th Infantry Regiment. The three combat platoon leaders were the key officers to provide engineer support to the regiment. The company executive officer was my second-in-command and took care of all of the administration and support. The company First Sergeant was the top enlisted leader and my constant advisor and helper.

The role of the 77th Engineer Combat Company in combat would be assisting the movement of our troops and impeding the movement of the enemy troops. Our tasks would include building roads, timber-trestle and Bailey bridges, floating bridges and ferries, and other structures; building obstacles, placing barbed wire, and blowing up bridges and buildings; and placing our mines and digging up and destroying enemy mines. To do this work the company had dump trucks, bulldozers, air compressors, other heavy engineer equipment, and hand tools. We could do a lot of different things well.

In addition we had the capability to reorganize and fight as infantry—a capability of which we were justly proud. Fighting as infantry would become necessary frequently in Korea. We had pistols, carbines, M-1 rifles, Browning automatic rifles (BARs), and .30 caliber and .50 caliber machine guns, for our own defense and for our infantry role. Although we weren't authorized to have them, we would also eventually have a pair of 81mm mortars and men who were expert in their use.

The usual relationship between the 77th Engineer Combat Company and the 24th Infantry Regiment was one of direct support. That meant that I, as the engineer company commander, took missions directly from the 24th Regimental Commander and staff but relied on the 65th Engineer Battalion for administrative and logistical support. When fighting as infantry, the 77th Engineer Company usually was attached to the 24th Infantry Regiment, which meant that all missions and support came from the regiment. In reality the 77th ECC was a permanent member of the all-black 24th Regimental Combat Team (RCT), which comprised the 24th Infantry Regiment and the 159th Field Artillery Battalion as well as the 77th. In combat, the all-black 24th RCT habitually operated together as a combined-arms team.

When I had assumed command of the 77th in Japan on 1

May 1950, the company was working at the Gotemba Training Area on Honshu. It had been at Gotemba for several months performing engineer work to keep the training area in good shape and to support training activities. This was good duty, and our time was taken up fully doing the work and coping with the soldiers. We left Gotemba for our permanent station on 26 May 1950.

The permanent home of the company was at Gifu. Our barracks were in the medieval Gifu castle. It was built of dark grey stones, which for the most part had been fitted meticulously together without mortar. There was a moat complete with alligators, and on warm afternoons an occasional python would crawl up to the parapets to sun himself. The castle was made to keep people out, but in our time it served equally well to keep people in. The ancient stables served as our motor pool, and the courtyard was our drill field. In all we fared well in the buildings, which had been designed for soldiers of a bygone era.

It was a good life. Little did we know that in just four or five weeks we would be in heavy combat.

The Officers

Attrition is always at work in military units. Death, wounds, illness, injuries, leave, and transfers impinge upon unit strength from day to day. The personnel pipeline is established to keep new people—soldiers of all grades—always on the way to combat units. It is always feast or famine. Either more good officers and men than you'd need, or pitifully short of those "granite blocks" and "keystones." Yet, it is the troops that do the work.

After the bridge-building episode had confirmed my command, I took stock of the officers and men I had inherited in the 77th. I was blessed throughout my tour of duty with the company in having wonderful officers to advise me and to carry out the duties we had as a unit. Every man in an organization must pull his weight, and every man did. The crew I had on board initially was first class, and I got some fine replacements later on in Korea.

When I took over the company, I had just two officers, Lieuten-

ant Benefield and Lieutenant Peoples. Lt. William Benefield led
one of the combat platoons. He was a Kansan, and a good man
to have on your side in a footrace or a fistfight. He was a superb
athlete, strong and aggressive. Although short in stature, he acted
like a giant. He played fine poker. He was a fine citizen, husband,
father of a daughter and two sons, and a good friend. He knew
his work well, having done several years as an enlisted man. A
tower of strength.

Lt. Hazael Peoples, also a midwesterner, led another combat
platoon. He was an ordnance officer, a good officer at what he
knew: motors and supply. He was a scrounger, without whom
we would not have been nearly as effective. I didn't understand
or fully appreciate him at the time; he wasn't aggressive enough
to suit me. Later on, there were at least two instances when he
didn't demonstrate the hard fiber I felt was absolutely essential
in the presence of our enlisted men. I couldn't handle his lack
of aggressiveness well at the time. Peoples stayed with the 77th
during the entire time I was in command.

When we moved back to permanent quarters in Gifu in May,
Lt. Chester J. Lenon, who had been running the post exchange
at the Gotemba Training Area, joined the company as a combat
platoon leader. Like Benefield, Chet was from Kansas, and the
two men became fast friends. Lenon was tall and slim, with bronze-
colored skin and a hint of freckles. He was strong and resourceful—
equal to the difficult circumstances in which he found himself
later. Chet Lenon was a man of impeccable manners and a soft
voice, totally out of character with the strength he showed in all
his endeavors. He was an asset to any organization or endeavor—
a giant.

Lt. James Wilson was also assigned to the company but was
away on temporary duty most of the time we were in Japan. He
rejoined the company just before we went to Korea and served
as a combat platoon leader throughout my tenure. Jim Wilson
was quiet and efficient. He was a very decent man, and I reflected
that society needed men like him to teach in schools, run banks,
and run society itself. It was a waste for a man like him to spend
his time fighting farmers halfway around the world from home.
Jim was wounded and won the Silver Star for his service in Korea.

The First Sergeant

Roscoe Dudley was the company First Sergeant. He did it all. Theoretically he commanded our rear echelon, but he was always a part of the action. In every respect he was the First Soldier. He was a quiet, highly perceptive man; positive, strong, every inch and pound a soldier. Deadly. Resolute. He won a Silver Star for his valor defending the Pusan perimeter. I should have somehow found the time and opportunity to have had him decorated for meritorious service as well.

When I took over the company, Dudley was a sergeant first class (SFC) in the platoons, and there were six master sergeants in the company. I interviewed each of them, and each had a cogent reason why he didn't want the job of First Sergeant. The First Sergeant's job is tough anywhere, but in that overstrength unit it was a nightmare. I talked to each of the officers, and each recommended Dudley despite his being junior in grade. I had an in-depth interview with SFC Dudley. He was the man. I talked again with my six master sergeants, and each expressed a willingness to work under Dudley, whatever that meant. So he got the job.

First Sergeant Dudley had an immediate impact. In Gifu General Wilson had advised me that my unit had the highest rate of venereal disease (VD) of any company-size unit in the Pacific theater, and that my success and tenure was predicated upon how effectively I reduced that VD rate. I put that monkey on the First Sergeant's back. Unfair, but one of my smarter moves.

He made a pronouncement at retreat formation on that first long day: "The next and every son of a bitch who turns up with a dose of clap, chancres, chancroid, or any other type of VD, I will stomp damn near to death. I will put a stop to your screwing for a while. Then I'm going to write to your wife or your mother or whatever woman whose name appears on your Form 20. I will tell that woman what a sorry disgrace of a man she sent to the U.S. Army. You've been told. Fall out!"

Sick call was at 0700 hours. My office was next to Dudley's and I was at my desk fighting the paper war. Through the wall I began to hear furniture being violently rearranged. Body blows, grunts, moans, epithets. I felt that I should intervene, but somehow I didn't. There are some things better not to know. It ran its course shortly. I didn't condone fights among the troops, but there are times when discretion is more valuable than policy. When it was over and quiet, I went to the First Sergeant's office and jumped him about his miscreancy. He sort of apologized and told me it was Sydney Thomas with his fourth dose of gonorrhea in the past six months. Dudley also said that it wouldn't happen again—neither the beating nor the clap. Corporal Harvey came in, and I left after a few more words. Harvey's typewriter became rapidly alive.

Soon, Dudley whistled for work call and announced the day's activities. When it was done, he called Private First Class (PFC) Thomas, "Front and center," and announced: "Men, yesterday I told you that the next man who disgraced our company with a case of VD I was going to whip his ass. Thomas here brought us a dose and I stomped all over him this morning."

Thomas stood there with a hang-dog expression, several knots on his forehead, lips busted, one ear torn down and greatly impaired vision in both eyes, a sorry sight. A spectacle. Dudley reiterated his promise and presented a letter to Thomas with instructions to place the letter, to Thomas's wife, in the company mailbox.

I observed the formation from my office. One month later in the same office, General Wilson visited me and presented me a letter of commendation for having reduced the VD rate to zero.

The First Sergeant got things done. A tall, tall man.

The Troops

There were dozens of outstanding enlisted men in our company, but I cannot include them all. I will mention some who were particularly close to me.

The position of field First Sergeant is seldom found in the official tables of organization and equipment, but in many engineer units, a field First Sergeant was appointed. The duties of the field First Sergeant are to help the platoon leaders and platoon sergeants organize and supervise the work of the troops on construction and engineering projects. The field First Sergeant also provides technical advice on how to do the work. Master Sgt. Andrew F. Walton was my field First Sergeant. He was probably the oldest man in the 77th, and he was the most respected. He was a big man in stature and in substance. His extensive knowledge of military engineering made him sought after on all of our field projects, and his extensive knowledge of life in general made him sought after for counsel on personal problems. I had considered him for the position of First Sergeant, but his preference was to work in the field. He was a mentor to the NCOs and a surrogate father to the younger troops. The unit's successes were based largely upon the skills and knowledge of our "Field First."

Sergeant First Class Lamont was skinny and tough; he never slept. A perfectionist. Our mess sergeant. His was a tight ship. There was never a moment when there was not fresh coffee and never a time when any man couldn't get a good meal. I liked it that way, and Lamont and I got along famously. When we were in Korea, in addition to preparing the poor Army chow well, he had a detail out scrounging for garlic, peppers, onions, and other seasonings and vegetables left behind by the refugees who had departed their homes and gardens in the face of friendly or hostile armies. There was no better mess in the division.

I didn't know until deep winter, as we came back off the rout in North Korea, that Lamont was also an accomplished vintner. He had made and stored numerous five-gallon crocks of raisin jack and prune, apricot, peach, and apple booze. Some of it he had even distilled. His output depended upon how much leisure time we had in different bivouacs as we moved northward. At −28°F to −30°F, when we were living like badgers, totally exposed to the weather without tentage and without arctic foot gear, the wine and raisin jack, judiciously dispensed, was a boon to us all. SFC Lamont was a definite and distinct asset to our unit. No one was more important.

I remember my jeep driver, Pinkney, best. He was always ready. He had a lot of guts. He looked out for me. He kept some clean clothes and shaving gear in the jeep. When I was stuck at one of the interminable meetings at higher headquarters, he would go into one of the vacant farmhouses along the roadside, build a fire, and heat some water for my infrequent baths, which were the sole luxury of my life. He was a good man to have along. We were an effective combat team. We could "unass" that jeep and go instantly into a firefight without a word being spoken. Like me, he'd grown up in the fields and ghettos. We were survivors. No one had to draw pictures or write stories for us to understand the rules of engagement or nature of life on the killing floor. It was always "green and go."

Of course, it was illegal to have an enlisted man take care of an officer's personal requirements. But without a little help I couldn't have done what was really required of me. Some clean clothes from the laundry and bath unit when I didn't have time to go there was wonderful. Some hot water for a shave and bath, when it was convenient along the main supply route, was my life's highest reward. Pinkney did these things for me without my ever mentioning or suggesting that he do so. I was grateful as well as needful.

There were numerous other noncommissioned officers and enlisted men who singularly or collectively contributed so very much. I had a profound love and respect for them: Master Sergeants Green, Wilkes, Knight, and Stallworth; Sergeants Walker, Davis, Jackson, Woods, Lee, and Brown; and many others. There was Corporal Fields and his sparring partner, Private First Class Van Ness, and Robert Semedo. American society owes them much.

Private Jack Beavers, 26 May 1950, Gifu, Japan

Jack Beavers wasn't a bad young man, but he was one of those who was contrary to authority. He was contentious. He always fought the problem.

Pvt. Jack Beavers had joined us at Gotemba, at the foot of Mount Fuji, when we were preparing to displace back to Gifu. The air around camp was charged because the troops were going home, and home always means renewal of relationships with wives, girlfriends, kids—being whole again. In due time we went home after securing the maneuver area.

Once we were back at the castle, we settled down to a routine, if you call a soldier's life routine, with its public toilets and showers. I was looking forward to some basic-type training. Our mission at the maneuver area was such that we did a lot of pioneer work, but we became very sloppy in basic soldiering. On the train ride going home, I worked out the schedule of activities for the ensuing months.

I'd had no problem with Jack Beavers, but I knew it was on the way. When you are a troop commander, you must on occasion assert yourself. It is mandatory that you be ready to support your troops, and that they know it. And sometimes you must discipline one of the troops a little to guarantee that everyone knows who is boss. Being new to the unit, I was waiting for an opportunity to be hardnosed.

Jack gave me the opportunity to be tough. I received a letter from a Mrs. Beavers, addressed to the commanding officer. It read as follows:

Dere Sir,

My son Jack Beavers is in your Company. Jack is my boy. I got 2 others and a girl. My girl is 13 and she is "big." My man got rumatick fever and is in bed. I do laundry and such—but can't quite make it. We nede ten dollars more a month. Am desperit. My boy don't rite no more. Can you talk to him. I nede help.

Thank you,
Jenny Beavers

I reflected upon the letter. Over the course of time a CO receives many such letters from families, girl friends, creditors, whomever. So I called Jack in and had him read the letter.

When he was through reading, I asked, "Is this letter actually from your mother?"

"Yes, sir, this is from my mother."

"Do the conditions set forth in the letter actually exist?"

"Yes, sir, things are tough at home. It's always been bad in

Louisiana, but since Dad's been down from the fever, it's still worse. Momma can't quite make it all happen."

"Well, can you send her the ten dollars per month that she requests?"

"No, sir, I can't spare it."

I was flabbergasted. I asked, "Why? You earn ninety-eight dollars a month. Quarters, clothing, and rations are provided for you. Surely, you can spare ten dollars."

"No, sir."

"Well, Beavers, I find that hard to understand. Did your parents abuse you as a child?"

"No, sir, they did the best they could. They loved me and did for me."

"Are you telling me that you refuse to help a mother who was good to you, who worked and sacrificed for you, a mother who needs one-tenth of your income in order to provide for the whole family?"

Jack responded, "Well, sir, you see, I'm setting up a house with this girl, and she needs a lot of things—pots and pans, radio, tatami, and all those things—and we're in love, and there just ain't no extra money. I'm sorry, but there just ain't no extra money."

I felt my hackles rising, and though family affairs, per se, are no concern of the Army, I was into this family's business. I remembered the struggle my mom had, even with total cooperation from all parties. I was incensed, and a man of Jack's stature and status could not deal with me under the condition I was building up to.

"Well, Private Beavers, I think you are a hunk of scum, an animal that puts his biology above the welfare of his family. I will crush you like the beetle that you are. I will not pay you until you decide that you can send some money home. I recognize that bringing you into line with the human race is not necessarily a part of my military duty, but that's how it is. I'm going to chew you up in small bites."

"Well, sir, you can't do this to me. I want to go to the IG. I have to have my money. I do my duty. Don't get into much trouble. I got a right to spend my money as I choose, sir."

"Very well, Private Beavers. Tell the First Sergeant that I want you driven down to see the IG immediately. Also tell him to send your Off-Duty Pass in to me. You will have no more passes until we have negotiated the disposition of your funds. Tell that to the IG also."

"Sir, I got a right to my pass. I do my soldiering."

"You are wrong, Private Beavers. A pass is a privilege, not a right, and you just lost your privilege. Understand that? Also understand that the Inspector General cannot—will not—change my mind. I'm going to crush you, as I said earlier. But you do have a right to see the IG. Move it."

Private Beavers made his trip to the Inspector General (IG). He had a good case. He garnered some sympathy, which materialized in the form of a hardnosed infantry lieutenant colonel whose mission, among other things, was to guarantee that soldiers were not abused and that their rights were maintained.

Lieutenant Colonel Hardesty came up to intimidate me by force of rank, which was considerable, and precedent, which was also on his side. But as the morning drifted along, Colonel Hardesty and I developed a fine rapport. He read the letter from Mrs. Beavers, and he agreed with me in principle, but he disagreed in practice. We drank a lot of coffee, and I introduced him to the practice of putting sharp cheddar slices into the coffee cup. It was great. We talked about World War II, and I filled him in on the techniques of dive bombing and all those things that nonfliers wonder about. He left without any threats and without any promises. He just left, and I felt that, with discretion, I could keep my foot in Beavers's behind. And I did.

I explained the situation to the First Sergeant within earshot of a couple of the troops, and the word was out. And ridicule set in, and that was part of the treatment—Beavers's and mine.

Well, payday came, and I had sent Beavers on a detail to the bridge-training site. I paid the other team members before they left. Beavers didn't get paid, and he hadn't slept with his newfound love since our initial confrontation. Rumor had it that someone else was solving his girlfriend's puzzles. The ridicule was relentless, and Beavers came in to plead with me. He knew that on the tenth of the month there was a supplemental payroll, which could and should provide a soldier with pay that was due. But Beavers was off on special duty when the supplemental pay became available. Beavers wanted to go to the IG and I gave him access to the telephone. He was told to call back if he wasn't paid by next payday. That gave me about twenty days for the pressure to build a little. My reputation for being tough and not to be messed with was well established, which made the job a little easier.

About 29 May, Beavers asked permission to see me, and I saw him in the office. Beavers was hurting—no liberty, no girlfriend, no money. He said in a wheedling, whining manner, "Sir, I'm ready to send the ten dollars a month home, starting next month."

I said, "Well, I see it otherwise; you don't need the money any longer. Without liberty and money, the girlfriend vanished, but your mom and family still need money badly. So you take the ten dollars and send the rest home."

Jack Beavers exploded into sobs, and asked if he could be excused. It was okay with me.

On payday he came to see me right after reveille. "Sir, I'm ready to send the money home. I'm glad you opened up my eyes. I've never had a real woman of my own before, and it sort of warped my thinking. I'm grateful to you, sir. I know what is right, and I'll do that from now on. Working for you is great. You're like my dad. Thanks."

I called Colonel Hardesty. He laughed, and said, "I thought you'd break him before we had to say anything about it. Good for both of you. Visit me when you're in the neighborhood."

"Thanks, Colonel. Out."

Colonel White and Me, 26 May 1950, Gifu, Japan

Every Wednesday evening I had supper with my officers and noncommissioned officers. We had standard fare, but the meal and the atmosphere gave us an opportunity to do a little pulling and stretching. It was pleasant and informative—good for the organization. On this occasion we resolved that we needed 16mm movies several times a week. We all thought it was a good idea, and I noted it for some study and presentation to Col. Horton V. White, the regimental commander.

A number of items came up, and there was some discussion and resolution. I thought the meeting was winding down, but I was mistaken, badly mistaken. Just as I was getting ready to announce the conclusion of a fine meal, the First Sergeant rose and addressed me.

"Sir, some of our NCOs and enlisted men have a serious problem. It's not a problem you can resolve alone, but we think if you pursue it, perhaps it'll work out. The problem is this: several of the men have applied to marry Japanese girls, some as long as two years ago. Some already have children, and they feel it's their right and responsibility to marry girls of their choice. We know the federal government doesn't want to import a lot of people with low morals into our country, but every one of the girls we're talking about tonight have passed their investigative examinations. There's no reason for these delays except for the standard prejudice of the State Department. It's no secret they always give us a bad time where it involves non-Negro women.

"We've investigated this thing under the table, and we know the applications were approved by the chaplains and signed off by Colonel White. So the problem's got to be at the State Department. We know the paperwork's just lost down there, and that it'll stay lost unless the Colonel leans on 'em. Maybe he doesn't want to press this thing because of the racial aspect, or maybe it's just that the military doesn't like to push the State people at all. We're desperate, and if nothing happens, we're gonna go to the NAACP. It's not the kind of issue they'd like to fight either, however, cause every Negro soldier who marries a foreign woman means some Negro woman doesn't get married."

I noticed a lot of "amens" in the body. "Anything else, Sergeant?"

"No, sir. You know the effect of marriage on soldiers: improved conduct, morale, and all that, and of course we'd like you to do whatever you can to help. We know how difficult it is to move a mountain like this, but please. . . ."

"I'll do what I can, starting tomorrow. I'll let you know as soon as I can."

I would rather have had most anything put to me than the racial thing. I got along well with Colonel White, but I'd never had this kind of difficulty to work out with him. I was acutely aware of the Jim Crow attitude of the Army in general, but they were cagey where women were concerned, even foreign women.

The locals had told Negro soldiers a thousand times about the comments that the majority of white soldiers passed along. The attitude of many Japanese reflected the enmity that they absorbed from the whites. Any fool could see the prejudice, the hatred, denigration, and the bigotry that existed. Of course that bigotry also existed, powerfully, against the Japanese. If possible, the hatred was stronger toward the Japanese, but they didn't seem to be aware of it. The Asia-Pacific war was just over, and that caused tremendous antipathy toward the indigenous people. There was no justification for hatred against Negroes; there had really never been a war or any real competition against Negroes. It was mostly habit, passed on from father to son, gifts along with religion, along with fresh air and blue sky. Having said that, I have to say that I'd known some damned fine white folks. In order for a Negro to retain his sanity in that idiotic white world, he had to learn to keep it steady as it goes, play the percentages, learn to accept his wins and his losses. Trust when you can.

I decided to trust the Old Man. He liked me, and I never dealt in foolishness where he was concerned. I decided to take the matter to him directly, without rancor or history. I felt that I could justify my position with respect to the marriages, but marriages are not a unit commander's business, really. Maybe I should say that too.

The next morning I called for an appointment and got one for 1300 hours. I was hoping that the colonel had had a good lunch with two large, chilled martinis. And it seemed to have worked that way. We had a lot of insignificant conversation, pleasant and mood setting. Finally, the colonel said, "You never come up here to b.s. with me. What's on your mind?"

"Well, sir, I have a problem. At least my men have. Some of them have had marriage applications in and approved for as long as two years, without final approvals. The marriages are vital to those men."

"Do you think those marriages will make your company better?"

"Yes, sir."

"I may or may not agree with you, but I'll get them pushed

through for you. And just for my entertainment, convince me."

"Well, sir, married men are happier. They don't chase around, no VD, and have improved performance of duty."

The Old Man laughed himself into a convulsion. "That is only funny because I know that you are married."

The colonel rose, and the confab was over. I was happy as hell. We went through the saluting drill. As I reached for the door, the colonel asked me, still in jest, "What do you think, really think, about these interracial marriages?"

"Well, sir, God must have willed them because the mechanisms work so beautifully together."

The bad part of this story is that even after the Colonel pushed the papers through, the State Department waited months to finalize the actions. Meanwhile the Korean War came along and swooped up some of the men who had so long ago petitioned for marriage. They were gobbled up in that war. The girls never became wives, and many children remained fatherless legally, reviled by the Japanese people, unborn as far as Americans were concerned, but nonetheless, sons and daughters of American fighting men.

Private Moorehead, 1 July 1950, Gifu, Japan

This is a story about a personnel problem, a human problem, a homosexual problem—a problem of towering magnitude. It's a problem I could well have done without. I won't guarantee that my method for dealing with this particular problem was the best, but it was humane, and it was in accordance with Army regulations. There were no books on the subject—then or now. I had to limp along on a short stick.

The problem was "Mabel." Mabel was a hyperactive homosexual male. Had he been a female, Mabel would have been considered a nymphomaniac and be done with the story. But Mabel was a male soldier named Private First Class (PFC) Artemis Moorehead.*

Private Moorehead was called Mabel at his specific request. Mabel was a cook and considered a good one. The problem with

---

* The name has been changed in this instance.

Mabel was his insatiable sex drive and his lack of discretion. In addition, he was an exhibitionist. Put that all together and stage it in an Army barracks, and you have insurmountable problems.

All of this information had come to me through my First Sergeant. Neither he nor I lived in the barracks, nor did either of us have to settle the fights among the men desiring to possess Mabel or caused by his desire to possess the troops. Mabel broke "dates," performed, and created one helluva nuisance.

The First Sergeant had brought this problem to me soon after I joined the company. He had wanted me to get my feet on the ground first. I asked him, "Why has this been allowed to exist, to continue?"

He responded, "Been goin' on for a year or more. Ever since the day he came here. We been tryin' to get rid of him, but division, Army, none of them will do anything about it, 'less we catch him in the act and someone will testify against him at a trial. Of course the man he's involved with goes to jail, too. The Table of Maximum Punishments in the *Court Martial Manual* says thirty years for sodomy. Bad news.

"There's a file in there, sir, you should read it. Then you'll see where we are. He applied for a discharge because of the problem, but Eighth Army headquarters figgers that he just wants out of the service. Hope you can do something about it. We got a bad problem."

"Well, Sergeant, how do the men feel about Moorehead's cooking?"

"Well, he's clean, or at least he appears to be, and he cooks damned well. He's accepted as a cook. As you know, that's one of the things fags do a lot in civilian life. But he causes problems with the men. Some guy is always beatin' on him, or they're beatin' on each other. Some men hate fags and just enjoy bashing them. We have a lot of that, too. Sorry, sir, I just don't know how to handle this. He's smart as hell and knows his rights, which are the same as if he were a real man. Sometimes he jumps on one of his lovers who has been out in the street and he 'spects him of playing with some woman out in town."

I had a sick feeling in my stomach. I could imagine nothing more repulsive than a man deliberately abandoning his normal sex drives to lay or play with another man. The practice is even castigated in the Bible. The touch of another man beyond a handshake produced negative—even hostile—feelings in me, and I considered that to be normal. I decided to read Mabel's file.

The file included a letter from PFC Artemis Moorehead to the commanding general requesting an honorable discharge from military service by virtue of a propensity toward homosexuality. The letter was neat and orderly, and it gave a long history of homosexuality, commencing during preschool, when Moorehead slept with his abandoned mother until he was ten years of age. The mother fondled and aroused her son sexually nightly. Mabel never knew his father nor any male members of his family. When the boy was ten, Mrs. Moorehead succumbed to an ill-defined malady, and her son was placed in a foster home. There the male adult recognized that Mabel had "round heels" and seduced him. From that time, men had been Mabel's thing. Not a matter of choice exactly, but now a matter of compulsion.

Moorehead was drafted into the Army in 1948 and had actively practiced his homosexual desires daily and even more often ever since. Private First Class Moorehead acknowledged that his actions created turmoil in the barracks, but insisted that there was nothing he could do to change his character. Moorehead stated—correctly—that release from military service would be beneficial to the Army.

The administrative wizards at the several headquarters through which the correspondence passed used the letter as a big joke. It was something for discussion at happy hour. The letter was circulated from office to office—an object of derision. It was also circulated through many homes as well. It provided a lot of exciting filth, the basis for sick humor with no concern for the good of the service or for the application for discharge.

At the end of several weeks, the letter had arrived back in the hands of Private First Class Moorehead. In essence, the high-level reply was a strong negation of Mabel's request couched in a cloud of drivel, undoubtedly written by a lawyer. There was an advisory—or threat—that the activity described in the letter constituted sodomy, the punishment for which was thirty years at hard labor, reduction to the lowest enlisted grade, and forfeiture of all pay and allowances. Hell, Mabel knew all that, as did his playmates.

As commander, I was completely deflated. Eighth Army knew the facts well. They had sent a senior field grade officer to investigate Mabel and his activities. He took many sworn statements, and he rendered an extensive report. I felt that in view of all the facts, Eighth Army should have made some disposition of Moorehead and rectified a difficult situation. Surely there were regulations that a board of officers could have used to get Mabel out of the service. As a minimum they could have transferred Moorehead out of a troop unit, where teamwork and coordination are so vital to mission accomplishment.

Sentiment had gone against PFC Artemis Moorehead, whose blatant, loose conduct had soured the troops. The troops looked at each other wondering who might become accomplices or witnesses. Time went by, and Mabel hung blankets down from the upper bunk, in order to screen his activities from the barracks' other occupants.

That was the situation I inherited. I toured the barracks, tore down Mabel's shrouds, and had him moved to a vacant room downstairs. Because of the deplorable condition of the area in which he had lived, I gave him nonjudicial punishment under the *Uniform Code of Military Justice:* restriction to quarters for thirty days and forfeiture of two-third's pay for one month. I charged PFC Artemis Moorehead with unbecoming conduct. I drew up a roster of noncommissioned officers, and one of the NCOs was on duty every night to ensure that Mabel had no visitors. I selected the duty NCO carefully. I didn't want any bashing under these conditions. I didn't want bullying or denial of civil rights. I knew that the restriction was not wholly legal, but it was the best I could do with an ugly problem. I was buying some time and clearing up the atmosphere at the same time. Mabel did his duty assignment and was allowed a few minutes in the library each evening with the duty NCO. The whole thing was made easier for me because of the Jack Beavers affair, which made Mabel feel that I really would lower the boom. But because Eighth Army refused to act against him, my hands were tied, and whatever I did was bluff.

The 77th Engineer Combat Company had other things to worry about. Our pleasant duty in the Army of Occupation of Japan had been interrupted by the actions of North Korea.

Going to War

10–11 July 1950,
Gifu, Japan, to Pusan, Korea

At 0400 on 25 June 1950, the North Korean People's Army (NKPA) launched a massive offensive across the 38th Parallel into the Republic of Korea. The attack was a complete surprise to the U.S. Army. Although the U.S. government had declared South Korea to be outside the boundaries of our vital interest, President Truman decided to intervene on behalf of the South Koreans. It was called a "police action."

However, the president's declaration that the U.S. Eighth Army was to become involved in a police action did not work out the way the Army expected it to. After all, it figured, when a policeman blows his whistle, the perpetrator climbs back over the fence. This did not happen when the United States blew its police whistle. Across the Sea of Japan, bugles were being blown by the North Korean People's Army as it advanced inexorably southward across the 38th Parallel north latitude. They didn't stop even when the U.S. Army intervened.

The U.S. Army occupation forces in Japan started getting ready to fight, and some units were sent to Korea right away. On 30 June 1950, following authorization by President Truman, Task Force Smith (essentially the 1st Battalion, 21st Infantry Regiment, 24th Infantry Division) arrived in South Korea to fight the invad-

71

ers. The remainder of the 24th Infantry Division landed in Korea starting on 1 July 1950, under Maj. Gen. William F. Dean. Along with the small Republic of Korea (ROK) Army, the 24th Infantry Division fought a series of delaying actions to slow the North Korean advance. The overwhelming combat power of the NPKA forced the combined U.S.-ROK forces steadily southward.

The 25th Infantry Division and the 1st Cavalry Division started landing in Pusan, Korea, on 10 July 1950. The 29th Regimental Combat Team from Hawaii arrived in Korea a few days later. Those U.S. Army combat organizations moved northwest from Pusan to help the 24th Infantry Division and the ROK divisions stem the tide.

At the beginning of the Korean conflict, the U.S. Army did not perform well. This led to much blaming. The Eighth Army blamed its debacles on the ROK divisions. The 25th Infantry Division blamed its inadequacies on its Negro troops. There was plenty of blame to be passed around. However, the performance of the U.S. Army in Korea, and particularly during the later great rout of the U.S. Army from Kunu-ri, could not be blamed on the blacks or the yellows alone. It was an integrated debacle with the whites doing just as well or just as poorly as the rest.

As soon as the war started, we realized it was just a question of time before the 77th Engineer Combat Company would be sent to Korea to fight. I turned my attention to getting the equipment and the troops ready. As usual in such situations, we did not know what was going on, but we knew that we had better be ready to move out.

Departure, 11 July 1950, Gifu, Japan

The Orient is unfathomable to the Western mind. In so many ways, no matter how intimately one is involved, events occur and information circulates in a manner totally incomprehensible to a westerner.

Most of the troops had "hooches," rooms in the village they shared with their girlfriends or their wives, mostly unregistered and unsanctioned by the U.S. Army and by the Department of

State. The hooch was as sacrosanct, and ostensibly as inviolable, as the legitimate domiciles maintained by men all over the world. It has always been the same. Soldiers of occupation have consorted with and bred with the women of all subjugated nations.

News traveled fast in the hooches. News of international significance circulated in the hooches, as did those of national affairs, military affairs, and even military secrets at times. Everything was public and trafficable.

Corporal Sledge, my communications chief, met me in the hall after dinner. As he braced against the wall for my passage, he said, "Sir, we're going to be ordered to Korea in a few hours. We pick up our TO&E* shortages at the RTO,** and proceed to Moji or Sasebo. We'll go to Korea from there."

I looked at him, with a lot of doubt showing. He said, "It's true, sir, the news is in the hooches. We're going!"

This brought me up short, and I conferred with the First Sergeant. He'd heard the word. He always had it; he was good.

The Army was silent. We'd had no word from higher headquarters for hours. I authorized open post until midnight against the possibility that the clandestine news was factual. There's always a lot of unfinished business when a man has to leave home for extended periods. Furthermore, I knew we could meet any movement deadline between midnight and departure time, whatever.

Sure enough, division called at 2330 hours, with the cryptographic identification requirement and hullabaloo, to give me the hyper-official information that the "mooses" had spread three or four hours earlier. With the troops on hand I started to saddle up. The word was that we would put up a show of force in the field in Korea, and when the enemy quaked and returned across the 38th Parallel—which was inevitable—we would return to home stations.

"Depart 0400 to RTO Gifu for 0600 departure. Full TO&E. Pick up shortages at RTO. Secure garrison. No, repeat, no rear security element. Additional instructions follow."

*TO&E: Table of Organization and Equipment.
**RTO: Rail Transportation Office.

I had forebodings of terror, fear, blood, and death in spite of the cavalier tone of the message. I was right on track. I just didn't reckon the horrible magnitude of it.

I called a hurried staff meeting about midnight, and we organized for departure at 0300 on 11 July 1950. Lieutenant Lenon went to the RTO to ensure that the railroad personnel were prepared for us and to locate our missing TO&E items, which included a D-7 bulldozer and a dump truck. He reported with our train make-up, location, car numbers, and track number, and we made ready for departure.

Never before had I dealt simultaneously with so many emotions—fear, happiness, uncertainty, concern for the lives and welfare of 250 men. I loved the company and the men as a group. They were my kids, my family, my life.

A company commander in combat has an awesome responsibility. He is father, mother, and big brother to every man in his command. His concern is the physical and mental health, morale, food, clothing, shelter, attitude, appearance, and every element of life of each man. He has to know their names, hometowns, family compositions, parents' occupations, religion, sex life, education, ambition, childhoods, likes, dislikes, and general dispositions. All or any one of these items may have a distinct bearing on the nature of the men's individual assignments, their daily or specific capabilities and duties, their performance potentials, and ultimately the success or failure of the unit.

Finally, the company commander has to know himself. He has to know all of himself, starting with the attributes stated above, and progressing rapidly to his strengths and weaknesses, and his faith in himself, in his unit, his country, and his God. Where he recognizes weaknesses, he has to shore himself up. He must be "tall," or the lives of the 250 to 300 men of his command will be forfeit. No level of fatigue, apprehension, or privation can ever be allowed to encroach upon the performance of a company commander. He cannot delegate his responsibility. He can only share it with his junior officers and his non-coms. But there is no hiding place for him. He must do the job.

The First Sergeant whistled up the troops and fell them in on the courtyard. I "eased" them and made something of a speech. I told them we were going to Korea, probably no action, just a show of force in the field, and then a trip back to Gifu. It was wishful thinking.

Over my talking, we could hear the "mooses" moaning and wailing outside the gate. They knew, I knew, and the troops knew that there was more in store for us than a mere show of force. The mooses knew that some of their lovers and husbands would never muster in the castle courtyard at Gifu again.

I talked to the company about the make-up of the train, about the hourly stops, the feeding schedules, the baggage list, the route, and the schedule of march. All the pertinent information incident to our move was passed out so that every man knew as much as I did, although that wasn't very much. I gave the men my final instruction, caution, or command, if you will: "Do not walk on the tops of railway cars. Wherever you happen to be when the train prepares to depart, remain there until the next stop. Dismount and travel on the ground to the car you want to visit, whether the chow car, equipment car, or wherever."

I made a rare explanation of my directive, because a commander seldom has time for random talk. "Before the Big War, the Japanese had started to electrify their railway system, and the catenary supports are still in place, although no wire is strung. The supports are one and one-half meters above the top of the cars. One and one-half meters is 59.4 inches, which is just a little less than five feet. All of you are well over five feet tall. At the speeds we'll be traveling, the support will cut off the head of any man in the company. Repeat, do not walk the tops of the cars."

Full instructions having been given, I brought the company to attention. I called, "First Sergeant," which automatically brought the First Sergeant directly before me as the officers retired to the rear of their platoons, and the platoon sergeants took their places. A brisk salute and I moved off the field. There was much yet to do.

The stand-off between me and PFC Artemis Moorehead had remained in effect and he was still very much a problem when the word came down directing us to move to South Korea. There was no way I was going to take a millstone like Mabel into a combat situation. There were too many other problems to attend to under the best of conditions in combat. Duty demanded that I use my time—all of my time—productively. There would not be one moment to waste on the likes of Moorehead.

Just before we got on the train to Moji, I wrote out a confinement order, which authorized the stockade commander to incarcerate Moorehead, with paperwork to follow. I knew that Moorehead's enlistment would expire in about forty-five days. I had no idea what Korea would be like, but I was willing to gamble that it would take some time for Moorehead to find us even if he tried. I wanted very much for Moorehead to serve out the rest of his enlistment somewhere else—anywhere else. He was out of sync with the Army. I wished him well, from afar—damned far.

By a quirk of fate, Lieutenant Benefield's wife and three young children arrived in Japan the very day we left for Korea. He wanted desparately to see his family. His youngest son was born after he had left home for Japan, and he had never seen the baby. I was sympathetic, but we needed him. After all, we were only going to be in Korea for a short time.

We departed shortly after 0300 that morning. The dew was heavy on the ground and on all the flat surfaces of our vehicles. The trucks were warm as we mounted, and the wailing of the "mooses" grew louder. For an instant I felt sorry for the girls and their children and for the men who left them. This was a modern reenactment of many long-past departures by soldiers; similar to the departure of Joshua for Jericho, or the departure of Napoleon for Waterloo. I thought of my wife and my wee ones safe and so far away at home, halfway around the world, and I wondered for a moment how my early morning departure would ultimately affect them.

"Move out!"

I looked into the predawn blackness as we rode past the rice paddies for the last time on the road into Gifu. We arrived at the RTO, loaded our equipment on the train, and settled into the coaches while the cooks prepared a 6:00 A.M. breakfast. We'd gone through the food preparation exercise many times traveling

to our training area in Gotemba. I thought fondly of Gotemba,
at the foot of beautiful Mount Fuji. Then I turned back to my
travel schedule and pondered the problems of shipping, ammunition issue, petrol supply, rations issue, medical support, administrative channels, tactical operations, and a thousand things that
a commander has to live with. I remembered that I'd had no
sleep for nearly twenty-four hours and decided to snatch a few
winks before breakfast. The nap was good to me and good for
me, and I awakened refreshed after twenty minutes. It was destined
to be a long, long day.

Our mess crew was well trained, with a good attitude about
their work. I had leaned on them about service. It had to be
good, or they were out of the kitchen and into the platoons.
Cooks traditionally don't like hard soldiering, dirt, and labor, and
the trade-off is to cook, bake, and serve in a creditable manner.
The mess and its personnel had to be hospital clean, and the
food had to be miles above the standards routinely established
for Army kitchens. To hell with the book! I demanded that the
chow be seasoned to suit the palates of the average soldier, namely
me. The chow had to be good, so that the troops enjoyed eating,
even as they would at home or better, more like a classy restaurant.
A man is only as good as the food he eats. That is axiomatic.

We re-inventoried all our tool and equipment chests to be sure
that we could perform all normal engineer company-, platoon-,
and squad-size tasks. We checked our weapons and our ammunition. It was best to be ready for anything. I had told the men
they were tough so many times and for so long they believed it,
and so did I. And we were.

There wasn't time for me to enjoy the beautiful Japanese countryside after dinner or the exciting seascapes. Japan is a fantastically
beautiful place. Totally manicured. But preparing a unit for combat and assessing unit capability are all-consuming tasks. I needed
to know our mission so that I could requisition quantities required
as soon as engineer dumps were available. I reviewed the personnel
forms to be certain that no man was assigned to a job he wasn't
currently fit to perform.

Suddenly the train began rapidly braking to a halt. I knew I had another problem, but I had no idea of the nature of it. When the train came to a stop, the brakeman came running up the track. As he approached me, he began to gesture toward the roof of one of the box cars. It was certainly one of the troops injured while walking the top of the car, and I was angered because I'd given explicit instructions against this very thing.

I climbed the ladder to the roof, and there was Corporal Summers with the back of his head cut off and blood and brains in splotches where the mess had landed on the walkway of the box car. He had been hit by one of the catenary supports while walking on top of the train. He was threshing around wildly atop the train and smearing his own brains on the top of the car.

Lieutenant Lenon climbed back down to get Private First Class Napoleon, our company medic, and some rope so that we could lower Summers to the ground. I was sick at the sight of him and hurt because a casualty at this stage of activity was so damned needless.

In my mind I wrote Summers off for dead. I saw no way that a man could live with so much of his head cut off. The catenary support had done a neat job on Summers as he'd walked toward the rear of the train while it sped toward Moji.

Private First Class Napoleon came up with his little bag. He looked at Summers, then at me, winced, and stooped for a closer look. He listened at Summers's chest and touched his carotid artery. Then Napoleon turned to me and said, "He's alive, sir, but I don't think he can live for long. It'd be better if we could get him down on the ground. I'll give him some morphine, but I don't think there's much that can be done for him. In fact, he doesn't even need the morphine; he's beyond that."

"How do you recommend we move him, Napoleon?" I asked.

"Rope sling around his chest, sir. I'll try to hold his head up while he's being lowered so's not to spill out any more of his brains."

We lowered him as gently as possible, after a bandage was wrapped around his head to hold what was left inside it and to protect that great gaping hole from the flies. Meanwhile he convulsed and flapped around a bit.

It was a pitiful sight, and Napoleon looked like he'd be sick. He'd never seen a real honest-to-goodness injured person. He was fresh from medical corpsman training. This was his baptism. He eventually became a master at the repair of damaged human flesh.

We lowered Summers away and put him on a stretcher in the baggage car where Napoleon had his gear. There was little to do but wait for him to quit living. I had the mess on top of the box car covered with straw as an absorbent and then cleaned up. I didn't call another formation. The word was out. There'd be no more top-walking. The troops really had the message now.

The train gradually accelerated, and we were on the way again. I had instructed the engineer to wire ahead for information about the closest U.S. Army hospital on or near our route and to advise me at our next scheduled stop. I asked him to advise the Japanese railroad authorities of the incident and to request the nearest U.S. Army hospital to send an ambulance and personnel to handle a partial decapitation. All the while I felt that only a hearse was really needed.

At our next scheduled stop, there was a wire for me:

108TH STATION HOSPITAL 45 MILES YOUR LOCATION. STOP. NO AMBULANCE AVAILABLE. STOP. NO PERSONNEL AVAIL. STOP. ADVISE. END.

I really had a problem: no hospital and Summers nearly dead or dying. I called Lieutenant Lenon over, "Chet, let's tie Summers gently on the stretcher. Hitch a ride for yourself and Summers to the 108th Station Hospital, Itamazu. Here's his Form 20. Stay with him until he dies. Do what you have to do. Join us as soon as possible. Don't know where we'll be—somewhere in Korea. We have no resources and no time. Good luck. God bless you both."

So we left Chet Lenon on the station platform with a badly injured soldier.

I had a moment's additional thought and numerous unspoken questions as we accelerated away from the RTO. How would Chet get Summers to the hospital? How long could Summers live? How would Chet catch up with us? And where?

Chet was totally resourceful, and I didn't worry. I looked out at the Japanese farms, and I said a fervent prayer for Summers.

> Oh, merciful God,
> accept the soul of our recently departed.
> Take him into Thy bosom.
> Forgive him of his sins, and
> provide him with eternal peace.
>
> Heavenly Father,
> protect us, your children,
> who know not whither we go.
> Give me strength,
> wisdom, and perseverance
> that I may prolong
> the lives of my men
> as we move amongst danger.
> Continue in the love
> and care of my family.
> And for all thy bounty,
> I thank thee.
> Amen.

When I opened my eyes, I had small tears, which were strange to me. A strong foreboding of danger and death, and silently I recited part of the Ninety-first Psalm.

> . . . Thou shalt not be afraid
> for the terror by night,
> nor for the arrow
> that flieth by day.
> Nor for the pestilence
> that walketh in darkness,
> nor the destruction
> that wasteth at noonday.
> A thousand shall fall
> at thy side
> and ten thousand
> at thy right hand,
> but it shall not come
> nigh Thee. . . .

I was greatly strengthened. The Psalms always reinforced me. I indulged myself with another nap as the afternoon wore away.

Soon it was evening. The chow was good, but I found little enjoyment in it. We were nearing the port of Sasebo, and I had very little knowledge of what to expect. What ship? Where? How would I move my equipment aboard ship? What about sleeping quarters for my troops? Questions tumbled endlessly in my head. Immediately before sundown, a tall, blond NCO swung into my car. He had an iridescent orange armband, which denoted some authority. He had all the answers, and thirty minutes later we were being hauled aboard the *Isikawa Maru* for our voyage to Korea.

Voyage, 11 July 1950, Moji, Japan, to Pusan, Korea

I shared quarters on the ship with its captain. It was an important feeling. On the pier I saw Lieutenant Colonel Burnette, executive officer of the 24th Infantry Regiment, to which we were usually attached. He had a lot of duffel and gear—too much for a combat situation. I invited him aboard and sent some troops down to wrestle up his bedroll, field desk, file cabinet, and packs. I was the troop commander there, so I had him bunk with my officers. I went to the captain's quarters. That was the protocol.

At midnight we mustered all hands, including 108 ex-prisoners from the Eighth Army stockade. All were black, and all were drug offenders released to go to Korea. It bothered me not at all. I'd known several of them in the past, and I knew—contrary to public opinion—that with no drugs there would be no problems. I created a 4th Platoon, reinforced my headquarters by redistributing personnel from the three original platoons, and distributed the drugheads evenly among the four platoons.

I designated SFC Collins A. Whitaker leader of Chet Lenon's platoon, and it was a damned wise choice. Whitaker was good.

Soon we cast off and slipped out to sea. A lot of the troops leaned on the rail looking back at Japan until all the lights faded away. Many of them were leaving the best homes of their lives.

I received a message advising me to proceed to Kumchon after debarking. I had no map except the one that had appeared the week before on the back page of *Stars and Stripes,* the official newspaper for the U.S. armed forces.

I napped fitfully during the night, and with daybreak I could smell the feces and garlic, or the garlic in feces, that was Pusan, Korea. The offshore wind was nauseating. I watched the horizon become a smudge, become a band, then become the shape of structures, a harbor, a place for debarkation.

Land of the Morning Calm, 11 July 1950, Pusan, Korea

It was hotter than the hearthstones of hell as we slowly rocked at anchor in Pusan harbor. The ocean was dead calm beneath us as we drifted into port and waited to be beached in Korea— the Land of the Morning Calm. The tides were favorable, and we docked at 0700. The light breezes we felt merely circulated the smell of garlic and feces. The sewers must have emptied into the bay.

The 25th Infantry Division, commanded by Maj. Gen. William B. Kean, had set up its initial headquarters at Yongchon, halfway between Taegu and Pohang, on the east coast. The division's mission was to block North Korean movement south from Chongju. Two of the division's infantry regiments were sent forward to contact the enemy and stop his advance. The 27th Infantry Regiment went first to Uisong, north of Taegu but moved later to Andong. The 35th Infantry Regiment was at Sangju. The 24th Infantry Regiment initially was placed in division reserve at Kumchon, ready to move either to Taejon or Chongju as necessary to support the overall defense.[*] The 77th Engineer Combat Company was to move to its designated area at Kumchon to support the 24th Infantry Regiment.

We did not know what to expect as we landed. It seemed as though we were blundering into a war which had no reason for us as outsiders. But in 1950 the time was right for satisfying the emotional needs I had not sated in World War II. Wars produced

---

[*] Roy E. Appleman, *South to the Naktong, North to the Yalu* (Washington, D.C.: Office of the Chief of Military History, 1961). Referred to in the text as U.S. Army official history.

promotions, medals, adrenaline, wounds, cowardice, hatred, heroism, valor, and above all, death. In all times men have gloried in war—young men out of stupidity, old men out of greed and lust for power.

The *Stars and Stripes* map was not good enough to fight from, but the town we were supposed to go to—Kumchon—showed on the newspaper map. I was itching to get there. Not only because duty demanded it, but since we were committed, I was anxious to get into action, get it over with, and get back home. There was living to do. I had two beautiful kids to raise, and once I got back in Japan, they would join me.

Immediately after the hawsers were in place, a pompous Korean gentleman came up the gangway and engaged the captain in brisk Japanese. The captain advised me in English that the longshoremen and stevedores were on strike, and would not off-load our ship. The captain was extremely unhappy because he had commitments back in Japan; I was disgusted because they were holding up our war. We'd been rushing headlong up to now, and I was anxious to get into action. It was time to apply the years of training.

I called a meeting of all officers and eight or ten key NCOs. We were all young, under thirty years old, skilled, smart, and tough. I gave the group my assessment of our predicament, from which, at the rate things were going, we could have been stalled for an eternity. Even at 1000 in the morning we were sweating in the damp, humid air. I raised some hell about the weather and ranted about being victimized by some oriental labor boss. I asked if anyone had experience in stevedoring or winch operations and, luckily, there were three NCOs who'd been in port battalions during the Big War. I made some notes.

It was time to act. I asked for locomotive operators and got some smarts on that also. I sent for the ship's captain, advised him that we were going to put our equipment on the pier, and requested his indulgence. When he was assured that we had skilled operators, he was more than happy to assist us. There was money to be made bringing more troops to Korea, and he wanted to get at it.

Meanwhile, I sent a brace of sergeants under Lieutenant Benefield to commandeer a train and an engineer with crew. I told him the train should have the same make-up as the one in which we had traveled from Gifu to Sasebo. I wanted it dockside so we could off-load directly onto the train from the ship. They moved out. I was excited about it. It is always exhilarating to break log jams.

I walked back out onto the deck and had the First Sergeant muster the troops. I always insisted that—to the maximum extent possible—everyone be informed. I gave the troops my plan, and I studied their faces as they assimilated the information. Much had happened in the roughly thirty hours since we left our home station. We'd picked up and moved to another country, another culture, another world. Soon I'd know whether we were made of "meat or dog food."

At 1130 hours Lieutenant Benefield waved to me out of the cab of a locomotive. His platoon sergeant, SFC Freddie Bardo, was the engineer. I was astounded, but I shouldn't have been. That was the kind of man Benefield was. There was a job to do, and he did it. That was the way he played basketball or poker, and that was the way he lived. Go for broke!

Sergeant Bardo was another good man to have around. He had served in engineer battalions in World War II. Although he was a quiet man of average size, he could operate bulldozers, road graders, cranes, and—apparently—locomotives. He did all this calmly and expertly. Bardo was long on guts, and he did whatever an engineer soldier had to do. He was the kind of man who made our unit successful.

My lieutenant colonel passenger was very antsy; he didn't approve of my action. He would have stayed on the *Isikawa Maru* forever. He had no guts for the war we were trying to get into. He'd become fat and complacent during the years of garrison soldiering. He was good on courts martial, boards, and inspections. He was a boozer. Wars are for young men, and he was no longer young. He warned me of possible ill consequences of my acts. I thought, to hell with it! I was the commander.

We had the ship's mules and winches operating, and the hatch-covers off. We began to off-load our equipment. At 1500 hours we were on the beach, checked, blocked, and ready to roll. That

lousy map from the *Stars and Stripes* had very few towns, no contours, no grids, no elevations, but it did show Kumchon.

I didn't know much about railroads except that other trains
ran on the same track, some going the same direction, some going
the opposite direction. This could be a problem. I sent Lieutenant
Benefield, "Benny," back to find an engineer and crew. I figured
the engineer would know the essentials, such as where and when
to go into railroad sidings to avoid trains coming the other direction. Thirty minutes later, Benny and Sergeant Bardo came back
with two Korean men. It is difficult, when a soldier carries a
carbine, to tell whether he is threatening with it or not. It didn't
matter; the two Koreans casually looked at the load, but gave
the engine a thorough "preflight," and we were on our way.

Lieutenant Colonel Burnette repeated his advice to me that I
was probably in deep trouble for kidnapping, larceny of a locomotive and rolling stock, and violation of countless labor laws. I
had to laugh in his face. He did saddle up with us, however. I
figured that the offenses of that day were nothing to the ones
I'd commit as time rolled by. I was right. To hell with local laws!
There was a war to fight. "Balls out for Kumchon!"

Well, we fooled around all night. Run ten miles, go into a
siding, wait an hour, run for twenty minutes, and go back into a
siding. We did meet two oncoming trains during the night while
we lay in sidings, so I didn't challenge the engineer's performance.
But I was damned unhappy at the slow advance we were making.

I drank a lot of coffee, which was always available in our mess.
It was understood that coffee and some kind of chow was available
to anyone at any hour of the day. I tolerated no hunger in the
ranks, irrespective of operating hours.

The night was long, and I welcomed the rays of dawn and
the promise of a new day and a new series of adventures.

About 0800 hours the next morning, we pulled into a station
labeled Kumchon. We switched down into the yards and commenced off-loading. The RTO was a crazy place. The Army had
kiosks and personnel giving confusing directions. I saw a man I
knew, and he directed me to a clear area near the 24th Infantry
Regimental Headquarters. My own reconnaissance team, under

Lieutenant Peoples, was already out looking for sites for bivouac, water supply points, motor pools, engineer dumps, and ration points. It was a helluva mess. My driver brought my jeep up in front of the station as soon as it was off-loaded.

I saw Lieutenant Colonel Burnette push his duffel and gear out of the train and onto the platform. He walked down to the bottom step, belly flopped onto his sleeping bag, and clutched at his chest. I looked at him with sickening disgust. He made a soft place to flop on and continued with his "heart attack." Someone called for a medic from the aid station, just setting up on the RTO. They finally evacuated that big, fat, lazy bastard. He went back to another cushy job in Japan, or maybe retirement.

Things were beginning to happen, and I needed Chet Lenon. I wondered if he was still in Japan; I wondered if he had been able to get Summers to a hospital in time.

Lieutenant Peoples reported the locations of the ration breakdown point, engineer supply depot, and ordnance small arms supply point. I told him we'd put our locators up. Lieutenant Wilson was supervising the off-loading. I told him, "When Benny comes back from his recon, set the company up, establish the water supply point with good security, and dig in. Put in foxholes and defensive wire. We don't have any intelligence, but I don't want any surprises."

Then I was on the way to report to the regimental commander, Col. Horton V. White. I liked the Old Man, and he liked me. He referred to me as "the Hot Shot." I never knew whether it was because I was a doer, or because I'd been in fighters during the Big War. It was alright with me either way. He liked action people. I found him in the shambles they called a command post. The headquarters company was in confusion, although the school they were setting up in was ideal for their purposes.

I checked in with Lt. Col. Paul F. Roberts, the new executive officer (exec). Lieutenant Colonel Roberts had been commanding an infantry battalion, but after Lieutenant Colonel Burnette got "sick" at the RTO, Roberts had come up to regiment to give the Old Man a much-needed hand. His new call sign was Lion Five. *Lion* was the regimental unit call sign. *Six* is the code designation for commanding officer. *Five* is the code for exec.

Lion Five was an old fightin' hand. He'd gone from second lieutenant to lieutenant colonel during World War II, and he was as tough as the men he fought. Behind his back he was referred to as "Terrible Tex" or "Tall Paul." I asked him about it once, and he knew and kinda liked the handles. He was a professional, and we got along well.

Colonel Roberts was straightening out the situation at regimental headquarters. It was good to see him there. I asked for the Old Man. Colonel Roberts gestured over his shoulder with his thumb, and I walked back to where Colonel White sat. He was suddenly tired and very old, and he looked sick. I asked him how he felt, and Colonel White said, "Hot Shot, I'm too old for this. I didn't realize it until this morning, but soldiering is for you young-uns. Mine is all behind me. I think I'll have to pack it in soon, but you give 'em hell."

I felt like crying, because I knew that he wasn't going to be there long. He'd aged in that God-awful heat, the mosquitoes, and the filth. There were no niceties out there—no booze and no comfort—and he was a man who was used to good living. We weren't whiskey-drinking friends; we had a sort of father-son relationship.

I excused myself and checked in with the S-3 and then the S-2. Regiment was not yet in touch with division, so they knew as little as I did. I said a few other hellos, reported the general location of my company command post (CP), made sure they were going to lay a telephone wire to my CP, and went about my business.

Lieutenant Wilson had been doing a good job of setting up. We'd made and struck camp so many times that all of our officers and NCOs knew how I liked things done. Always fundamentally the same. Kitchen and sleeping areas near the road, but out of the dust patterns, on high ground with good drainage. The security was out and it was all coming together well, and the evening meal was nearly ready.

Lieutenant Benefield briefed me from a map he'd improvised. He showed me the relative locations of elements of the division, the regiment, and the artillery and engineer battalions. The water point was in business, and he had nailed up locator signs. He had made arrangements for ration pickup, POL allocations, and numerous other unit necessities.

He gave me a rumor he'd picked up: "13th Field Artillery Battalion had been overrun the night before; lost all guns and all troops. The 23d Infantry Regiment from down south, was routed with extremely heavy casualties; unit presently ineffective." I looked at him in stark disbelief.

He said, "Chief, we're fighting some mean sons of bitches. We ain't going home soon. We've got some real fightin' to do. This ain't no Gotemba maneuver. Trouble is the Korean soldiers wear the same white rags the farmers wear. Farmers by day; soldiers by night. Russian weapons, mostly automatic .28 calibers. Damned good soldiers."

And still no word from Lieutenant Lenon.

The wire was laid. We had communications and almost instantly the phone was jangling. I was called to regiment for a meeting. I told Jim Wilson to have some weapons maintenance done, issue hand grenades (with some good instruction), and place some trip flares and antipersonnel (AP) mines on the perimeter along with some more wire. "Get set up for the night."

Things were better organized at regimental headquarters, but their sorry kitchen still hadn't gotten their miserable field rations ready to eat. I'd have scuttled the whole bunch.

Colonel Roberts ran a good meeting. He set up a tentative move for the following day: north to Sangju and west about twenty-five miles, where we were to tie in with Leopard on the left and Lynx on the right. *Leopard* and *Lynx* were call signs for our sister regiments in the division. He outlined my tasks, which were routine. I gave him the status of the unit, engineer supplies, mines, barbed wire, demolitions, sand bags, and other items for which I was responsible. We were heading for some action, I could feel the flesh crawl between my shoulder blades, eerie but exhilarating. Combat!

The move was later postponed, and the regiment sat.

C H A P T E R 6

Desperate Intervention

12–25 July 1950,
Kumchon, Korea

It was truly a desperate intervention. The news was bad. The *Stars and Stripes* spoke of catastrophic losses: the 24th Infantry Division is defeated at Pyongtaek, the division artillery loses all guns; fierce fighting occurs at Taejon; there are severe losses of personnel and equipment at Taegu; the 21st and 34th Infantry Regiments routed and ineffective, after serving vigorously.

Our Army was ill prepared to fight using the individual and organizational tactics forced upon us by our enemy. Our mentality was the same as that used at San Juan Hill, St. Mihiel, and Normandy. We certainly hadn't trained for night fighting. The soldiers were not physically fit for combat in that hostile environment. We had not trained to change our tactics from mass attacks to guerrilla warfare from one day to the next and from massive tank actions to individual combat with handmade knives from one hour to the next. We were blundering, befuddled clowns, posturing, mouthing, stumbling, losing, criticizing our allies, blaming others for our indecision and errors. We were pitiful.

The U.S. Army's problems in Korea didn't start in Korea. The problems started back in Washington, D.C., with the attitude that "we won the last war; we've got the bomb; and these gooks won't

89

give us any trouble. We'll show some force, and they'll go home." This attitude pervaded the minds and attitudes of our political and military leaders. They all grossly underestimated the serious intent and full capability of the North Korean People's Army (NKPA). The motivation, level of training, and logistics system of the NKPA were stupidly underestimated. The Soviets had equipped their North Korean protégés well for their mission and for their enemy.

Our divisions were sent to Korea lacking intelligence about the enemy and about the terrain. There were no good maps, and this lack made it virtually impossible to travel prudently, communicate, or fire artillery effectively at the elusive enemy. The maps that were available had neither contours nor grid systems and were printed in the Korean language and calligraphy. At best, the maps were crude sketches. The troops and their leaders had no knowledge of their enemy's capability, his strength, nor his determination.

The U.S. Army and the allied forces were not prepared to coordinate their activities closely with the Republic of Korea (ROK) Army, nor were they willing to trust each other. Most of all, they did not understand the politico-military status of the South Koreans, particularly in light of the invasion from the north. The "No-Win" policy of the United States defeated our forces even before the first American soldier arrived in the Land of the Morning Calm. What had our State Department and our intelligence agencies been doing during the five years between the end of World War II and the North Korean invasion?

A new and ugly pseudo-military term, "bug out," was born. Bug out implied that troops abandoned their positions without a fight, or yielded to the enemy without a struggle, or fled out of control in the face of the enemy. This term was used by those military personnel and civilians who were not under the pressure of assault by a determined enemy. It was a term used by headquarters' troops, reserve forces, and newsmen who commented from safety miles to the rear of the fighting.

The news remained bad. The 19th Infantry Regiment sustained severe losses after joining the 24th Infantry Division; the 5th RCT was battered, bruised, demoralized, and rendered ineffective for some time. The days were hot and miserable; the nights were murderous. The nights were spent vying feebly against a tough, fiercely determined, motivated enemy, who caused casualties never anticipated nor even imagined by the U.S. command. The 24th Infantry Division lost its commanding general, Maj. Gen. William F. Dean, who was taken prisoner on 25 August 1950, south of Taejon. Entire battalions of the U.S. Army broke ranks and ran. The North Koreans enjoyed phenomenal success against the U.S. forces.*

There are several conditions that constitute losing in the military sense. In a defensive situation, one indicator of defeat is the loss of men. When a platoon of forty men is assaulted by a vastly superior force and dwindles down to eight to twelve fighting men; when the crew-served weapons fall silent; when one's buddies are screaming and dying from wounds; when no reinforcements are imminent; when the enemy is storming, yelling, and blowing bugles in an obviously vigorous onslaught; and when the enemy continues his encroachment with heavy supporting fire—the chances are good that the platoon is lost whether those remaining men stay in their foxholes or not. This is particularly true at night and even more so if the troops are "green." When troops are entering combat for the first time, and the lieutenant is down, and the sergeant is dead or silent, they will be sure losers. Chances are good that the enemy will continue to gain ground and kill the men remaining in their foxholes. When the enemy gains his objectives, his morale is improved, and he becomes difficult to dislodge.

These conditions become fact when the enemy is determined and has the overwhelming strength, when the defending forces have neglected to fortify or are lacking in barbed wire and other barrier materials. If communications are not established and functioning, and if the leadership is not in complete control, we have a loser. Radios or telephones are a must. God help the soldier if the next higher echelon (company or battalion) is not responsive and responsible.

---

* Clay Blair, *The Forgotten War: America in Korea, 1950–1953* (New York: Times Books, 1987), 139. Chapters 5 and 6 deal with the early days of the war.

The leadership of each echelon of command must know their men. They must know which are capable, which are fighters, which bleed readily, which love to fix bayonets and fight hand-to-hand, and most important, which are the runners without an appetite for combat. The leader must know which soldiers have to be paired with a stable warrior in a foxhole when the enemy storms at them with epithets, threats, bugles, and bullets. The leaders must know and they must lead, and sometimes that is tough—damned tough.

No matter what, the troops must be fed, protected from weather, allowed to bathe with some frequency, and provided with changes of clothing, particularly socks. This is necessary to keep the troops effective. This is the responsibility of the rear-area logistical personnel, who frequently are insensitive to foxhole concerns or are incapable of responding.

Particularly strong judgment in the art of pairing is essential to success. This involves identifying the weaklings—the men who are all mouth and no production—and teaming them with men who believe in themselves and their weapons and have the desire to use both. The fighters will demand performance of the weaklings, and the weaklings will attempt to measure up to the strong men. Strong, formidable teams often are formed in this manner, and the unit is improved significantly by this practice. Small, tough teams can make a unit more effective, proud, and mean—winners with towering morale.

Morale is the *sine qua non* of successful combat. The U.S. Marine Corps has demonstrated that hundreds of times. When a fighting man thinks he is tough and really believes it, then he is. He will prove it repeatedly, given the opportunity. The Marines had a chant: "We gonna win, by God, we gonna win." The belief in the chant sometimes produced a win when some or all of the negatives were present. And fighting men must win to stay effective. They can live with incidental setbacks, but only incidental setbacks.

In order to win, soldiers—like all other competitors—must be trained. Training—long, hard, pushing, stretching, tooth grinding, gut wrenching—is the essence and substance of soldiering.

Training is strength, and strength is soldiering. This applies to all ranks from generals to grunts. Big bellies reflect the absence of training in all ranks from generals to grunts and all jobs from cooks, to bandsmen, to 11-Bravo infantrymen. We humans are characteristically lazy, but without that hard training and conditioning we will lose before we start. The North Koreans showed us that in 1950.

The platoon example set forth above can be expanded three times, twenty times, or five thousand times, and catastrophes of increasing magnitude will result until finally not only losses of handheld weapons ensue, but losses of artillery pieces. Then we talk shamefully and ominously not of platoon defeats but of the defeats of divisions, corps, and armies. This happened to the French Army in May and June of 1940. It happened to the North Korean Army in September and October of 1950 after the Inchon landing. It happened to the U.S. Army in the ignominious rout of United Nations (UN) forces from North Korea during November and December 1950.

The fundamentals apply both to white soldiers and black soldiers, to French, Korean, and American soldiers. The press and the historians, however, have made much more out of those defeats involving black troops than the greater number of defeats involving white troops. Bugging out by black troops implied a racial defect, while bugging out by white troops was ascribed to other reasons.

Devil's Workshop, 12 July 1950, Kumchon, Korea

I had some firm rules, which I stated from time to time at company formations. One of these rules was that there would be no fighting among ourselves without the approval of the First Sergeant. The First Sergeant would give permission for fighting only to men of similar grade, and under no condition would noncommissioned officers be involved. It was beneath the dignity of NCOs to fight. All fights were to be held publicly for the whole assembled company to watch, especially the commanding officer.

Most fights would never occur except when one man could

throw a "Sunday punch" at an unsuspecting soldier and thus win the fight by default. One protagonist or the other often was unwilling to lay it all on the line and put up or shut up on an even basis in front of the troops. The rules were inflexible, and fighting within the company was held to a minimum.

We were living in a schoolhouse in Kumchon, and I happened to walk around the corner of the building just in time to see two soldiers explode violently out of the second story of the building. Private First Class Fields saw me and had just enough time to shout, "We ain't fightin', sir!"

Then Private First Class Fields and Private First Class Van Ness crashed out on to the walkway from the second floor. I ignored the two of them. I knew damned well they were fighting, but the beating they took hitting the ground was enough punishment for their crime. "We ain't fighting," indeed!

I told the First Sergeant to have the medics check them over and patch them up as needed. It turned out that the two battlers were in good condition, but I remembered an old saying of my dad's, "An idle mind is the devil's workshop."

That saying translated in my mind to, "Keep young men busy, and they will stay out of trouble." Dad was always right—always. Busy and tired young men rarely stray into mischief.

Not just because Dad said it, but from my own personal experience, I knew that mind and muscle must always be active. We were laying around in Korea waiting for something to happen, and I hadn't gotten into the rhythm of the war. So I started some work.

I ordered a series of reconnaissances of the road network in and about Kumchon. We checked the roadbeds, shoulders, culverts, and the bridges—beams, decking, and even the handrails. We checked whatever was needed to make all the roads passable to Class 60 vehicles. There was no immediate requirement to do this, but we had heard rumors that the 24th Division had needed good roads, and the same condition could prevail with the 25th Division. I made it a practice to keep the troops busy, and I created some tired soldiers, but for as long as I was in Korea there was never—well almost never—any misconduct in the company.

We had no construction material, so we had to rely on the local lumberyards. These lumberyards were always privately owned and always full of lumber stamped UNRRA.* Although the material was donated to South Korea, it seemed to end up in the hands of the local politicians somehow. We helped ourselves and issued blood chits for the value of the misplaced American property. I never knew whether the local yard owners were paid, but I assume they were because they always managed somehow. Had the lumber in those lumberyards not been available, we would not have been able to provide the support the infantry so desperately required.

Our few days in Kumchon waiting for action turned out to be very valuable time. I had time to formulate and inculcate procedures for securing job sites and establishing outposts, which made it possible to accomplish road and bridge maintenance and construction without combat casualties. The policies and procedures developed in those early days of the war were to sustain us throughout the conflict. After several days of hard work at Kumchon, we were prepared to face the troops of the North Korean People's Army, who were themselves hard, tough, resolute, and probably some of the best fighting men in the world.

Visions of Home, 15 July 1950, Kumchon, Korea

I was ready for action. I stood five feet, eleven inches tall and weighed about 180 pounds, but I felt a lot bigger. I was in good physical condition, and mentally I was strong and resolute. I prided myself on being tough and durable. Mean but fair! I considered myself a good man to have on your side in a footrace or fistfight—or in combat.

I had been away from home too long, and there appeared to be no chance of getting back for many months, if ever; but I had infinite confidence in my survival. I frequently wondered about the growth and development of my son, Charles, who was

---

*United Nations Relief and Rehabilitation Agency. Headed by Fiorello H. LaGuardia, former mayor of New York City, the UNRRA sent building materials to underdeveloped countries.

a toddler when I left and who had now lost his first teeth. I thought of my baby girl, Fay, who was in a crib when I left and who now walked and talked. I had missed so very much of their development. I had lost so much of them. To them, I was a beautifully framed picture named "Daddy."

My wife Thelma had been supportive when I rejoined the Army, and she was happy when I was ordered to Japan not in flight status. Little did she realize that the hazards I was to face as an engineer officer were far more dangerous than those of a routine flier.

My family had been scheduled to join me in Japan in August 1950, but the outbreak of the Korean War changed all that. Correspondence replaced our normal relationship. All went well for the first few months, but letters are a poor substitute for conversation. I noticed, too, that more frequently in our mail there was disagreement between Thelma and me. Our viewpoints were moving further and further apart. Mail, though cherished and vitally essential, was woefully inadequate. There's no substitute for eye-to-eye contact—the tactile relationship.

Thelma mentioned in one of her letters that she wanted to buy a television set. She felt that it would be good for the kids—educationally and so forth. I heartily agreed. I had never bought a television set, and I had no idea about their specs or cost. A couple of weeks later I got a letter describing that beautiful $500, 19-inch television set. I was deflated. That TV cost me two months of hard pay, combat pay included. I knew damned well that the kids could be entertained at a lower cost—a cost consistent with a captain's wages. I let Thelma know how I felt in no uncertain terms. My response resulted in several weeks of no mail. We were growing apart.

There was no way the folks at home could understand any part of my life. They knew nothing of my dreams, my fears, my longings, my needs. They, fortunately, could not conceive of my life on the killing floor. I lived daily a whole life alien to their experience. Their lives seemed tender, mundane, and childish to me.

I wondered often if I could ever really go home, and diminish the scope of my being, to shrink my mind into synchronization with the humdrum mediocrity that was civilian life—working 8:00 A.M. to 5:00 P.M., washing the car, mowing the lawn, grocery shopping. I had grave doubts. How could I learn to live without my cherished guns and aircraft? How could I live with men who respected themselves very little and other men not at all? I had real fears about cleansing my mind of war and war making. Soldiers of all wars must have had the same questions.

There was very little time, however, for reverie and reminiscing. I turned my mind back to the very real problem at hand—survival.

Trauma, 16 July 1950, Kumchon, Korea

Malaria hit me like a ton of bricks. One moment things were normal. I was planning and calculating my mine storage, and a moment later I was staggering and suffering a terrible headache. Hallucinations began leaping through the pain; then came the fever. I felt my body temperature go up intolerably, then it plummeted as though I were facing a blizzard. Then up again. Control of my body was lost to a shivering fit. I trembled and rattled in every joint. The joints became sore from drumming on the packed ground. Someone, several of the troops, picked me up. My weight wasn't a problem for them to handle, but the twitching and shivering made it difficult for them to carry me.

In the back of my mind I knew that it was malaria, my ancient enemy, which I'd known and feared of old. It was a souvenir of my service in the Mediterranean theater in World War II. The wild hallucinations took control of me; my gyros (equilibrium) tumbled; and a vicious, nightmarish experience seized me.

Private First Class Napoleon was bathing my head, neck, and chest in cold water, but I was barely aware. He dissolved one of his "horse pills," and between vibrations I choked it down, and the gyrations and headache slowly—very slowly—subsided. As the pain receded, so did the hallucinations—the visions of carnage, violence, and death; the purple, orange, and reds.

I'd been wrestling with the malaria attack for about three hours according to my watch, but there was plenty of daylight left. Cautiously I tried my senses and my legs, which responded with great reluctance. Another horse pill, and my driver took me up to regiment for the next round of activity. I was embarrassed to have that malaria fit in the presence of my men, but it couldn't be helped. I vowed to stay on those pills.

Life and the war went on. I had things to do, and never mind the malaria.

I got the reenlistment papers for Cpl. Jerome Barnwell, all 280 pounds of him. He was the heaviest, strongest, and most jovial man in the company. I swore him in, paid him his $400 reenlistment bonus, and made a silent memo to have him promoted at the first opportunity. I offered to keep his money in the company safe until he had an opportunity to buy a money order and send it to his mama. I'd like to meet her, to tell her what a fine young man she'd loaned to the military service. He was a rare one. Then I "ground him down" for the "run-over heels" of his shoes. He was congratulated by 250 men—fellow soldiers, and his friends—on his reenlistment.

The 3rd Platoon, Lieutenant Lenon's, was ready to go to Yechon—another town and another adventure.

Yechon

20 July 1950, Yechon, Korea

Exodus 20:13, "Thou shalt not kill."

The first combat engagement between the 25th Infantry Division and the NKPA occurred at the town of Yechon on 20 July 1950. The NKPA had taken Yechon on 19 July, and the regiment was ordered to retake it. The 3rd Battalion of the 24th Infantry Regiment, under Lt. Col. Samuel Pierce, Jr., attacked on 20 July and took the town back from the NKPA. This was the first major victory for the U.S. Army in the Korean War. At the time it happened, this important victory was hailed in the press and in the U.S. Congress.

I will remember Yechon for another hundred years. Even in my nightmares I've never seen carnage, death, and destruction to equal—even to approach—that of 20 July 1950. But I'm ahead of the story. Let me go back a ways.

Whenever a task force is put together, there are always the engineers. It has always been so. In antiquity engineers were called "sappers" because we sapped the enemy's strength. We removed stones from the foundations of his castles and fortresses. We drained his moats, poisoned his water supply, and otherwise weakened him so that he could be assaulted effectively or starved. Later we were called "pioneers" because we went ahead of the infantry to clear the path. It is the same thing now. We help our forces move and try to prevent the enemy from advancing.

In modern times we purify and provide potable water instead of poisoning it. Water is the *sine qua non* of soldiers' lives. There ain't no combat without water!

Most combat commanders are commanders because they win battles, damn the cost. I understand, and I agree. I was a combat commander. It was time for me to deliver.

Lieutenant Lenon joined us and reported that Summers was still alive when he left him in the hospital. It didn't seem possible, but Summers was expected to live. Lieutenant Lenon took over his platoon after he had been briefed on our situation. It was good to have him back.

Chet Lenon gave me an account of his time. He'd taken Summers to a Japanese medical facility, and the Japanese had transported Summers and him to an American hospital, where a series of operations was performed. Finally a metal plate had been fashioned to cover the gaping hole in Summers's head, and skin from several parts of his body was grafted to cover the metal plate. Lieutenant Lenon had left Summers alive and improving. He would live.

I felt for Summers. I knew very little about him, but I valued him and regretted his loss. The fact that his injury was because of his misconduct made no difference. It was a weird situation to record on the morning report. It was even more strange when Summers reported back for duty with the company in November 1950, when we were at Kunu-ri, North Korea. It was an amazing end to that story.

Regiment called, and Lieutenant Lenon's platoon saddled up to accompany the 3d Battalion, 24th Infantry Regiment, to Yechon. After a brief shakedown, the platoon lined up and swung onto the rear of Item Company, 3d Battalion in the first section of the convoy. It looked like any other milk run, and I sent them off with casual blessings, as the sun baked their truck tops. I located Yechon on my situation map, and in the total absence of intelligence I wondered what the hell they were going to Yechon for. I wonder still.

Things at regimental headquarters were in a typical state of disorder, and I waited impatiently for something—anything—to happen. This was thoughtless; I should have welcomed any opportunity to be relaxed and go with the flow. The voracious mosquitoes chewed me through the long night. I was up and checking security every fifteen to twenty minutes, a habit that was to last a lifetime. Even when security was not a problem, my sleeping pattern was forever altered by the habits I established in those days.

The next day, our first mail since we arrived in Korea came in, and morale was lifted immeasurably. Only another soldier knows the value of mail. Receiving letters from home is by far the most pleasant event in a soldier's life. I decided to check on Lenon's platoon and take their mail to them. I cleared my trip with Colonel Roberts, the regimental executive officer.

My jeep was prepared for combat. A .30 caliber machine gun was mounted on a post on the right side immediately in front of my right leg, an idea I got from the regimental intelligence and reconnaissance platoon. I kept a Browning automatic rifle close at hand in the back seat of the jeep for use if we had to leave the vehicle to fight. I also had installed a barbed-wire buster— a notched piece of two-inch angle iron mounted on the front bumper of the jeep extending up about four feet. We all drove with our windshields down for better visibility, and occasionally the enemy would stretch a length of barbed wire at Adam's apple height across the road at night. Without a wire buster, a man riding in a jeep could easily be decapitated, so the barbed-wire busters were essential.

The countryside was pleasant with kelly-green rice paddies stretching for miles. We passed many groups of able-bodied Korean men walking along the roads and doing farmer-type things in the fields. I wondered how many of them were farmers by day and soldiers by night. I kept a watchful eye out in case some of them wanted to be soldiers by day also. They all behaved, so the trip was uneventful. I was admiring the countryside, when abruptly the 3d Battalion's signs indicated a turn off the main road, and we were on a levee that was one-vehicle wide. The road ran a mile or so to the village. We drove along until we came upon the last transport vehicle of the convoy that had brought the battalion to Yechon. I dismounted and approached a group of soldiers who were lollygagging at the rear of the column of vehicles.

Hell was breaking loose in the town up ahead, at the levee's end. I asked a sergeant where the 77th Engineers were, and he replied, "They're spearheading the attack, sir."

We'd been had again! We were supposed to be in support.

The village of Yechon was cradled deep in a buttonhook mountain, which nearly ringed it and loomed above it. The enemy had fallen back, climbed part way up the mountain, and was raining fire down into the town.

I assessed the situation from the rear of the vehicle column. There was no possibility of turning the column, or even individual vehicles, around. The levee was too narrow. If one of the rear vehicles were destroyed, the column would be trapped. The battalion was out of touch with regiment, and there were no other American troops within forty miles. An attack on the rear of the column would be disastrous. In very hostile country, with no support, a force capable of putting up the fire that I heard coming off the mountain could effectively chain up the entire battalion.

My heart grew to the size of a football, and adrenaline flooded my blood supply.

Immediately north of the rear of the column was a small hill, about three hundred yards high, that commanded a view of thousands of yards of rice paddies ranging toward the mountain to the north and toward the village to the east. I climbed the hill and had a good long look with eyeballs and with binoculars.

About a kilometer to the north I noticed a large body of men coming out of a defile and heading toward the rear of our vehicle column, which was at my position. I scuffled down the hill, commandeered a dozen of the lollygagging infantry soldiers, and had them carry a .50 caliber machine gun and ground mount, plus one of their water-cooled .30 caliber machine guns, and all the ammo we could carry in two trips, up the hill. I set the guns up about 100 feet apart and watched the group of white-clad men moving purposefully toward my position.

As I waited for them to close in, I made certain that the .30 caliber machine gun was mounted and ready for action with gunners. I sent the sergeant and six men back to the convoy for more ammunition.

I watched the group of farmer-soldiers coming ever closer and reckoned that farmers scatter and run if you send a long burst of machine-gun fire over their heads, but soldiers flatten out like quail and await orders or signals from their leader.

It was a beautiful plain, and the rice paddies were a deep shade of green. It was too nice a day to die and too nice a place for any man to die in, but c'est la vie. I was born to be on that hill that day. Destiny dictated it.

I sent a burst from the .50 caliber machine gun dangerously close above the heads of the approaching group, which was moving in a loose, hustling, route-step doubletime column astride the levees in the gigantic mire of the rice paddies. True to the form of soldiers, they flattened into the paddy as the bullets flew past them. A whistle was sounded and an arm raised to signal a movement to the west side of the check (or ridge of soil that helps control water, where the irrigation is controlled by flooding). My next burst was not just dangerously close. The signalman and those close to him were broken up like rag dolls in the mouths of bulldogs. The .30 caliber machine gun joined in. Bullets raked and chewed them up mercilessly.

The advancing column was under tight observation from somewhere on the mountain because large mortar rounds started barking at us like a giant dog—long, then short, then overhead. I was knicked by a fragment. The gunner on the .30 caliber machine gunner was hit badly, and his assistant was killed. The enemy mortar was accurate. The shells were bursting about twenty to forty feet overhead, showering us with shell fragments. And we were now drawing small-arms fire from the rice paddies below.

I was locked in and totally committed, but at intervals I wished I was almost any place else. I was hunkered over that gun. My assistant gunner was damned good, and I chopped the North Korean troops to pieces.

I called to the sergeant to bring up a lot more ammo, but he was cowering behind the trucks and pretended not to hear me. I still had ammunition and I continued to depress the trigger, systematically sawing down the levees and turning the area into a bloody mire.

We continued to rain heavy fire from our hilltop. The enemy mortar stayed close on us, dumping shell fragments all around. I was ashamed of the slaughter before me, but this was my job, my duty, and my responsibility. I stayed with it until not one white rag was left intact. One mortar fragment had cut my right wrist, and another had driven a splinter into my cheekbone. I was spitting blood.

I felt deep animal emotions within me that I had known in lives before, in the trees, in the caves, in holes, in vertical cliffs, in chariots, and in modern war machines. The gore, the smashed bones, the grinding and crushing of skulls, the horror, the mortal dread, the smell of blood, the smell of death—cold, blatant, demanding death. It was red and orange, and it was purple, and it was death. And my gun was overheating.

For the first time in this firefight, I felt fear. Without my gun, I was impotent, and death would surely swallow me up as it had my enemies.

I moved over to the .30 caliber water-cooled machine gun and lifted the assistant gunner away. The young gunner was paralyzed, hunkered in his place, struck dumb and rigid by the events around him. I kicked him hard, twice, three, four times, until the glaze left his eyes. I moved him over to the assistant gunner's place.

"Feed it," I told him, and he did. I activated the bolt, and the .30 caliber machine gun was alive and destructive. I was grateful. The assistant gunner tried to show me his shattered arm, but I continued firing. I fired bursts of two rounds, of three rounds, and sometimes of four rounds. The mortar shells barked overhead with their terror and destruction, but there was much less activity down in the rice paddies. I was patently secure in my mind. I could feel convulsions in my intestines, but I knew that there was no death for me that day. I was the dealer.

I continued my grisly chore with a vengeance, with furious dedication. It seemed like eternity plus eleven days, whereas it was only a few minutes. Dedication to what? Vengeance against whom? But there was no time to think. The handler fed, and I fired, and life fled from those bundles of white, linen, muslin, cotton farmers, fathers, citizens—men.

An arm extended from the slime terminating in a hand reaching to God, in supplication for life or supplication for death.

I would like to have had a moment for shame, but there was no time and there was no shame. Only duty. This was the killing floor, and I knew it well. I'd previously seen and smelled the bloody mire somewhere: Jericho, Thermopylae, Belleau Woods, or was it with Ghengis Khan at Cologne? No matter! I was a soldier, and gore was the hallmark of my trade. Death stomped on through the rice paddy on bloody feet.

Finally there was no more movement, and the carnage ceased. There was nothing left to kill. The gentle breeze of early evening bathed us all. It chilled me as perspiration evaporated on my spine. The handler looked at me, and he was afraid—not of what he'd seen, but of me. For a moment I was afraid of myself. Never had he seen a man do what I had done for the past fifteen minutes or so. He'd only known death from movies and adventure novels. It had always been heroic, grand, noble, piteous. Now he knew that it was cold, ugly, totally insensitive, and inconsiderate. There were no heroics. He started to cry, and I envied him. The mortar had stopped. I bandaged his arm and told him that he had done well. We carried his dead friend back beyond the brow of the hill. He felt better for it, but it really didn't matter.

We went down the hill to muster the help we needed to recover the dead and our guns. Even with the guns silent, the sergeant and some troops were creeping around the rear of the truck column. I told them we had to go back up the hill to retrieve the guns. They moved up the hill with great trepidation.

I looked out over the plain of young rice at the levee where the eternal willows were growing moments before. Now there were twigs and shards of wood and blood. I wondered if the willows would grow there again. Part of me died there also.

There was neither movement nor life remaining in the plain before us. It was nearing sunset. I had the sergeant bandage my arm. I rounded up the lollygaggers and stragglers. I issued each of them a bandolier of ammo and directed them to shoulder their weapons. We moved northeast of the hill onto the plain. There were a few of the enemy badly wounded, mortally wounded, but still clinging to life by less than a thread. There was no doctor or hospital within thirty miles. I saw indescribable pain and misery in the rice paddy. With great pity and sorrow for the enemy and myself, I did the merciful and the only humane thing that I could: we shot the nearly dead.

We counted the enemy dead. In that plain were 258 dead men in large and small pieces. The rice paddies were now crimson and green. I was sick, sicker than I'd ever been in life. We moved back to the vehicle column. I climbed the hill again and took a final look at that valley. The valley of death.

Gradually, the firefight in the village slowed down, and the battalion secured the area for the night. It was sunset and then dark. I was ashamed and sick and sore. I forced myself to think of the consequences that would have befallen the battalion and my platoon if I hadn't been there to do that butchering. That didn't make it right, but it did make it necessary. The engineer platoon remained with the battalion combat team.

We got ready for the return trip. We put the .30 caliber machine gun on the hood of the jeep. It wasn't much security for a night ride in the Korean countryside, but it was all we had. As we rode along back to camp, my mind raced and retraced the events of the day. I had never known a time like that. I chose to think of the killing later.

This episode was the plot and scenario of ugly dreams for me for many years. I had nightmares with those guns rattling and lurching and killing, but such is a soldier's lot, such is a soldier's duty, such is a soldier's life. Oriental soldiers stomped on my grave in my dreams every night for fifteen or twenty years.

I had no real grievance with the bodies in that bloody mire. They should have been home tending their crops and raising their sons. The same was true of me. I knew that the world was not going to be a better place because of the death of those white-clad men. In my way and in my time, I weep for them and all of their kind, which is my kind. I asked God for forgiveness, but God was mute.

I was raised to be a Christian, and I tried to be. I tried to live by the Ten Commandments. One of those commandments stated "Thou shalt not kill." No qualification, no rationalization. No ifs, ands, or buts. As a youngster, I used to wonder if the directive extended to animals as well as humans. In any event, duty had demanded that I do a mass killing, and I had complied. The conflicting claims of duty and religious principle grate against each other in my mind and in my soul.

Moses laid down in Numbers the law pertaining to the raising of armies for war. Maybe that made it all right.

That is my story of the Battle of Yechon. I was there, and it was a battle as far as I was concerned, and it was a victory, too.

Most historians of the Korean War have either dismissed this combat engagement or termed it a disgraceful defeat for the black troops. The U.S. Army's official history implies that there was no victory or even a real battle at Yechon.* Despite evidence to the contrary, including first-hand reports by Associated Press (AP) correspondent Tom Lambert, this error has been perpetrated over the years by historians too careless to search out primary historical sources. It was not until Clay Blair published his *The Forgotten War* in 1987 that the facts about Yechon came out.**

The Army and most historians assert that Negro soldiers in black units did not fight very well in the early days of the Korean War and were prone to run away, or bug out in the jargon of the time. That is true, but white soldiers in white units also did not fight very well at that time. It was desperate combat. Bugging out was common for troops of all kinds and colors. The reality is that the entire Army—white and black—did not fight very well initially, with some notable exceptions. One of those exceptions was my 77th Engineer Combat Company.

In my opinion, the primary reason for success or failure in

* Appleman, *South to the Naktong,* 190–91.

** Blair, *Forgotten War,* 147–53. This presents another account of the treatment of black troops and of the Battle of Yechon.

combat in Korea was the quality of leadership at the battalion and regimental levels. Good leaders had units that fought well; bad leaders had troops that bugged out. Unfortunately, there were many bad leaders in the U.S. Army in the Korean War. Fortunately, there were a few good leaders, too. The original commander of the 24th Infantry Regiment, Col. Horton V. White, was competent, but he soon became exhausted by the demands of combat and left the regiment. The next commander of the 24th Infantry Regiment, Col. Arthur S. Champeny, was incompetent and lasted only a few weeks before he was wounded and evacuated to Japan. Then Col. John T. Corley, a highly decorated combat veteran of World War II, became the regimental commander. The 24th Infantry Regiment performed extremely well for Colonel Corley. He was Irish, and leadership seemed more important to him than skin color in determining success in battle.

It is hard for me to understand how the U.S. Army's official history could say that the Battle of Yechon simply did not occur. I was there when the 25th Infantry Division Commander, Major General Kean, came to the regiment and pinned a Silver Star on my chest for my actions at Yechon. He told me it was a down payment on the highest medal. I doubt that the general did that for an imaginary battle.

Certainly, Colonel Corley, the regimental commander who took over command on 6 September 1950, thought it was a victory. His rallying cry to bolster the morale of the troops was "Remember Yechon!"*

---

* Blair, *Forgotten War*, 245.

Desperate Combat

23–30 July 1950,
Sangju, Korea

I had been to regiment to receive our orders. The 24th RCT had been assigned to defend the general area northwest of Sangju. At this time all of the U.S. and ROK forces were attempting to stabilize a defensive position generally along the Naktong River. The 77th ECC was to operate in direct support of the 24th RCT. I realized early that being attached or being in direct support was purely an administrative distinction. Our job was to support the regiment, and we were part of the team. We were moving northwest of Sangju within the hour.

The day had been spent maintaining vehicles and equipment. When I got back from regiment, I had the troops mustered. It's bad to be near a tactical operation and not know what's going on. I filled them in with everything that I knew and even passed along the rumors I'd heard, mostly about the losses in the 24th Infantry Division.

I gave another caution, "Do not, repeat *not*, under any circumstances, ride on a trailer." I explained why in detail. "Trailers do not have the suspension of trucks and tend to bounce hard when striking rocks or pot holes. The impact is sharp and will throw a rider off onto the ground; sometimes it will throw the rider forward so the trailer runs over him."

109

Finally, "The last time I gave a caution, it was ignored by Summers, who's probably dead back in Japan someplace now. *Repeat, again,* do *not* ride trailers."

We saddled up at the appointed time to fit into the regiment's order of march. On the way up we passed hundreds of farmers in those white clothes, and I wondered how many were soldiers by night. I was slightly paranoid about those uniforms. This war was definitely not like the one the U.S. Army had fought in North Africa, Italy, France, Bougainville, or Tarawa. This was something else. The trip was without incident until late morning, when the long column stopped short in response to the tattoo of small automatic-weapons fire that was pouring down on the convoy from the brush above, high on the hillside. I walked past the stopped vehicles, which I kept between me and the source of the gunfire. When I got up to Colonel White's jeep, I overheard the last part of a conversation between the Old Man and Lieutenant Gilchrist, a black officer from the 1st Battalion. The colonel was old, tired, and exhausted; he wheezed at Gilchrist, "You take some men, go up that hill, and get 'em."

Gilchrist said, "That'd be suicide, Colonel. Let's get some heavy-weapons fire up there. You ain't going to get me killed."

I was sorry that I had heard the exchange. The colonel turned to Lt. Ransome Holt, another black officer, and said, "Take some men, and go get 'em."

Holt said, "Yessir," and moved out.

The colonel looked back at Gilchrist and said, "I'm going to court martial you. You are relieved of duty and are under arrest. Report to me when we arrive in Sangju."

Both officers were lying tight to the overhanging bank for protection from the gunfire. Lieutenant Holt and one of his squads climbed the steep embankment and headed up the mountainside. The gunfire ceased before they had climbed 100 yards. The North Koreans fled rather than face capture or death.

The convoy rolled again, generating a nimbus-type cloud of dust. God, it was hot!

Later, Lieutenant Gilchrist was tried by court martial, convicted, and sentenced to death for refusing to obey an order to engage the enemy. President Truman reduced the sentence to twenty years of confinement. Gilchrist actually served five years in a federal prison. There were some alleged irregularities in the conduct of Gilchrist's trial. Some or all of his witnesses were not allowed to leave the combat area to testify for him. In a capital case, that was unconscionable. It gave the trial the appearance of a "kangaroo" court. When added to the numerous unfair trials exposed by Thurgood Marshall, Negroes were further denigrated. The Army's disciplinary system was reminiscent of the Scottsboro case, which occurred in Alabama in 1931.

I was bitter about it. Gilchrist brought his trial upon himself, which was his privilege, but his action hurt every Negro officer in the theater of operations. The senior (white) officers made the worst of it, and the white press had a field day. Gilchrist's action placed an inferred stigma of cowardice on all Negro officers, particularly those in the 24th Regiment.

We passed the site where the 13th Field Artillery (FA) Battalion had gotten its baptism. The troops had been overrun and lost all their guns. Their 105mm howitzers had been destroyed by the North Koreans. They had loaded the guns and then jammed a round, fuse first, into each muzzle. With an extended lanyard, they had fired each gun. The resulting explosion in the barrel had caused the barrel to split.

The war seemed real now. Garlic and gunpowder. A number of vehicles had been destroyed by mines along the roads. I don't know why, exactly, but I was surprised to find such active and effective land-mine warfare. From the damage, I judged that the mines contained from six to eight pounds of TNT—tough on wheeled vehicles and occupants.

The country was rugged. The hills were steep and utterly barren. The natives cut the trees for firewood for the long, cold winters. There was no cover for fighting; we were always exposed. The valleys were lush, green, rice paddies. The inhabitants invariably fled when the war became active in their area. Marijuana grew wild along the roadside. The old men in the villages smoked it incessantly. So did some of my people; I smelled it at night when the air was still. I worried a little because I knew there was no way to stop it. I hoped no inefficiency would result from overindulgence.

My bigger worry was the men in the long white drawers—our enemy.

Trial by Fire, 25 July 1950, near Sangju, Korea

Colonel Roberts called me and asked that I send my 1st Platoon to be attached to the 1st Battalion. I rogered. Each of my platoons, by number, supported one of the three battalions of the regiment by corresponding number. It was all worked out so that my platoon leader's personality jibed with that of the battalion commander he supported. Otherwise there were sparks. Sparks I could do without.

It was always touch and go because the engineer school doctrine was vastly different from that of the infantry school. We were always one breath away from a flap. The infantry loved to push the tough, killing jobs off on the engineers. We engineers always insisted that the infantry should "buy" the real estate, and we engineers would develop or destroy it. That is gospel, but there was always haggling about who would do what for whom.

The 1st Battalion got hung up in heavy fire west of Sangju, and there were mines in the road that kept the tanks from advancing. Lieutenant Colonel Miller, the battalion commander, called Lieutenant Benefield in for a conference on the predicament. After a heated discussion, Benny decided to acquiesce and remove the mines. This was a very dangerous mission. The enemy had those mines covered by withering small-arms fire.

It was the Infantry battalion's responsibility to neutralize the enemy fire before Benny started to probe for the mines, but the shabby Infantry battalion commander talked Benny into probing the minefield right away so the battalion commander could run his vehicles into the enemy. Benny tried it. He took Sergeant Bardo, and Lieutenant Wilson went along to help. They didn't have a prayer. Enemy fire cut them to ribbons.

Finally, the battalion commander called up his 81mm mortars and destroyed the enemy covering force that was protecting the minefield. But it was too late.

By the time I arrived, the medics had evacuated Benny, Wilson, and Bardo to the regimental clearing station. I got there soon after they did. Although Sergeant Bardo and Lieutenant Wilson were destined to live in spite of their wounds, Benny was all torn up in the abdomen. There was a hole in him that I could have put both fists into. He suffered terribly. There was nothing the field medics could do for him. He needed a well-equipped surgical unit to give him the necessary support. That miserable Army, of which we were a part, had at that time no qualified doctor or medical unit within fifty miles that was capable of helping the seriously wounded.

I prayed silently for Benny,

> Oh, Father in heaven,
> accept the soul of this valiant soldier
> who has come to thee for his rewards
> and the eternal refuge of thy bosom.
> Forgive him his sins, I pray.
> Replace the guidance and protection
> he provided for his loved ones
> only with thine own.
> Amen.

We waited nearly six hours for his evacuation to a higher-level medical facility. Benny said to me, "I can make it if I can get sewed up and get a transfusion."

I believed him, but the aid didn't come.

Benny lay and suffered in agony from gross gunshot wounds from about 1330 hours until 1900 hours. He muttered, fingered his rosary, and died. I wept for Benny. His was a great loss. His three children would have to survive and mature without him. I was selfish in my attitude. I'd lost a friend and colleague. We all were poorer for his sudden and needless demise. I was deeply hurt and angered.

I recommended Benny for a Distinguished Service Cross. He earned it, and he received it—posthumously.

Lieutenant Benefield should not have been committed to such a suicidal mission. The infantry is committed to buying real estate and silencing enemy small-arms fire before the engineers are used. There should have been competent medical backup.

It was the first of numerous instances of incompetence by field grade officers that I was to see and be adversely affected by.

Lieutenant Wilson and Sergeant Bardo were taken to a field hospital and treated for their wounds, which were quite serious. After several days in the hospital, they had a short leave in Japan and then returned for duty with the company.

I talked to Colonel Roberts about the minefield incident, and I was contumacious. I raved insubordinately about a sorry officer four grades senior to me, and the Army does not tolerate that from its lieutenants. The colonel let me blow it off. He knew the impact that the loss of an officer like Benny had upon me.

I gave Benny's platoon to SFC Collins A. Whitaker, an outstanding soldier. "Whit" was a platoon sergeant, and an exceptional one. I was desperate for an officer, but there was no one in the pipeline for us. There were plenty of engineer officers, but no black engineer officers. I considered our unit predicament carefully and in great depth. Finally, I settled on applying for a battlefield commission for Sergeant First Class Whitaker, subject to his own desire in the matter. He was reluctant to accept a commission in the same company where he'd served as an enlisted man, but we talked at great length, and he finally agreed that he should do it. I had no doubts about his ability to make it all happen. I knew that he had only finished high school and that academically he had a deficiency that would make it difficult for him to advance beyond company grade, but that was another set of problems for another far-off day. His acceptance was announced. The officers and enlisted men supported Whit, and we were a strong, combat-ready unit again. In a very short period his commission was approved, and he moved into "officer country," where he performed commendably throughout the war and into years of garrison duty.

Every Man's Price, 27 July 1950, Near Sangju, Korea

All my life I'd heard that every man had his price. I'd heard that with some significant gain every man's integrity failed and left him a coward or a thief. No one told me that sometimes the price was not in money. Sometimes the price was in values. Rarer, but the possibility existed that the price was in negatives. So it was with me.

I have always taken an extreme pride in being a Negro. I enjoyed accomplishments of any magnitude, particularly so when the accomplishments happened against obstacles. The more difficult the obstacle, the greater the pleasure. The greatest pleasure, of course, came from success in spite of racial barriers.

I hated the imposition of hardships that had racism as the originating or causative factor. Fate dictated it, and I learned to live with it. My price was the realization that we Negroes were destined to be denigrated, besmirched, abused, lied to, lied about, and used as whipping boys on a continual basis in spite of Truman's edict that called for integration.

Although the Gilchrist affair was over and done with, the press did not let it die; neither did the Army. The entire Negro regiment was denigrated, lied about, and the 25th Division commander, Major General Kean, who had deliberately or inadvertently sabotaged the regiment with his personnel policies, attempted to have the regiment removed from active service. Fortunately he failed in this action. General Walker denied his request.

The treatment of us Negroes as second-class citizens with poor leadership, poor training, and abuse in white-controlled courts should have been enough, but there was more. They debased us in the white press, and they flaunted it to the entire world. Propaganda continually decried the quality of service performed by the black soldiers of the 24th Infantry Regiment. I watched them poorly officered, poorly led, dying, and dead—and all the while maligned unfairly.

After a top-flight commander, Col. John T. Corley, assumed command of the 24th Infantry Regiment in September 1950,

Negro officers were assigned as company commanders but not to higher positions. The exception was Maj. Richard Williams. Although fully qualified to become a battalion commander, he remained on the regimental staff. Corley and all the commanders back all the way to the Pentagon opposed using Negro officers above company command level.

This was not my personal problem because I knew that troops are as good as their leaders. I had a ton of confidence in myself, my officers, and my noncoms; my troops were good. My company was one of the most decorated company-size units in the Eighth Army. I was a patriot in spite of the bigotry and duplicity of the country I served. I had never been allowed, or allowed myself, to feel or act otherwise. I loved my country for what it *could* be—far beyond what it was.

Let me get to the point where my price was established. My price, which caused me to abandon my moral principles and abrogate my legal principles, my oaths, and the tenets of my religion, was a negative one. The company's mission west of Sangju was to mine the roads with antitank mines and the foot approaches with antipersonnel mines. It had been hard work, taking two days and one night. I was sitting in my jeep with a sheet of heavy corrugated board in my lap, completing minefield reports. Minefield reports are extremely important because, at some time in the future, my people or some other troops would have to remove every single mine and its activating mechanism. Without reports, some GI, farmer, or child would probably die for each emplaced and unrecorded mine. So I did the reports with meticulous— no, religious—care. I was parked beside a "cut" in the road, and on my right there was a bluff twenty to thirty feet above me. The bluff was of no importance to me. I was totally engrossed in my paper war.

Then I heard a voice above me ask another person, "How far away do you figger that ol' muthuhfucka is?" It was unmistakably the voice of a black American soldier.

"Oh, I'd say six hundred yards," was the response.

"Ten dollars says I can hit him."

"You got a bet!"

Like the crack of doom the M1 rifle went off. As my eyes suddenly, attentively, swept the horizon, an old man tumbled off a bluff about six hundred yards down the road. I recognized the inverted hat that the patriarchs wore. The lifeless tumbling of the body told me that murder had been committed.

My duty was explicit: apprehend the man who had committed the crime, arrest him, and turn him over to the MPs; accomplish the paperwork; identify witnesses; and eventually testify against the perpetrator.

Those were my own men up on that nearby bluff. Duty demanded that I do what was legally, morally, and religiously right, but I could see the press and the holier-than-thou rear-echelon officers browbeating another "nigrah soljuh" and smearing this crime on every other Negro in the theater of operations.

I was convinced that the Army's policy was to punish Negroes more harshly than white soldiers. The record was hidden, but it was common knowledge that Negroes went to trial for offenses that were only winked about when perpetrated by white soldiers. Punishments for Negroes were usually the most severe found in the Table of Maximum Punishments in the *Uniform Code of Military Justice*. Whites were punished less severely.

My belief was supported later, in February 1951, when Thurgood Marshall, special counsel for the National Association for the Advancement of Colored People (NAACP) visited Korea to investigate charges that convictions and punishments were more severe for Negro soldiers than for white soldiers. Marshall, who later was appointed an associate justice of the United States Supreme Court, produced a report that was highly critical of Army justice. He found that there was an unusually large number of court martial cases against Negroes. He found blatant cases of racial discrimination in both the nature and severity of punishment that had been handed down. Marshall's report resulted in reversed convictions or reduced sentences for most of the thirty-nine Negro soldiers of the 24th Infantry Regiment who had been convicted for serious breaches of discipline.*

I couldn't pay the price. It was impossible for me to turn my man over to the system, to be used as an object to further denigrate

* Blair, *Forgotten War*, 683–84.

all Negroes. I couldn't do it. I felt for the old Korean man lying dead in the road ahead of me, but in my order of priorities it was his life against the lives of ten thousand black soldiers who didn't deserve the ignominy.

I finished filling out the minefield report.

ROK Troops, 28 July 1950, Near Sangju, Korea

Korea presented thousands of new problems for the U.S. Army. Our Army was oriented toward, trained for, and totally involved with the previous war—World War II. When problems arose that hadn't been mulled and tugged over in the service schools and academies, commanders in the field often were ill prepared to deal effectively with the new problems and even with the new solutions.

One such problem was how to use the Republic of Korea troops, called ROKs. Because the local troops were recruited faster than they could be trained or used against a well-trained, disciplined enemy, some U.S. personnel came up with the idea of integrating the South Koreans into Eighth Army units. They were willing to integrate the ROKs, even though most Negroes were still segregated.

An abbreviated ROK engineer company of approximately one hundred foot soldiers was assigned to my company. It was a noble experiment, albeit naive. None of the Korean officers, NCOs, or enlisted people could speak one word of English. None of my troops could speak any Korean. It was one helluva mess. Integrating people who could not communicate was difficult—if not impossible.

We were building some culverts and small bridges, trying to use my new charges. It was impossible to communicate with the ROK commander, and the problem multiplied in geometric proportions from that point.

Without any consultation, the First Sergeant solved the dilemma, as first sergeants are wont to do. First Sergeant Dudley assigned a number to each Korean soldier and assigned the same number to a designated soldier from our ranks. Numbers were painted

on helmets. Names were impossible, but the Koreans could handle
the numbers and were able to identify their American counterparts. Mass instruction commenced, making the integration and
utilization of the native troops a reality. Our troops learned many
words of the Korean language, and some fine—although short-
lived—friendships bloomed.

An interesting incident took place on the first morning of the
ROK assignment. We were having hotcakes, among other things,
for breakfast, and the fare excited the Koreans. Each of them
loaded his mess pan with the half-inch thick hotcakes. They
drowned the hotcakes in the heavy syrup, poured an inch of
sugar over the entire area of their mess pans, and wolfed down
the whole supersweet glob. Half an hour later there were one
hundred writhing, bellyaching Koreans on hand. Some were
agonizing on the ground; others were doubled over heaving up
that sugar. It was a helluva mess, those Asians attempting to
ingest all those Western carbohydrates. Private First Class
Napoleon, our medic, advised me that there was nothing he
could do about it. He recommended that we put them to work as
soon as possible. The ROKs had learned their lesson, however,
and from that moment on they ate exactly as the GIs did—no
excesses.

The ROKs were willing to work, but we had to overcome the
communications obstacle for our relationship to be effective. It
was obvious to me that we needed several interpreters—soldiers
who could speak both Korean and English. I spoke to Colonel
Roberts about it, and he assured me that he could obtain some
Koreans with the required linguistic ability. Late that afternoon,
the interpreters arrived, and after a short period of indoctrination,
we were in business. We taught the ROKs some basic soldiering
and how to use hand tools. They were eager to learn, and things
went smoothly after the interpreters arrived.

One of the most effective of the Korean interpreters was Pak
Mal Tom, who, of course, was called "Tom" by the troops. Tom
was a brutal and ruthless man who had served as a marine in
the Japanese forces in World War II. With his rugged personality,
military experience, and knowledge of English, Tom practically

took over the ROK unit. I could see it happening, but lacking the ability to understand Korean, there was little I could do but wait.

Together, we accomplished a lot of badly needed road work, and the training went well. I noticed, however, that the ROKs were not well trained in marksmanship. There had not been enough time for the Korean army to really make fighting men of these recruits. I applied to Colonel Roberts and the regimental operations officer for permission to conduct some small-arms training for the ROKs. They thought it was a good idea, provided the training was well supervised, other troops in the area were notified, and security against North Korean attack was adequate. We laid out a small-arms range, firing into a small hill. It turned out well, for some of the ROKs had no proficiency in firing their weapons at all. We conducted live firing with rifles at ranges of fifty yards and one hundred yards from the targets. Time and space limitations would not permit firing from longer ranges, but I figured that nearly all of the firing that these troops would do in real combat would be at close range.

During the markmanship training, I saw Tom putting the boot to one of the young ROK soldiers for some minor infraction. I took Tom aside and chewed him out. I reiterated his job responsibilities. I advised him that he was to interpret, facilitate communication between the U.S. and ROK soldiers, and make suggestions regarding training and operations, all under the supervision of the field First Sergeant. Under no circumstances was he to make policy in any matter or to impose discipline on anyone—ever. I left no doubt in Tom's mind about his job and his authority. After that, Tom stayed out of my way.

The regiment was west of Sangju. We were in direct support, but I didn't know what I was in support of. No one seemed to know what it was all about. There was no sustained contact with the enemy, but there had been some clashes in the area. Lieutenant Benefield had been killed, and Lieutenant Wilson and Sergeant Bardo had been wounded in one of these clashes. I had been hit by a mortar fragment from a proximity-fused mortar. The shell had cracked about forty feet above ground. I had heard or felt it, and ducked with my hands over my ears, and the fragment had driven into my wrist. In all, it was a bad situation. The lack of information about the enemy and about what we were doing was bad. Very bad.

Colonel Roberts called me and said, "There's enemy troops holed up in the huts and warehouse five hundred feet west of regimental headquarters. Get 'em. Alive if possible. Burn all buildings."

"Yes, sir. Wilco. Out."

We moved out smartly. The 1st Platoon surrounded the huts, and Tom, the interpreter, called for the occupants of the building to surrender or die in the building, which was about to be burned. No response. The building was torched. The same procedure was used for three or four more buildings.

As we progressed through the huts, lighting them up with thermite grenades, we began to collect prisoners. Realizing that they were hopelessly surrounded, the North Korean soldiers and some nurses lay on the ground, face down and spread-eagled. When it was all over we had thirty-six prisoners and some massive fires. The warehouse was full, or nearly full, of rice. Lord, how it burned. What a waste!

At Tom's direction the prisoners arose and formed three ranks, with hands palms-down upon their heads. We searched them and found nothing of a contraband nature. I reported to regiment with the prisoners, who were forced to sit on their haunches to wait for some indeterminate fate. When the regimental S-2 finished his cursory and nonproductive interrogation, he called G-2 at division and promised him sixty-one prisoners. The other twenty-five had been captured by other units of the regiment. We ordered the first thirty-six into a waiting cargo truck. They filled it up.

The S-2 told the truck driver, "Give them the treatment." At this command, the driver pulled ahead a hundred yards or so, turned the truck around, and accelerated rapidly toward us and the other prisoners. When nearly abreast of us he slammed on the brakes, which caused the thirty-six bodies to move forward. The compressing effect on the prisoner cargo created plenty of room for the remaining prisoners. The two jeep escorts formed front and rear of the cargo truck. Each jeep had machine guns mounted so that escape attempts were considered futile. All prisoners were delivered safely to division headquarters.

Later that day the troops brought in two more prisoners who were trying to steal a drink at the water point. The temperature was well over 100°F, and it was brickyard dry. The prisoners were docile, but Tom treated them as though they were war crimes perpetrators. After a little jabbering between Tom and the prisoners, Tom declared, "This one's an officer; he has a lot of information on troop disposition."

Although I knew better, I reluctantly went along with Tom and left him to his informal and unauthorized interrogation. I was gone for a couple of hours.

When I left, Tom really did a job on the prisoners. He placed them in a sitting position on their haunches. That was typical of the Koreans. It depicted servitude and humility; it was an indication of inferiority. From his vantage point, Tom asked the prisoners numerous questions my sergeant didn't understand, nor did he understand the answers.

When Tom became bored with this mild form of interrogation, he quickened the pace. He determined that the younger prisoner had no information, but that the older one had valuable intelligence, which Tom was going to extract. He placed a small log, perhaps two to two and one-half inches in diameter, behind the prisoner's knees and directed that the prisoner sit back on his haunches. The prisoner could no longer do this, so Tom jumped on his shoulders, which popped both knees out of socket. The prisoner shrieked with pain. He was beyond giving information if he had any. But Tom was not through, not by a long shot.

Tom broke out an EE-8 telephone, skinned back the insulation on each wire, jammed a wire into each of the prisoner's ears, and directed an onlooker to crank the telephone. The prisoner, with blood gushing from both ears, lost his mind upon receipt of the electric shock. He rolled over in merciful unconsciousness. When Tom saw no further sport in the matter, he took a hatchet and chopped into the prisoner's temple. Death was instantaneous.

Upon my return, the body was lying where it had expired. I got the story pieced together. I sent for Tom and directed that he dig a six-foot grave for the body that he had violated. He started to give me some sass, but I jacked a .45 caliber shell into the receiver of my automatic pistol, and he allowed as how he guessed he could do it. I allowed as how if he didn't get it done within the hour I'd bury him in the hole also. I put him under guard, and he got the grisly job done.

When the burial was over, I threatened to shoot Tom if I saw him again, anytime, anywhere. With only those items of clothing that he joined us with, I headed him up that dusty road. He was in a hurry to be gone, and dust flew from his hasty footprints in the loose soil of the road back toward Sangju.

That prisoner of war had his rights, and I felt that his fellow men owed him reasonable treatment. I will not budge from that position.

Captain Jackson, 29 July 1950, Near Sangju, Korea

Capt. William Jackson and I became good friends when we were stationed together at Gifu early in 1950. He was a senior black infantry captain in the 24th Infantry Regiment. Bill was a genuinely nice guy. His wife and kids were great, too. His wife was a fine cook, and I ate a lot of weekend chow at the Jackson home. Bill and I were avid coon-can players. Coon-can is a kind of rummy, involving taking ten cards and trying to make eleven. We spent a lot of our leisure time in Japan trying to catch eleven.

We spent a lot of time, before Korea started, jawing about politics, religion, economics, and race relations, particularly as pertinent to the Army. We were in it, and it was lousy. But if one was a Negro and wanted to serve for either patriotic or economic reasons, one had to choke down that racism. It meant second-class citizenship and, in some cases, no citizenship. It meant substandard quarters, inferior training, and poor morale and facilities. Worst of all, it meant being subject to a gross lack of leadership from inferior officers.

Jackson was a cool, intelligent man. We always had a lot to talk about. The Jim Crow practices always came first, but more significant and most ignominious were the discipline and morale problems. The 24th Infantry Regiment in Japan was loaded with cowardly and inept officers who were not acceptable in white units. Some of them should not have held commissions in the Army at all. There was also a group of West Pointers and other Regular Army officers who occupied favored command positions at company level.

Inasmuch as all Negro officers had to be assigned to Negro troop units, they were given only the "dog robbing" assignments, such as theater officers, athletic and recreation officers, assistant supply officers, and sometimes no assignments at all. There were only four Negro company commanders in the entire 24th Regimental Combat Team (RCT) while stationed in Japan. There were a few outstanding white officers in the combat team and, inevitably, there were a few piss-poor Negro officers.

After the 24th RCT arrived at Kumchon, Korea, things had changed. Company commanders and platoon leaders began getting killed in significant numbers, and suddenly, these company-level command jobs became available for Negro officers. No matter how well qualified, however, there still were no Negroes commanding anything above company level.

A Negro officer commanding troops had many problems that white officers didn't have. The troops did not communicate extensively with white officers. They expected little or nothing from these officers and concentrated only on their own survival. Certainly, there were some exceptions to these conditions but not many. On the other hand, Negro troops expected miracles of Negro officers. They expected superior leadership, sympathy, and involvement in situations outside the officers' areas of responsibility.

A soldier once asked me in a sidelong manner, "Sir, why should I follow you and possibly get myself killed? When I get back home to Mississippi, I won't be able to vote or go to a decent school. Why, sir?"

I responded, "If you follow me you have at least a remote chance of survival while we accomplish our mission. If you don't follow me closely, you will get killed. That is for sure. As far as Mississippi is concerned, I recommend that you find a better place to live."

We had to know and understand the problems of Negro life. We had to know the mire and muck that was life in the dark lane. We had to work the troops through it. We did.

After we went to Korea, I didn't see Jackson for awhile. When we did meet again, it was under adverse circumstances. I almost killed him by accident.

The 77th Engineer Combat Company was given a series of missions to protect elements of the 25th Division, which were moving back from the Sangju area into the Pusan perimeter. Our first mission was to blow a crater in the main supply route (MSR) to the north that would preclude passage of tanks; the selection of the site was optional. The second mission was to perform a rearguard action at the crater for twelve hours. The third mission was to destroy the throughput capability of rail traffic and demolish all switches, frogs (track-switching devices), and rail necessary to deactivate the Sangju rail yard. The fourth, and final, mission was to destroy the three southern spans of the bridge across the Kum River to include the south abutment. I was to report to the division engineer upon completion of these missions.

We selected a site on the MSR where we could blow an inside curve with no possibility for bypassing and little possibility for combat-quality repair. A Lieutenant Zandis from the infantry was designated to be the last and final contact person; his arrival at the demolition site would signal that all elements and individuals of the regiment would have evacuated their combat sectors. This would be my authority to blow the crater. Lieutenant Zandis was due at the crater site at 0400.

He was on time. He assured me that all 24th Infantry personnel had cleared the area and that I could blow the crater at any time.

It had taken ten hours to place nearly fifteen hundred pounds of TNT deep into the mountainside. Zandis had a cup of coffee as dawn crept over the barren hills. I looked down the long empty back road, then walked over the site of the crater with the generator, or "hellbox," in my pocket. I connected the box to the electrical blasting wire after "proving" the circuit with the galvanometer.

"Fire in the hole! Fire in the hole! Fire in the hole!"

I vigorously twisted the T-handle on the generator, and the whole world blew up in a cloud of rocks, dust, and cordite. It was the crack of doom! I felt a surge of elation as we awaited the settling of a virtual cloud of dust. I wanted to inspect our handiwork.

When I arrived back at the crater, day was breaking. Nobody was to be seen on the back road. I prepared to send most units to Sangju and beyond and to man the roadblock with one of Lieutenant Lenon's squads across the arroyo.

High above me on a cliff overlooking the crater a soldier yelled down, "Sir, you blew up two men in that blast. They were coming up the road when you blew it. They were at the edge of the crater. See their shoes and belts and carbines? That's them laying against the bank, down there about one hundred yards."

I looked, but there was a slight bend in the road that blocked my vision. That was how the two people had been able to move up to the site of the crater without my seeing them. I could feel the gates of Leavenworth clanging shut on me. With a couple of my officers, I hurriedly climbed the hill, skirted the bend, and descended toward the victims of the blast.

The sun was casting long horizontal rays over our heads as we climbed down the hillside. At the level of the back road, I was looking into the eyes of my dear friend Jackson. He wasn't focusing well, but he knew it was me. So he asked, "Tryin' to kill me, Hoss?"

"God, no, Jackson. But it was still too dark to see you, and Zandis was my contact. He got here about a half hour ago. He was supposed to be the last man out."

"Well, it was a typical snafu. We had a short firefight as we were disengaging. I think I've got a concussion. My eyesight comes and goes. You may have done me a big favor, Homeboy. Five thousand men and their vehicles and equipment were supposed to pass this point. Two men late ain't too bad. Sorry I'm one of them, though."

I looked over at Jackson's companion, a Lieutenant Morgan, who was silently crying. He looked at me as if I was the personification of death. I had been, nearly. I sent for some stretchers to carry the two of them back over the hills.

Jackson asked me, "Where's my shoes, my web equipment, and my carbine?"

"Don't ask me how, but all your stuff is about two feet from the edge of the crater. I'm glad you weren't one step farther to the east or you'd be dead and I'd be on the short end of a court martial."

Jackson and Morgan both had concussions and were evacuated back to Japan, but not for long. Personnel were in short supply. Injured personnel were returned from the hospital to the combat zone as soon as possible. So both of them were back to duty in about two weeks.

Crater Fight, 29 July 1950

I had done the first part of the mission by blowing the crater. Now I had to secure it for twelve hours. First, it was about time for breakfast, and the food went down well.

After breakfast, I carved up the company mission among the platoons. When all was well, the company, minus the squad remaining with me, fired up their engines and motored down the road to the city of Sangju.

During the preceding day and night, we had prepared foxholes. We moved into them as the morning began to heat up. It was yet another day when the temperature was going to climb to 110°F by noon. We waited and waited. We had been issued 3.5-inch bazookas, which were touted to be tank killers—real effective hell busters, the living end. I believed it all. I was manning one along with Corporal Barnwell.

The enemy came. They moved cautiously up the road, and our boredom ceased. Adrenaline began to tighten us up. First, there was a squad or so of infantry on the road. Then came a small Russian-built tank. The temperature grew hotter, and the enemy task force came closer. As mortal combat deliberately comes closer and closer, an attitude of dead seriousness overtakes the protagonists. A pain rises out of one's spine, a tightness grows between one's shoulder blades, and the stark reality of imminent death intrudes on one's consciousness. The question of fight or flight arises. But there is no possibility of flight. A sense of patriotism takes control. It justifies whatever killing is to ensue—the possibility of one's own demise or the probability of the enemy's. "America, America, land that I love." Nothing else matters except the killing—powerful, glorious, bloody, overpowering killing.

We hunkered down in our foxholes, and the enemy drew ever closer. The game plan provided for no firing of small arms or automatic weapons until the bazooka had eviscerated the tank. We waited and waited still more amid the ever-mounting tension, and the adrenaline flowed, charging our bodies higher and higher and still higher.

The enemy infantry arrived at the crater. Animated conversation and gesticulation took place. After sizing up the situation, they began to survey the terrain. We were hunkered well down into our foxholes and were not observed. So the enemy squad leader radioed to the tank. It lumbered up the grade to the point of impasse—literally and figuratively. The tank could not negotiate the crater.

The tank crawled right to the edge of the crater. I was tight as a cat on a rail fence. I touched the trigger of the bazooka as the sighting hairs steadied right on the guts of the tank. Blam! While the missile was still in flight, Corporal Barnwell reloaded. As soon as he touched my helmet, I fired a second round. Double-hell broke loose.

There was no doubt that two direct hits had knocked out the tank. Through smoke and dust my men had begun firing. They were chewing up the startled enemy infantry all around the tank. Some who weren't hit manged to rush to the cover of the tank itself. Although it had lost its tracks, it was still intact.

But the tank was not dead. Ponderously, that giant 89mm gun started to swing onto our bearing. Blam! I fired a third missile. It exploded in virtually the same armored spot as my first two.

Suddenly Corporal Barnwell yelled, "Look behind us, sir!"

I jerked my head around. Up the hill to our rear, a huge gray-white arrow had been gouged out of the dirt by the bazooka's backblast. It pointed directly into our foxhole.

Goddamn, I thought.

The snout of the 89mm tank gun stopped dead on us. KA-WHUMP!

The whole world moved at the first impact and kept on, registering 10s on the Richter scale, through a total of forty-seven rounds. I shivered as I counted the rounds.

Scared shitless, we hunkered more and more deeply into the foxhole as frantically we tried to prove that a man-size object could shrink through sheer willpower into an infinitesimal point. We were trapped, shivering, and that bastard across the arroyo was trying to dig us out or to eliminate us altogether. Dust and cordite began choking us to death. I managed only enough awareness of our predicament to continue counting each successive earth-shattering KA-WHUMP! I kept saying over and over, "Damn, Bussey, you screwed up again!"

First, I had trusted our ordnance people's assessment of the enemy weapon. Second, I had overlooked entirely the backblast characteristics of my own weapon. Third, I had been overly eager to engage the tank. After all, it couldn't go anywhere or do anything. I should simply have left it alone. Finally, I should never have emerged from my mother's womb.

At some point the enemy tank's machine gun opened up on my troops. They had continued to fire on the enemy infantry. The 89mm tank gun finally slowed its cyclic rate of firing. Either it was overheating, or the crew was running out of ammo. Finally it stopped—almost.

I looked over at Barnwell. His eyes were red. His face was totally begrimed in tannish, grayish dust. I had to laugh. Looking at me, he laughed also. Owlishly, we blinked. Tears cleansed our eye sockets. We both raised up a little to assess our situation. Unfortunately, the tank was ready to resume.

KA-WHUMP!

There was hardly any time between the gun's report and the shell's explosion beneath our foxhole. The sun had kept doing its thing, and it became stiflingly hot as we approached midday. Shaking, grimy, disgusted, the corporal and I shared a K ration. We stayed well down in our hole for fear we couldn't duck fast enough the next time. We had reached an impasse. Stalemated, we waited in the stifling noonday.

Fortunately—through pure happenstance—I had spaced our foxholes so that we had extended coverage of the main supply route. We covered one thousand yards or so of the road and bordering hillsides. When a company-size enemy force came into view, we could let them advance into extreme BAR (Browning automatic rifle) range but no farther. Fortunately, also, two of our foxholes were out of view of the crippled tank.

Seemingly, only darkness would afford us a means of safe escape. By 1600 hours I would have fulfilled my assigned mission, and we would be free to leave. In tactical language, we would be able to disengage from the enemy. If, that is, he would permit us to do so.

The day wore hard on us, but not as hard on us as on the tank crew. We kept them bottled up tight. No matter how many tank ports might be open, there was very little ventilation. That enemy endured a very hot and long afternoon.

Time passed. Sixteen hundred hours came and went. About 1630 the sun had declined to an angle that brought some respite from the burning, blistering heat. The barren hills began to lose some heat, and it became slightly less miserable. The corporal and I shared a C ration. We drank the last of our water. A thought came to mind: I didn't need to be here at all. After all, I was the boss of the 77th ECC and, as such, I could have (and perhaps should have) been back in Sangju in some shady place. Any of my lieutenants could have handled this roadblock just as well and probably better. But I was a slave to my convictions. One of them was never to send my men into a situation I would not go into myself. So, at this time, at this place, here is where I belong and here is where I should be.

We waited. I assumed that the tank, though crippled, could still function, and that its crew, not crippled, was still alive. Like a great rattlesnake, it waited also for a final, mortal stroke. Gradually, almost imperceptibly, evening came on. I hissed to the holes on my right and then on my left.

"Ssssst! Split in fifteen minutes. Pass it on."

"Roger!"

"Roger!"

As the tank began to lose definition in the poor light of dusk, I tested things by raising up halfway out of the hole. Nothing happened. So I hissed again. On my left and on my right, men slowly lifted up and step-by-step began to tiptoe away. We all crept away from our positions. Our weapons carrier and my jeep were about a half mile away. Camouflaged, they were still under guard. When we reached a position about a hundred yards from the vehicles Corporal Barnwell began to sing a little barracks ditty in English and Japanese together:

> I was on my way to town
> When Moosy-May sounded me down.
> Ah-no-nay! Ah-no-nay!
> Coco dozo ee-lay shay?

My guards on the perimeter of our bivouac knew that it was our squad finally returning. The ditty was a hallmark. They knew that the long day was over and that the mission had been accomplished as ordered. The company saddled up and moved eastward to Sangju, on the way back to the perimeter.

The next afternoon I was sacked out along with most of the unit, after having been up for two full days and nights, when Lieutenant Colonel Rivers, commanding officer (CO) of the 65th Engineer Battalion, visited me. That meant rousing me from some beautiful sleep. Colonel Rivers was escorting a tall, slim, blond young man, two weeks out of the Citadel: Lt. Carroll LeTellier. I assigned LeTellier to the 1st Platoon, which was asleep. In combat you sleep when you can. I explained to LeTellier what we'd been doing for the past two days, excused myself, and crawled back under the mosquito net. We'd have a lot of time to become acquainted. We did.

After a couple of weeks, I recognized that this was the best lieutenant I'd ever known. He was complete. He had learned his technical and social lessons well. I wrote to his father, Col. Louis LeTellier, head of the engineering department at the Citadel. This was totally irregular, but I felt that a man who had so obviously put so very much into his son should know how effective his training and upbringing had been. I told the colonel, and he was mighty proud. I didn't feel bad about Carroll's combat exposure. He needed it and thrived on it. He wasn't just a "war dog" but a damned good officer. The best!

At about the same time, we were also joined by 1st Lt. Paul D. Wells, an infantryman, and a good one. Wells was a product of Texas A&M College. I never knew why a white infantry officer was assigned to the black 77th Engineer Combat Company, but I was glad that it happened. Paul Wells became my company executive officer, or second-in-command. We worked well together, and he was highly effective at taking care of the necessary company administration, which made it possible for me to spend more time in the field. Wells would be the one to develop our good, although unauthorized, 81mm-mortar capability. He used infantry mortarmen, who had been released from the hospital but who weren't able to perform the duties of a full-fledged infantryman, to man our unauthorized mortars.

Rain of Stones, 30 July 1950

No matter the hazard, if one works at an occupation or chore long enough, there's a strong tendency to become a little careless on occasion. We were moving back into the Pusan perimeter, withdrawing from Sangju. Division sent down a demolition plan and made the explosives available to carry it off. We burned the rice warehouses at Sangju and destroyed the switches and frogs in the rail marshaling yard. Theoretically we were denying the productive systems to the enemy. This was farcical in the extreme because the enemy had no trains or rolling stock of any kind, and if they acquired any, our Air Force would've had a field day with it. Ours was not to reason why! Systematically we accomplished the demolition plan—burning and destroying as we retreated.

We practiced the engineer school guidance on demolition techniques with strong emphasis on safety. I always carried the generator, so there could never be an accidental firing. All charges were prepared both for electrical firing and for fuse firing. On those rare and dangerous occasions when the electrical firing failed, we waited the prescribed period, gingerly lit the fuse, and then ran as though pursued by the devil to be out of harm's way when the demolition exploded. It was exacting and dangerous work.

We fired bridges, dams, electrical transmission stations, railroads—everything in the demolition plan. Any equipment or installation that could be beneficial to the enemy had to be destroyed. It all went well—until our last target.

The countryside was peaceful. The rice paddies were green. The weather was hot and dry as we prepared our last bridge for destruction. The 2d Platoon placed the charges three spans out: deck, pier, pier, deck, and abutment. The rest of the company, except for the security element, swam and luxuriated in the slow current of the Kum River, which was wide, shallow, and warm at that point. We leisurely inhaled the cans of 3.2 beer that the American people deigned to allow us over the violent objection of the Women's Christian Temperance Union (WCTU) and other do-gooder outfits.

When the charges were all placed and wired, we ate the evening meal and got the trucks up on the road heading south. Sergeant Woods and I went back to the bridge to set off the charges. Sergeant Woods was a favorite of mine. I guess it was because I understood him so well. He came from Pittsburgh, Pennsylvania, and he was a hell-for-leather guy. He gave the impression of not giving a damn, but in reality he cared. He loved a challenge, and he was strong, tough, and ghetto smart. There was nothing he didn't know about fighting, and there was very little he didn't know about equipment operation and field engineering. He was rare. I had served with him in the 74th Engineer Battalion in the States. He was not very popular there, because he was considered to be a know-it-all, and he was. I had no problem with him because he was a top-flight soldier. He was also reliable and loyal. Whenever there was anything difficult, dangerous, or urgent, he came to mind. So I was glad he and I were working together on this demolition job.

When we got back to the bridge site, I connected the action wire, which ended close to the abutment charge. We played out the reel of wire after getting a positive reading on my galvanometer. I paced off the distance as the wire played out: exactly one hundred yards. I made a rapid calculation, which indicated that for the amount of TNT in the abutment, the minimum safe distance was one hundred eighty yards. But there was no more action wire, and I was in a hurry. Sunset was nearing, and what the hell. I looked at Woods. He shrugged his shoulders, and like a damned fool, I abandoned caution, cleared, and connected the hell box.

"Fire in the hole! Fire in the hole! Fire in the hole!"

With the twist of the little, black handle, the whole world erupted. We started to run away from the bridge, but looking up I could see that the sky was full of boulders in a trajectory already descending well beyond us and where we'd be if we continued to run.

I knew we couldn't run out of the danger area, so we ducked and drew ourselves up into tiny knots and waited, looking up into a sky full of boulders, some as large as a jeep. They landed all around us with sickening thuds. It was a rain of stones, and I tweaked as they landed around us. I knew that a boulder the size of my fist could be lethal, and lo and behold, it was raining stones of two-ton size. They were burying themselves in the turf around us. I gazed upward all the while, ostensibly to duck away from stones that might have endangered us. Finally, the gigantic stones stopped falling, and only gravel and dust remained. Woods and I looked at each other, silently acknowledging our stupidity, but most of all our good fortune at being alive.

I placed my life in jeopardy through my stupidity; I did the same to my sergeant. For that, there is no forgiveness.

The Pusan Perimeter

1–19 August 1950,
Haman, Korea

During August 1950, I took part in some of the most vicious fighting of the war. We were defending the southern part of the Pusan perimeter. It was a period of constant combat and work for the 77th Engineer Combat Company.

As the North Koreans advanced in July 1950, the U.S. and ROK forces were forced to retreat to the southeast to form a defensive position around the port of Pusan. This was truly a last stand. If the U.S. forces were forced to evacuate Pusan, the North Koreans would win. Pusan was a big port and the second largest city in South Korea. It had to be held.

Initially, we fought in the south-central part of the country near Sangju, but on 31 July 1950 the 25th Infantry Division was shifted suddenly to a new defensive sector in the southwest near Masan in order to stabilize the defensive position securing Pusan against a new NKPA threat from the west. The NKPA forces had broken through in the west and were threatening to outflank the UN forces in the south. The 24th Infantry Division, reinforced by the 27th Infantry Regiment of the 25th Infantry Division, was already fighting in the area but losing ground steadily. In a brilliant move, the 25th Infantry Division moved 150 miles in two days to arrive just in time to hold the line.

The 24th Infantry Regiment was deployed on Subok-san, an imposing piece of high ground running across the corridor leading from Chinju through Masan and into Pusan. The enemy needed that high ground, which was its stumbling block on the way to Pusan. Subok-san was a steep, treeless mountain. The terrain was rugged. Vehicles were confined to the roads, which were poor. The temperature was 110°F. The tactical plans were inept and poorly suited to the terrain. Barrier and field fortification materiel was in limited supply and often simply not available. Our personnel were not conditioned to cope with the harsh terrain, the heat, and the shortage of water for bathing and drinking.

Shortly after the 24th RCT closed in on the southern end of the Pusan perimeter, our first regimental commander, Col. Horton V. White, was sent back to Japan. I liked Colonel White. He had always been a fair man, and he was a good commander, but he was fifty years old and Korea was not a place for a man his age. Colonel White was an intelligence officer who had previously worked for General Willoughby, General MacArthur's G-2, so he went back to Tokyo.

Colonel White was replaced on 6 August 1950 by Col. Arthur S. Champeny. Colonel Champeny was fifty-seven when he assumed command; he was four years older than the 25th Division Commander, Major General Kean. I found Colonel Champeny to be biased, gutless, and totally inefficient. The regiment did not do well under his command.

During the defense of the Pusan perimeter, the 24th Infantry Regiment lost its position only once when they evacuated Subok-san under heavy pressure from the enemy and with a lack of reinforcement by friendly troops. On this occasion, the regiment withdrew under the supervision of its white officers, who must accept a large part of the responsibility for the performance of the troops. It is inconsistent to attribute only the defeats of the 24th Infantry Regiment to its black troops. Officers accept the glory of success; they must also bear the onus of defeat.

Gradually, the Pusan perimeter became stronger. More UN troops arrived, and the gaps were filled. The line became better fortified and took on aspects of trench warfare. Small attacks regained some ground from the North Koreans. The line stabilized. The North Koreans still pressed the attack, however, and the fighting was fierce. The issue remained in doubt until our amphibious landing at Inchon took the North Koreans by surprise and cut their supply lines. Our job during this period was holding the line.

It was early August, and the mosquitoes were at the height of their growth and vigor. The roads were at their dustiest. The Land of the Morning Calm was not at all calm. There was a lot of activity on the small community farms. There was a lot of activity to the front and rear of the infantry positions at night. It was a busy war, which our president called a police action. Bullshit! Damned good men were dying every night.

I shot two guerrillas at our water point when I was checking my security. By daylight they turned out to be kids not more than fourteen or fifteen years old, but they could kill a GI just as easily as their fathers could.

I remember a prisoner interrogation conducted by the regimental S-2. He extracted from a couple of Korean kids the fact that they'd been pressed into service from the Kaesong area just south of the 38th Parallel along with fifty or sixty other youngsters. They'd received about seven days of basic training and were taught to use some crude knives. They were told to climb the hills where the Americans were by night, an inch at a time, so as to detect the trip wires for mines or flares. Slowly, groping, feeling and slithering, listening, and feeling and slithering. They were taught that when one hears snoring, one moves into position behind the GI, mugs him, and slides the knife swiftly down into the esophageal area, holding the mouth to prevent any sounds; then waits a few seconds for death; warm, final, cruel, gurgling death. Then one withdraws the knife, crawls into the foxhole, places the rifle or carbine on the parapet, and removes the shoes from the still-warm corpse. If the shoes are too big, as most of them are, leave them. But if one kills enough soldiers, eventually one finds size 5 or size 6 shoes, then one crawls silently back to one's unit—a hero of the people. A North Korean soldier with American shoes and an American weapon is honored by his peers.

Naktong River Bridge, 6 August 1950, Near Masan, Korea

The war was becoming habit and, God, what a grisly habit. We were a generation of ghosts. We had never had an opportunity to build, to create, or to structure. We went from college directly to combat, from Sunday school to slaughtering shed. We were blessed, I suppose, to have had a five-year interlude of peace— long enough to sire two or three children, many of whom were to mature fatherless.

We were quartered in a schoolhouse in Masan. We'd been there for several days. The regiment and division were in and around the town also. We weren't doing much, and we needed the time for maintenance of equipment. We'd been mighty busy, first at Yechon, then at Sangju, and then during the withdrawal into the Pusan perimeter. So maintenance it was. Early in the morning on 6 August, a message came in for a platoon-size recon up to the bridge on the Naktong River. "More instructions after arriving."

Platoon-size reconnaissance always interested me, so I decided to add my jeep to the small convoy carrying Lieutenant Lenon's platoon. We left about 0930 hours. The trip to the bridge was uneventful, and I called and reported this to division. The G-2 type responded that a battalion-size North Korean unit was approaching and was about two miles from the bridge.

He instructed us, "Hold at all cost. Deny the bridge to the enemy until relieved."

This didn't worry me much because it was still in the forenoon, and denying the bridge wasn't difficult, even with only one platoon.

I could see the elements of the enemy battalion moving toward us. Thousands of refugees were on the road in advance of the battalion. It was always the same. When the enemy moved, the civilian populace scurried before them. There were thousands of white-clad women, carrying suckling children on their hips and huge bundles of household goods on their heads. Once in a while one of the women would have a radio in that bundle to advise the enemy of our strength, weapons, locations, and general disposition. We were wise to that, and the few men we left with our meager trains were to look for women using radios. If any were found, they were summarily shot. No radios on this occasion, however.

There were numerous foxholes on the bank facing the oncoming battalion. The plain was flat. The river banks were twenty to thirty feet higher than the plain and roadbed. The enemy approached. We waited. And waited. The troops became antsy.

It's better after the firefight starts because once you're in action, you function with a certain amount of automatic reflexes. I planned to let the battalion's point come to within 600 yards. Six hundred yards is good killing range when there's no cover, and it was far enough away, under those conditions, to make the enemy pay dearly for any advance. I knew we'd kill his point and make it impossible for him to advance in the daylight.

Eventually the enemy point came up to my estimated six hundred yards. We opened fire on the hapless enemy. We hit them with .50 caliber machine guns, .30 caliber BARs, .30 caliber water-cooled and air-cooled machine guns, and rifles. The point dissolved into masses of rags and bloody members of bodies. The enemy battalion stopped cold. There were some ditches and other small depressions that provided some safety for the enemy, but the move toward the river was stopped positively. We fired sporadically whenever one of the enemy moved.

I became a little concerned when, at 1500 hours, we were still at our point of impasse. I called G-2 and was advised that a battalion of the 27th Infantry would relieve us in about thirty minutes. Good news. Then I heard a whale of a firefight a couple of miles away toward our rear. I was afraid that somehow we'd been out-flanked, but I could see the battalion position in front, and they hadn't moved since the initial engagement.

The firefight to the rear stopped, and the battalion of the 27th Infantry Regiment moved up to the river. I explained what had happened and gave the disposition of the enemy battalion, which was well dug-in by then. I was relieved, and the 27th began to use their 81mm mortars on the enemy with great success.

It was now about 1600 hours. We saddled up for home base.

I remembered an abandoned house on the roadside about five miles back. I sent Pinkney, my jeeper, back to hustle some water and build a fire, so I could steal a bath, which I needed desperately. I could even smell myself.

Pinkney was back in about twenty-five minutes. He had the additional duty of collecting spices for the mess hall, so he raided abandoned gardens along the roadside for peppers, garlic, onions, celery, and other things Sergeant Lamont used in his gourmet kitchen. He did a masterful job. Sometimes he caught fowl, which were left running free as people from the countryside fled south ahead of the enemy.

I told Chet Lenon to take the platoon back to the shed, and I stopped off for that overdue bath. I luxuriated, cut my toenails, shaved, spent a fabulous half hour on personal maintenance, and then headed back to Masan.

Valley of Fear, 6 August 1950, Masan, Korea

When I arrived back at the company about 1700, Chet's jeep driver told me that General Wilson stopped my 3d Platoon on the road near Haman, unsaddled them, and attached them to a small task force he'd put together under Captain Daley of Item Company of the 24th Infantry Regiment. They were to open a trail to Masan for the 24th to link up with a beleaguered element of the 5th RCT near Chindong-ni. We should expect them back that evening because they had no rations and only their canteens of water.

I hated the sound of it. I had the utmost confidence in Lieutenant Lenon. He'd fared well at Yechon and everyplace else, but rear guard for Item Company? Appropriately, I started to sweat. The evening wore heavily upon me. I tasted trouble, deep trouble. And it came.

About 0200 on 7 August I was checking the security and heard a commotion up front. I went up and there were about twelve men from the 3d Platoon, all trying to talk at once. There were six or seven walking wounded, who'd been helped in, but Chet Lenon was missing, as was Corporal Barnwell, PFC Robert Semedo, PFC Robert Cunningham, and several others. I got the whole bloody story.

General Wilson had designated my 3d Platoon as the rear element of Daley's task force. The first mile or so was routine, if you consider walking into a death trap routine. The route of the task force was into an upsloping valley, rimmed by a horseshoe of crags, where the enemy patiently waited until the entire task force was inside the dish-shaped valley. Then they riddled the valley with plunging fire. Daley, at the head of his column, was able to go over the crest, and about half of his task force got out of the valley. The remainder, including my 3d Platoon, was left to fare as best they might. Most of those left were dead or dying. The ex-task force, instead of forming and fighting after reaching the crest, bolted down the escarpment and continued to haul ass until overcome by fatigue and utter exhaustion when the enemy was no longer in range. What a debacle.

I could find fault with my people, too. They should have rallied and returned some fire when they were on the high ground, rather than follow Daley. I was shattered because no one could tell me where the valley was or how to get there directly from Masan. I went looking for Daley.

When I found him down near the RTO, I felt sorry for him. His eyes were begrimed, and he was dirty from head to toe. Direct spatters of blood, shed by one of his helpless wounded, covered his shoulder. His troops were sprawled out on the ground more like cattle than men. The harsh taste of death and the long march without food and with very little water had turned a company of fighting men into a group of rabble.

I asked about the valley. Daley couldn't get there. He told me that there was no way to get firing positions inside the valley. "We came out through a hole-in-the-wall," he said.

"Exactly where is this valley?"

"Not positive, but the open end is about one mile south of the Engineer Road that you built. Not a road entrance, but a trail enters there through heavy underbrush."

"How can we get to the hole-in-the wall from here?"

"I'm not sure, I headed southeast, but I don't know the distance, what with carrying the wounded and all, but there's a range of mountains perpendicular to the hills at Chindong-ni, it runs for maybe twenty miles or so. But I don't know where the opening is from here."

"Is there any chance of my men being alive?"

"None. The fire was devastating. I heard it long, long after we cleared the hole. No one could possibly have survived it. No way."

I left Daley there without any animosity or rancor whatever; I figured that he had done his best. But the loss of these men hurt to the bone, particularly the loss of Chet Lenon. Men like him were rare. And Benny, too?

I knew that we couldn't just sit in that perimeter. Soon we would have to go for the enemy, or he would drive us into the sea. I located about five hundred oil drums, and I had outboard motors for twelve assault boats. I made a sketch and estimated the lashing required to make one or several rafts of oil drums to float my people back to Japan if we had a Dunkirk. Fortunately that didn't come to pass.

Sugar Loaf, 7–8 August 1950, Chindong-ni, Korea

Sugar Loaf (Hill 255), just east of Chindong-ni, was the site of one of the first engagements between the U.S. Marine Corps and NKPA troops on 7 and 8 August 1950. I happened to see the attack on the Sugar Loaf.

The corridor from Chinju across Subok-san (Hill 738) and on to Masan was the grand objective for the NKPA forces at this time. This corridor led directly to Pusan, and the capture of the port city of Pusan would have been the supreme accomplishment. It would have denied ingress and egress to the UN forces. It would have been a resounding defeat for the UN and the United States. The 25th Infantry Division was responsible for the defense of this sector of the Pusan perimeter.

It was a time of task forces. Troops from several organizations were joined together under a task force commander to accomplish specific missions. Of course, the units had no knowledge of each

2nd Lt. Charles M. Bussey at graduation from the Tuskegee Army Flying School in May 1943. He soon saw combat for the first time, as a P-51 pilot with the 332d Fighter Group. *U.S. Army*

The Korea of 1950. *A.
Spencer/77th Engineer
Combat Company*

Bridge over the Kum River and North Korean tank destroyed by the U.S. Air Force in July 1950. *A. Spencer/77th ECC*

Men of Bussey's 77th Engineer Combat Company probe for a booby trap under a mine near Haman in September 1950. From the left: Lt. David Carlisle, Lt. Collins Whitaker, and Cpl. Paul Witt. *U.S. Army*

Prisoners of the 77th Engineer Combat Company, near Pyongtaek on 15 September 1950. *A. Spencer/77th ECC*

The 77th constructs a vital twin-span railroad bridge on the main supply route at Pyongtaek on 1 October 1950. *A. Spencer/77th ECC*

Lieutenant LeTellier officially opens the Pyongtaek bridge. *A. Spencer/77th ECC*

3 October 1950. Captain Bussey dedicates the bridge at Pyongtaek, dubbing it "LeTellier Bridge" for its designer and construction supervisor, 1st Lt. Carroll LeTellier. *R. Dudley/77th ECC*

LeTellier (left) and 1st Lt. Paul D. Wells with Bussey at the Pyongtaek bridge. *R. Dudley/77th ECC*

Soldiers of the 77th sweep the road near Kunu-ri for mines. 28 November 1950 *U.S. Army*

The 77th transporting elements of the 24th Infantry Regiment across the Congchon River northeast of Kunu-ri in December 1950. *A. Spencer/77th ECC*

Troops of the 24th Infantry Regiment leaving the Kunu-ri area in December 1950 for the Congchon River bridge to confront the Chinese. *R. Dudley/77th ECC*

The mass grave at Yechon. *A. Spencer/77th ECC*

other or of their commander. At the battalion level, a typical task force might include an infantry battalion, a battery of field artillery, some antiaircraft artillery, a platoon or company of tanks, and a platoon or more of combat engineers. At the division level, a task force could include several regiments and supporting units. The effectiveness of these impromptu organizations was highly questionable. The impromptu task forces faced poor communications, nonexistent roads, a clever, shifting, and determined enemy well fortified on difficult terrain. This often led to distress and defeat.

Task Force Kean was formed to make a major counterattack on enemy forces opposite the southernmost part of the Pusan perimeter. The objective was to take and hold the town of Chinju about twenty-seven miles west of Masan. Task Force Kean included the 25th Division with the 5th RCT and the 1st Marine Provisional Brigade attached to it. The 27th RCT had been taken away from the division and placed in Eighth Army Reserve.

My 3d Platoon was supporting Lt. Col. Sam Pierce's 3d Battalion of the 24th Infantry Regiment at Chindong-ni, which was only a short distance from my command post in Masan. I dropped in to visit the platoon shortly after breakfast on 7 August. I found Lieutenant LeTellier and Colonel Pierce in close conversation. I joined them. It had been the first time we'd been able to have a powwow since Yechon, and Lieutenant Colonel Pierce congratulated me on my impromptu action there. He mentioned that he had heard a rumor about the award of the Congressional Medal of Honor for me.

As the talk wore on, the colonel required that we provide him with a water supply point, and I marked it paid. I asked the colonel, "Why Chindong-ni, and why no fighting? What is the significance of the Sugar Loaf?"

Colonel Pierce told me that the enemy had sneaked around behind our forces and occupied Sugar Loaf, Hill 255, just north of Chindong-ni along the road to Masan. Their roadblock on Sugar Loaf cut off communications to Masan, and we had to take it back.

He continued, "Well, we're here to do some killing, so we fired

1,600 rounds in preparation. We assaulted the hill, but we couldn't move the gooks; the devils gave us a bad time. Division has pulled us off. Now we're waiting for the Marines. They landed a day or so ago, and they're going to show us how it's done. That's a tough enemy. The only way we'll get them out of there will be by digging them out with bayonets one foxhole at a time. And unless I'm wrong as hell, the school solutions the Marines'll bring with them from Camp Pendleton or LeJeune or wherever will add up to a big flop. Both the Army and I personally will look bad, but we couldn't dislodge those North Koreans and neither will the Marines. The press'll give the Marines credit for winnin' the whole war out here, but it'll be a big farce."

The rumble of tank tracks told us that the Marines were nearing our position. The morning calm wasn't going to be calm much longer.

Accompanying the tanks was a battalion of Marines—young, healthy, motivated, starched, and loaded for bear. I was proud of them, but I hadn't forgotten Colonel Pierce's prediction. The tanks carried bundles of sandbags on their left sides. They moved up to a line of departure and turned left parallel to the Sugar Loaf, dropping off sandbags and Marines. The hill was silent; there was no enemy visible and no action. The Marines filled their sandbags at their leisure and placed them so as to protect the men from any fire from the hill.

The assault was scheduled to start with the arrival of Brig. Gen. Edward A. Craig, commander of the 1st Marine Provisional Brigade. General Craig showed up in well-starched eminence, stepped into his slightly fortified position, and postured for a few minutes for the benefit of the cameras and sound equipment. The tanks nosed into the hill, and upon a signal from someplace all hell broke loose as the tanks opened fire. The tanks bombarded the hill; in fact, they post-holed it. It seemed that no inch of the Sugar Loaf was not scarred and blasted.

Then the Marine infantry fixed bayonets and charged up the hill chanting, "We gonna win, by God; we gonna win!" The charge became bloody. The NKPA troops rose up to their parapets and sprayed the charging Marines with their automatic .28 caliber grease guns. These were cheap weapons any American mechanic could manufacture in his garage, but they were deadly nonetheless. The kids from Camp Pendleton withdrew in good order. The medics were damned busy. What a waste!

There was a period of hustle and scurry. The staff and commanders went through all the drills that the manuals prescribed, and the general made terse comments. The audio-visual equipment caught it all, including the instructions to make the whole thing "Caesaresque," and General Craig ate it up in huge gulps. Meanwhile, another Marine battalion lined up with the tanks, and the walking fire exercise began. The tanks first crawled up the slopes, firing their 90mm guns and their machine guns just above the heads of the advancing Marines. "We gonna win, by God. We gonna win. . . ." And the kids advanced halfway up the hill. They used those bayonets, and they dug out a lot of the enemy, but eventually it was obvious that their losses were greater than their gains.

The Marines withdrew again in good order. The medics and the Marines who were still in good health removed the wounded and the dead. The losses were great. They didn't win, by God.

Lieutenant LeTellier and I walked over to the area where the medics were working on the wounded and dead, and for the first time I noticed there were black Marines. I noticed one man in particular. One medic was giving him a morphine shot, and another medic had his finger hooked under a badly smashed clavicle to stem the gush of blood. The young Marine was still mumbling, "Gonna win. . . ." His eyeballs were chasing each other around in their sockets looking for a focus. He didn't find it. He shook violently, relaxed, and was dead. The medic checked the dead Marine's dog tag and told me, "That's Jim Reedy. He was our middleweight champ." That was the end of another battalion that was less than successful—severely chewed, mauled, and bloody. The medics and the grave registration people were busy.

Another Marine battalion came up and went to the original sandbag fortifications, lying prone while they waited. Then the Marine air support came in on the target.

As the fighters flew overhead, Carroll asked me, "Make you homesick?"

I responded, "Well, it's a better way to fight than what the ground pounders have. Low-altitude flying is damned dangerous 'cause any good pheasant shooter can knock you down, there probably won't be enough altitude for you to bail out, and in this terrain, bellying in isn't too safe either. But every flier has a bed to sleep in; he just has to get back to it. Always has good chow too, if he can reach it. I'd gladly trade places with any one of them up there."

The prop-driven fighters were making their first pass with napalm. The fliers knew their business, and they blackened the Sugar Loaf. The busting canisters of liquid soap and gasoline spewed forward of their points of impact and burned every twig, every blade of grass, and the flaming jelly burned a lot of enemy, too. Foxholes provide a lot of protection, but liquids find their way in, and the occupant usually jumps up out of the hole screaming, crying, running, wallowing, and rolling in the dust in the most excruciating pain. The enemy suffered like the damned, running helter-skelter over the hillside. Napalm is merciless—the most dreaded implement on the killing floor.

After numerous passes, the charbroiling was over, and the 'birds left the scene. I could not imagine any survivors on that hill. Even from my safe vantage point, the heat was intense.

So the Marine infantry had another go at the Sugar Loaf. "We gonna win, by God. We gonna win." But in spite of the mass killing by infantry, artillery, and napalm, much of the enemy force was still alive and well, and dangerous. They were still well enough to repel the Marines, although the last battalion nearly gained the hilltop before retreating.

The following morning, Lieutenant LeTellier brought his platoon back to our bivouac area. After greeting him, I asked, "What finally happened after I left out there?"

"Well," LeTellier replied, "it turned out exactly like Colonel Pierce said it would. The Marines called it a gigantic victory, with a lot of handshaking and picture taking. They headed this way with a lot of jubilation."

"What about today? How'd you get loose from Colonel Pierce?"

"Last night around midnight, the Intelligence and Reconnaissance Platoon showed up with Lieutenant Teague. They rested 'til first light, then they and King and Love companies went around to the back side of the hill. They climbed and trekked the whole range. The enemy was gone and had taken their dead and wounded during the night. There were scraps around. You could tell there'd been a fight. The North Koreans probably claimed victory too, because they sure didn't give up that hill; but I'm also damned sure they couldn't stand another day like yesterday."

"Yeah, Carroll, and I'm sure you're right. This is a crazy damned world we live in. I remember all those fine young men who died yesterday. Just big kids. They should all have been home driving fast cars and planting babies in the local girls."

Old Friends, 9 August 1950, Masan, Korea

A military policeman was directing traffic at the intersection in the middle of Masan, a dirty little town at the head of a bay opening onto the Korea Straits. It was home for the time being. I was in a hurry to move along and unhappy at being detained so long. As the MP stopped the crossing traffic, a jeep rolled up beside me, and a raucous voice called out, "Fathead!"

I recognized the voice and the face from which it came. It was George Gray, a classmate of mine from flight school. We exchanged greetings and friendly epithets, and the MP became unhappy because we were holding up traffic. We rolled through the intersection and continued the conversation.

George was a captain then. He gave me a bad time because I was still a lieutenant and more because I was still making like a ground pounder. George was with a group of P-51 pilots. They were flying off a pierced-steel plank runway down the road a mile or so. I followed him to the airfield and met a host of the old Tuskegee hands: Peepsight Smith; Red Jackson; my old squadron commander, E.J. Williams; Dudley Watson; and several others from the 332d Fighter Group. They were flying P-51s against the NKPA troops. They had been in Korea long enough to realize that the enemy was dangerous and well equipped to shoot down propeller-driven aircraft.

It was good to see my old friends and to be reminded of our

past association. Despite bigotry we had gone into combat and had fought well. These were my friends from combat, and no other activity or environment forges stronger relationships. I hoped that their hunting would always be good and that they all would survive. I envied them. Theirs was a far better way to fight a war. Dough footin' ain't nowhere.

We had one helluva visit until I had to get back to work. Duty consumed me for the next several days, during which George was shot down by small arms fire and killed. E.J. Williams also was killed. "Peepsight" Smith was shot down and killed. Red Jackson was shot down, but he survived.

I was crushed. It is painful to lose old friends. In my misery, I pondered the life-death cycle; I had hours, long hours, and thousands of hours of thoughts and remembrances of the guys, of our days as aviation cadets at Tuskegee, and as young, black lieutenants in the hate-filled environment of the Deep South. I remembered flying combat missions from Italy. Mostly I thought about "Skeegum," our nickname for the place where they hid us black pilots in Alabama.

I was still in the Jim Crow Army, still suffering from the physical, emotional, and mental privation and the denigration that accompanies that condition. But I knew of survival, and I didn't allow myself to be weakened by Jim Crow. I knew that I would not only survive, but that I would thrive.

Back to the work at hand!

French's Ridge, 13 August 1950, Masan, Korea

I sat around and chafed and galled about the loss of Chet Lenon and his men. I talked to Lieutenant Colonel Roberts about it and asked for permission to go after my men, but he was negative about it all. "Wars are like that," he said.

I had been promoted to captain on 10 August 1950, and General Wilson had personally brought my orders to me. I felt good about that, but I worried about the men in my 3d Platoon. I figured they would only last about seven days without food or water.

It was easy to know what to do if the men were still alive: go in after them. But one can't risk the living for the dead. I had an idea about the location of the ambush, and I knew that area belonged to the enemy.

In the meantime, I found a road close by in bad need of repair. The road was really none of our business, but I needed work to keep my people busy and tired. We went to work building four large box culverts and a short timber-trestle bridge. We continued to improve the road network during the following few days. We were bored, but we were tired-bored. Tired soldiers sleep at night.

About 0300 on 13 August 1950 my phone rang. I hadn't gotten back to sleep since a check of security at 0200, so I wasn't at all disturbed. The call was from a medic at the RTO, who advised me that Private First Class Edwards, one of Lieutenant Lenon's missing men, was there, nearly dead. The medic said, "Edwards insists on talking to you. Recommend you come as soon as possible."

I hustled down to the RTO to talk to Edwards. He was an absolute wreck. A bullet had cut across the bones of his left foot, and the heavy muscles in the sole of his foot had contracted and doubled the foot under and downward. He'd crawled and otherwise dragged himself for at least twenty miles. He wore off his clothes and the skin of his hands, knees, elbows, and thighs. A snake had bitten him on his right cheek, and his entire face and head was swollen, completely disfiguring him. But he could talk.

As soon as he saw me, Edwards began, "Five more of us, including Lieutenant Lenon, are still alive out there where Item Company left us. They're all badly wounded in both legs. None of them can walk. Jerry Barnwell, Bob Cunningham, and Billy Lewis are all dead."

He told me what had happened. They had been rear guard for the task force, and had all been hit. After the enemy took off after Item Company, Lieutenant Lenon had dragged each of them into some tall bushes. He'd found a stream near where they were hiding, had dug a little depression, and collected water for them. Edwards said, "That water was all we had to keep us going. We were real hungry for the first three days, but after that the hunger wasn't so bad. I was better off than the others, and after the third day, I asked Lieutenant Lenon to let me go so I could come back and tell you where we are. I thought I could make it, but the Lieutenant thought it was his job to get the help, and he was gonna go for it in a few days. He knew you'd come for us eventually. Anyway, I finally decided to come back and tell you where we were."

Edwards kept on talking. He told me how to get to the valley and how to find the trail to the hole-in-the-wall. He said, "I saw hundreds of enemy soldiers on the high ridgeline. That ridgeline will be on your right all the way. I know, because I kept it on my left coming out. I came right by that Sugar Loaf mountain. I forget the number of that hill, but you remember."

I replied, "Yes, son, I remember the hill well. I can find the way to the ambush site. I'll go for Lieutenant Lenon and his people. I'll take care of the ridgeline. Glad you came in, son. We'll do the rest. Relax, the medics'll take care of you. Thanks."

Edwards was in terrible shape, he'd become insensitive to pain, and he seemed almost oblivious to the snipping and cutting the medics were doing on his feet, face, and limbs. He was tired and eventually drifted off to unconsciousness or sleep. The war was over for him. Later, I recommended him for the Silver Star to go with his Purple Heart.

Day was breaking as I drove back to our bivouac area. I decided to go out to the valley, find the hole-in-the-wall, and bring in our wounded and bury our dead. If there was some fighting to be done, so be it. I was aware of all the risks, all the hazards, and the possibility of disaster. But in my mind there was no alternative to disobeying Lieutenant Colonel Robert's direct order in order to rescue my troops.

I studied the poor map I had and planned the day's operation. I knew I couldn't take all my men, 'cause there was still work to be accomplished in Masan, and there were a few men with minor injuries and other problems. I decided to take three of my four platoons—about 150 men—with some extra automatic weapons. Securing the ridgeline would be the critical task. My plan was to put a platoon on the ridgeline to protect the main body in the valley below from enemy fire. I also decided to ask for volunteers rather than select men from specific platoons.

At morning work-call formation, I told the assembled troops about my conversation with Edwards earlier that morning. I gave the troops all the details Edwards had given me. I felt a strong surge of enthusiasm flow through the unit. I explained my plan for rescuing our wounded. Then I asked for volunteers. As if on cue, every man in the unit raised his hand and shouted emphatically. I was overwhelmed. I made the cut and dismissed the men who were not going. I advised the troops in the rescue party that we would depart at 0830 and dismissed them to make their preparations. I scrounged some stretchers from the medics, and they gave me a large bag of candy bars for the wounded who had not eaten for nearly seven days.

I picked Cpl. John French to be in charge of the group on the ridgeline. French was young and ambitious, and he had stamina. I knew that nothing would deter him. I selected Cpl. Lavaughn Fields to help French, back him up, and prevent straggling. I called Corporals French and Fields aside and went over the details of their assignment. I told them they were to climb the ridge where it rose from the valley floor near a place called Chindong-ni. Fields remembered the place. As the main body of the company moved along the road in the valley, the ridgeline group was to proceed slightly ahead of the main body, so that no gunfire could be brought to bear on us. I told them that theirs was a tough and vital assignment.

Corporal French expressed some reluctance to assume such responsibility because there were so many senior noncommissioned officers in the company, including men with World War II experience, who outranked him. He said, "Sir, I'm just a corporal, and we have master sergeants and sergeants first class—all of them outrank me. You have plenty of men with more experience than me."

I replied, "French, that ridgeline must be kept clear at all cost. If the enemy holds that ground, we can't move. But move we must. Go up onto those hills, always keeping us in sight. Use your radio and advise me of anything at all that I need to be aware of. I want no ambushes. My experience is that the enemy leaves small detachments of their troops on the hills. Just enough men to exercise the advantage of high ground. Just enough men to create havoc among soldiers walking on the road. When we put a force up on the ridgeline, they'll probably run without a fight. It'll be tough. You men'll get tired, and you'll have to push them. If the main body's moving too fast, tell me, and I'll slow down. I picked you for this job because I want it done properly. I picked Fields for the same reason. Get it done!" We saluted, and I went about my duties.

The company moved out right after breakfast. I told the First Sergeant to tell any callers that I'd taken the troops out on a road repair job and would be gone all day. I was sticking my neck out a mile. A company commander does not have the authority to use his troops except as directed by higher authority. I knew I couldn't get permission for this rescue mission, so I was departing on my own initiative. If the mission failed, if I lost a lot of men, or if I didn't come back with Lieutenant Lenon and my wounded men, I'd be in deep, deep trouble. But trouble be damned. I felt compelled.

I followed Captain Daley's instructions, but tempered it all with Edward's details. We drove north to Chindong-ni as far as I felt it to be safe. Then we dismounted, camouflaged the vehicles, and set out a small security force. Then we started walking.

When we got to the point where the ridgeline rose out of the valley, French's group climbed up on it. The main group moved along the valley road. As we moved ahead, I saw enemy soldiers on the ridgeline running well ahead of French. I called French on the radio and advised him of this. The enemy troops were of no consequence to him. They abandoned their positions because they were too few in number to cope with a platoon-size force of about forty men.

American troops had been ambushed many times because they tried to move along the valleys and roads without also owning the high ground on the sides of the valleys. Admittedly, it was hot, and it was tough climbing hills in the sweltering heat, but it could be done, and doing it saved a lot of lives. French and his men covered us from the ridgeline both going into the valley and also on the way out. Three or four times I saw enemy soldiers moving back, away from French's group, but they didn't bother us.

After seven or eight hours on the move, I began to recognize the landmarks that Edwards had mentioned. We were nearing our objective—the hole-in-the-wall. An ancient lava ridge about forty feet high—almost a vertical wall of stone—ran along the side of the valley. The hole-in-the-wall turned out literally to be just that—a twenty-foot gap in the lava ridge leading to a smaller valley off to the side. Foliage hid the gap, so that it would have been easy to pass the hole-in-the-wall without seeing it. But we were looking for it, and we had landmarks to guide us. We also began to smell the odor of dead bodies decomposing.

As we approached the gap in the wall, we saw many, many bodies of American soldiers. It appeared that the soldiers had bunched up when they attempted to flee through the gap, and this had made the slaughter easy for the enemy, who knew the terrain and capitalized on their knowledge. It really had been a debacle. And it could have been prevented if the high ground had been secured.

French divided his force at the hole-in-the-wall and covered the main body as we descended into the small, horseshoe-shaped valley. I concentrated on finding our own people, both living and dead.

I called, "Chet Lenon. Chet Lenon."

As we approached a copse of willows, I heard a voice.

"Over here! Over here!"

It was Lenon. I followed the sound of the voice. He sounded good. Chet Lenon was a damned good man, and I was glad to get him back among the living. We found four other men still alive but with serious leg wounds.

Poor Corporal Barnwell's body was there; he'd been hit many times. I was saddened. He still wore his shoes with the run-over heels. The wallet containing his reenlistment pay was missing. Cunningham and Lewis were also dead. We gave the three of them a hasty burial—enough to protect their bodies until the grave-registration people could return to retrieve all the bodies and start them through the long process for final burial at home.

We placed the five wounded men on stretchers and started them on a diet of candy bars. Their wounds were badly in need of attention, and Private First Class Napoleon was busy with his patients, who were all in good spirits. As we came back out through the hole-in-the-wall, Private First Class Semedo said, "I knew you'd come for us sooner or later, and when I woke up this morning, I knew that today was the day."

It was a long walk back to our vehicles. French was still on the ridgeline covering us. We returned without incident, the way I hoped it would be. I was blessed, and so were my men. When we neared our parked vehicles, someone starting singing our company song, and he was joined by many happy voices: "I was on my way to town when moosie mae. . . ." The security force knew that the company had returned and had been successful.

We arrived at our bivouac site late that evening. Lieutenant Colonel Roberts was pacing up and down in front of the company command post, fuming.

"Did you lose any men?"

"No, sir."

"Did you find Lieutenant Lenon?"

"Right here, sir," Chet said.

"Good. Don't ever do that to me again. You broke all the rules, but lost no men, recovered your wounded. Thank God! You should be in deep trouble, but I'm glad we have guys like you. You get things done. Thanks again. Good night." Lion Five moved out into the night.

We turned our wounded in to the medics, and the war was over for them. They needed surgery and months of rehabilitation to heal those shattered legs and recover from exposure and neglect. Chet Lenon and the others were evacuated to Japan. They never came back to the company. I had lost my strong right arm, my ace platoon leader, and my friend. But at least he and the others were alive. For his heroism in keeping his men alive during their days in the valley, Chet Lenon was awarded the Distinguished Service Cross.

That night, for the first time since I'd been in the combat zone, I slept all night and slept well. I felt good about myself and my men.

Big Gun, 14 August 1950, South of Haman, Korea

I usually had crews working on the road south of Haman, almost down to Chindong-ni. The road was really the MSR, except at each end of the Haman north-south road there was a road to Masan. The problem was that either road could be interdicted at random, and the roads were frequently interdicted—almost nighly—by mine warfare and guerrilla operations.

Early in the morning of 12 August 1950, elements of the 6th North Korean Infantry Division overran the 90th Field Artillery Battalion and captured five 155mm howitzers. A howitzer is a fieldpiece that fires at high angles, enabling it to hit targets that are over hills and cannot be seen by the gunners. Observers on high vantage points overlooking the targets direct the fire of the guns by radio or telephone to the gunners. The 155mm howitzer can throw its projectile about twenty miles using charge seven—the maximum powder charge. Although classified as medium artillery, the 155mm howitzer is a big gun.

The North Korean troops had taken these weapons in operating condition, complete with the trucks used to move them and trailers with a supply of ammunition and powder. Apparently, they had hidden one of the weapons about five miles south of Haman. The gun was up a draw on the south slope of Subok-san. The stream in the draw produced heavy foliage, so it was a perfect place to hide the gun. From that hiding place the enemy could effectively use the gun to blow the 24th Infantry Regiment off Subok-san as well as Hill 625.

Fortunately, as it turned out, we were repairing a small bridge on the MSR in that vicinity. For whatever reason, some time after 12 August one of my men ventured up the draw and discovered the big gun. He returned to the work party and reported his find to one of the sergeants. The word spread through the work party and through the company, and soon the gun became a *cause célèbre*. Everyone knew about it except the officers.

The troops decided to keep the howitzer as their toy. Some of them attempted to fire the weapon. They tried to fire it with charge three and even up to charge seven. Fortunately, none of them were able to fire the howitzer. This went on for several days.

On the morning of 16 August, when I went out to my jeep, my driver handed me a note. It was marked, "Urgent. Please read at once!" The handwriting on the inside was poor but legible.

Dear Sir, I can't just walk up to you and say what is happening. Finks get into bad trouble, but you need to know about the gun hidden up the draw where we been working on that bridge on the MSR south of Haman. There's this big artillery piece up in the draw about a hundred yards. They been trying to shoot it just for fun, but it should be turned over to someone. Just thought you ought to know. That ain't no toy.

I called Lieutenant Whitaker, and we went down to the work site. I chose not to make a big deal of the incident. Otherwise, I'd probably have to rip some stripes off some otherwise damned good men. I didn't know how the gun got to the site or if the enemy was guarding it. We approached the draw cautiously and uneventfully. Two things were obvious. One, the howitzer didn't belong there. Two, it was placed there to kill American soldiers.

I asked Whitaker to go over the equipment carefully to be certain there were no booby traps in or around the gun or the ammunition. My troops had played with that monster for several days. If there had been booby traps, some of the troops would have been dead already, but it always pays to check.

While the inspection was going on, I went to regimental head-quarters and talked to Lion Five. At first, I joked about it, offering the regiment a 155mm howitzer as a gift. Then I assured him that it was no joke and asked him in all seriousness how he recommended I dispose of the weapon.

He responded, "From what you've said, the gun isn't far from here. I remember seeing your people working on the bridge. I want to be damned sure that no one fires it at us. Why not bring it up here? We'll all be safer."

We dragged the trailer out with our dozer. Then we brought the gun out and finally the truck, the prime mover. We joined the members together and fired up the prime mover. It was some operation. When we got our dragon train back to regimental headquarters, there were some criminal investigation people there to ask me a lot of inanities. There were also some ordnance and artillery people. They were glad to get the gun back, but they also appeared upset at me for bringing it in. It was obvious that no one knew how or when the big gun was brought into the 24th Infantry sector. I left regiment, my responsibilities discharged—almost.

I sent for all my NCOs after work that evening, and I gave them hell—individually and collectively. I told them that every one of them was guilty of hiding the gun instead of reporting it. I chewed them out for not recognizing the potential hazard of the unreported weapon. I didn't actually communicate any threats, but it might be said that I implied some.

Engineer Road, 14 August 1950, Haman, Korea

Upon arrival at our new location in the southern part of the Pusan perimeter, I made a reconnaissance of the area and started a program to improve the roads, culverts, and bridges. The work kept the troops occupied and ensured the 24th Regimental Combat Team of clear passage on the MSR and auxiliary roads and trails. We stayed busy. I established priorities for work to be done in infrastructure, field fortifications, and other engineer works.

When I had gone over all of the 24th RCT area, I assigned a high priority to developing an access road to eliminate the bottleneck where the MSR dead-ended in front of the 24th RCT command post. The MSR ran for about three miles southeast from the town of Haman, and if the enemy ever cut that road, there was no way the troops could leave their positions by vehicle.

I discovered a trail about fourteen feet wide that led off eastward from the MSR. The tracks indicated that it was used by farmers with their ox-drawn carts. The trail led up to a row of low hills and ended at a shale hogback, which precluded passage by vehicles.

As the main roadwork wound down, we went to work vigorously on the trail, while another crew worked on the hogback. It was hard work because the shale was too hard to move, even with our bulldozer. I posted daily reports of our progress on the regimental situation map. Removal of the hogback would allow the trail to extend uninterrupted for several miles and finally rejoin the main supply route. This would give the RCT another vehicle road to get supplies in or to move out.

I was concerned about the RCT being hemmed in with no roadway out of the Battle Mountain area. The 6th North Korean Infantry Division was exerting extreme pressure on the RCT, and the pressure seemed to be increasing from night to night. Our work on the trail intensified, and eventually we removed enough of the overburden to place a large demolitions charge deep enough to remove the shale or at least to loosen it up.

I was a bit concerned. Shales and slates are difficult to blow because they're stratified, or layered. The spaces between the layers often contain water and fine silts that cushion the effects of a demolition shock, dampening the explosion so that it's ineffective.

Not so that time. After careful preparation, we blew the obstruction. We blew it well, leaving only a lot of loose rock, which the dozer could handle.

Shortly after the big blow, a jeep rushed up to the demolition site, and a very excited colonel got out. It was the new regimental commander, Colonel Champeny. When he saw me, the Old Man puffed up the hill, shaking his finger at me.

He coughed, "I thought that noise was artillery. What are you doing? I told you that we didn't need another road."

I advised the colonel that this was just a training project and that the notice of the blow was on his situation map and had been for two days.

Colonel Champeny took a long, mean look at me and said, "I'm unhappy with you. You just do things the way you want."

I replied, "Sir, I serve the regiment well."

I was careful not to become contumacious, because it was easy to do with him. His face had become florid, and he turned and went down the hill. Fortunately, he had not told me not to open the road. His parting remark was, "I don't know what we'll ever need it for."

I beckoned for the troops to continue their work.

It was my duty to maintain and construct roads in my area of responsibility. I always did that, and it was always good for the regiment that I did. I, too, hoped that the infantry would never need that narrow, slightly improved dirt strip that we named "Engineer Road." But it was available if and when.

I announced that the road was completed at the next regimental staff meeting, and Colonel Champeny glared at me in his ugliest manner. He advised his commanders and staff that the road was of no significance, and it would neither be needed nor used. He was wrong. Engineer Road proved to be invaluable in the fighting for Battle Mountain.

Battle Mountain, 18 August 1950, Near Haman, Korea

Pound for pound the North Korean soldier was as good as any in the world. He was wily and tough. He was tremendously motivated and probably the best mortarman on the planet. The North Korean was trained to a razor's edge. Through the glasses I once watched an NKPA soldier dig a foxhole. He dug into the hillside with a crude half-shovel, deposited the spoil into a large kerchief, and then moved away a few yards where he meticulously distributed the soil and gravel. When he finished, it was barely visible. The NKPA soldier was arrogant, confident, and highly capable. He was at home in the heat, the dust, and on the barren mountainsides.

For some reason our northern enemy wanted possession of Hill 625, which became known appropriately as Battle Mountain. NKPA units attacked the hill nearly every other night, and on the odd night the 24th Infantry Regiment took the mountain back. It was dirty, bloody, hot.

The 24th Infantry Regiment lost and regained that hill for nearly forty-five days. They had no baths, very little drinking water, and seldom did they have clean clothes. Sunset provided the only respite from the hellfire of the sun. It was a stinking conflict, with numerous changes of commanders at battalion and company level. It was impossible for the troops to identify with their officers or vice versa.

On the other hand, there were some dedicated and highly competent officers who led their men brilliantly, officers who respected the troops and were respected in return. Such an officer was Capt. Laurence Corcoran, the commander of Charlie Company.

Larry Corcoran was a good-size man with determination showing in hard blue eyes. He was blond and strong, and he knew his business. A no-nonsense type of man. I had last seen him back at Gifu, a light year ago, and I noticed that he had lost a lot of weight. The same was true of most of us.

Larry mentioned his need for installation of mines, barbed wire, and trip flares. I knew he needed those items to help solidify his position. I could have provided the engineer support, except that I normally performed my activity at the request of the regimental plans and operations officer. However, I arranged to wire in Larry's Charlie Company anyway.

We set out a concentrated minefield, interspersed with trip flares, and antipersonnel mines to include bouncing betties. Lord, it was hot up on that hill—hotter than the hinges to the doors of hell. It was slow and difficult carrying mines and rolls of wire up those hills, particularly in that heat.

The troops were neither trained nor conditioned to function efficiently in the prevailing high temperature and humidity or in the rough terrain. It was particularly difficult for American soldiers to occupy hilltop positions where food, water, ammo, barbed wire, and other heavy items of equipment had to be manhandled. Somehow it had to be done; the stuff had to be transported and installed. There had been a time when Army tables of organization and equipment called for mules, but modern technology won out over common sense. Accordingly, beasts of burden were no longer authorized, whereas soldiers were authorized to be beasts of burden. So enterprising soldiers used cows or other indigenous transportation devices whenever possible.

When the regiment occupied Battle Mountain and its environs, the engineer commander was directed to round up and corral all the livestock the natives had left behind in their flight from their homes when the enemy came near. We rounded up cattle, pigs, and chickens. We corralled the animals where pasturage and water was available. Then I got a bright idea.

I realized that in many other parts of the world cattle were beasts of burden. Why not in Korea? Why not use the beefsteaks to carry significant loads up hills? One cow would carry the load of four or five soldiers without griping or bellyaching. I had two A-frames secured together and hung over the backs of the cows. We found that if we used the rings in their noses that the cattle wouldn't resist doing our bidding. We led the burdened animals up to the mountaintop positions. I'm sure that the animal lovers from home would take a dim view of the use to which we'd put the beasts, but in combat, only the soldier is significant. From that day onward I expanded the use of the animals. They were used to transport all of our field fortifications, water, and ammunition to the line companies of the 24th Infantry Regiment.

The field fortifications stopped the enemy from storming Charlie Company's positions. The antipersonnel mines interspersed in the barbed wire wounded or killed NKPA soldiers who came crawling with great caution or recklessly hurtling through the wire. The riflemen and machine gunners did their slaughtering under the eerie light of the trip flares. It became extremely difficult for the NKPA to dislodge the GIs from that hill. Our enemy paid an awesome price for every inch of Battle Mountain. That was probably the most expensive real estate in the world.

However, on 22 August 1950 things turned from bad to worse on Battle Mountain when a hellfire 120mm mortar round came in. The big mortar round exploded about forty feet above the deck with a KA-WHUMP! Lieutenant Mathis and four good soldiers of the 24th were cut down. With Mathis down, Larry Corcoran was the only officer left for duty in Charlie Company until 30 August. Those were hard days and hard nights.

The casualty rate was devastating, and the replacements were kids, most of them eighteen to twenty years of age without combat experience. Most of the replacements were not infantrymen. They came from the technical services: signal corps, ordnance, medical, whatever. The lack of combat training rendered the replacements less than fully effective.

The Army's personnel assignment and utilization policy specified only that replacements to the 24th Infantry Regiment be Negroes. It didn't matter if they were properly trained or were qualified in the proper skills. It only mattered that they were black. That policy guraranteed the weakening of the 24th Regimental Combat Team.

Immediately following the loss of Mathis came the loss of Lieutenant Anthes and another officer from Easy Company. These losses left a terrible leadership hole in the 1st and 2nd battalions. The shortage of experienced junior officers, together with the rapid turnover of senior officers, really created a hole in the "Main Line of Resistance."

Wounded men who were ambulatory were of necessity returned to their units, often too soon—before their wounds were healed properly. That created a terrible morale problem, which militated against organizational efficiency.

In spite of all the negatives, however, Captain Corcoran and a few other fine company-grade officers hung on, as is the hallmark of infantry officers and noncommissioned officers. One night Larry Corcoran lost his position when the NKPA overwhelmed him. He yielded, regrouped, counterattacked, and retook his position— all without the knowledge of battalion or regimental headquarters. For his outstanding leadership at Battle Mountain, Capt. Larry Corcoran was awarded the Silver Star Medal.

The troops complained bitterly about the presence of decaying bodies in front of their positions in that withering, rotting environment. The regimental commander ordered the engineers to obtain quicklime and provide it to the line units immediately. The lime was used to decompose the enemy bodies. What had been bodies a few days ago were reduced to a few long bones, some rags, and some grease spots. It was grisly business, but it satisfied the troops. Somehow, it seemed demeaning to the fallen soldiers.

On the night of 31 August–1 September, the 6th North Korean Infantry Division attacked in force and moved the 24th Infantry

Regiment off Hill 625. Colonel Champeny was one of the first people to leave through the cut we had blown to create Engineer Road. He was followed by at least two of his infantry battalions. The road Colonel Champeny had derided had saved him and his troops.

Later, the regiment came back to take Battle Mountain by way of Engineer Road. One battalion of the 27th Infantry Regiment reinforced the 24th RCT in retaking the hill. The NKPA suffered great losses in taking that hill from us the first time and much greater losses from our counterattack. There were no more mass attacks by the North Koreans on Hill 625 after the night of 31 August 1950. We paid a price also. Over five hundred American casualties were suffered on Battle Mountain during the month of August 1950.

Once Hill 625 was properly fortified and we had a tight grip on it, the mountain was never lost again. Superb duty performance by a few officers and some valiant enlisted men made it possible to retain our positions until the Army broke out of the Pusan perimeter in mid-September 1950. We held because of some tough NCOs and a handful of dedicated officers—Capt. Larry Corcoran of Charlie Company; Capt. Charles Piedra of Heavy Weapons Company, 1st Battalion; Capt. Roger Walden of Fox Company, 2d Battalion; and Capt. Mike Keiler of Heavy Mortar Company. All of these fine officers contributed to making good things happen in spite of the very transient leadership at regimental, battalion, and company levels.

The great pity of it all was that so many good men had to die needlessly because the U.S. Army refused to send qualified white combat soldiers as replacements to a black infantry regiment, even in desperate combat.

Battle Mountain was certainly one of the most fought over and exchanged pieces of real estate in the annals of American military history. Pork Chop Hill, later on in the Korean War, and Hamburger Hill in the Vietnam War were also scenes of intense combat. There is no use in arguing over which was the hardest; they were all hard.

The Captain's Tomb

20–21 August 1950,
Haman, Korea

We were a s
worn, with no r
a pair of umma
foot, and a size 1
available. The won
of the violence, carr
This was a war wh   ....s.
war of conflicting p   ....d. It was a
win a physical victor)   ... Koreans intended to
a retreat, a withdrawal, a defeat at every encounter. Up to 20
August 1950, he'd enjoyed considerable success.

this chapter is very difficult to read EMOTIONALLY — you may want to skip it …

We had no cots, no bedding, no mosquito netting, no tentage.
The canned food we were issued left much to be desired. But
we did have ammunition and demolitions in abundance. Such
was the lot of the U.S. soldier in Korea in the summer of 1950.

I guess soldiers are always tired. Combat is not a restful business.
I watched the shipment of land and antipersonnel mines being
off-loaded in the schoolyard in which we were bivouacked. The
mines made a small mountain. There was enough explosive in
that pile to destroy the town of Haman and all of us with it.

At nightfall I lay down to another fitful night of sleep, fighting

165

gigantic and voracious mosquitoes. I had been at it for several hours, when, at the stroke of midnight, artillery rounds started coming in. The rounds were bursting short, then long, then shorter. Even as I awakened from slumber, I realized the danger of a shell bursting in the demolition dump and those tons of mines exploding.

I aroused the troops, dispersed them outside the walls of the school and into the combat area, where the prepared foxholes were. If the mines exploded, they would be safer in the foxholes. I waited to make certain that the last man had run through the gate at the rear of the school, then I followed. As I went through the gate and started a step in a turn to my right toward my foxhole, I heard and felt the crack of doom.

A shell hit a stack of land mines, and it exploded with a tremendous force. A ten-foot–high fence of rocks and soil blew over on me. In my last moment of consciousness, I realized that I was being buried under tons of rubble. Although it was a totally unlikely place, that was my tomb.

Some time later—I'll never know how much later—I slowly and painfully gained consciousness. I was in a sitting position. I tried my damnedest to arise. I came to the abject awareness that from a sitting position I had almost no strength with which to overcome the burden of soil and stone. My left arm was pinned underneath my body, and the earth was compressing my right arm across my chest.

I struggled until I became exhausted. Then I became totally and uncontrollably fearful. I sensed a level of fear that I had never known. I was trapped, and—subject to a miracle—I was going to die. I was sorry for myself, and I struggled some more, with a sense of rapidly growing futility.

Fortunately, I was able to breath adequately due to air pockets in the rubble under which I was pinned.

I was terribly uncomfortable. My left arm had gone to sleep. Thousands of needle-like pains told me that my arm was still alive and that there was at least slight circulation. My helmet was still intact on my head, but my neck was twisted and the heavy muscles on the right side cried pitifully. A dizzy sensation originated above my right shoulder and ran up to my ear. The more I struggled the more oppressive became the pressure on my chest, neck, and legs. A large boulder with a sharp point was bearing on the inside of my right thigh. I hurt. I struggled some more until consciousness and hope ran out.

I regained consciousness and became aware of my situation. I attempted to divert my mind. Then I realized that it was cold— the cold that comes with dawn. I must have been out for several hours. My eyes and nose were filled with dust and small granular particles.

An insect crawled along the shell of my ear and finally into my ear, and the sensation of minuscule feet entering my ear canal was the most devastating experience of my lifetime. Each foot clawing in the surface of my middle ear was like murder, and I was powerless to scratch. I waited to be bitten. I knew that I could handle no more pain or frustration. At some point that tiny insect, which felt to me to be the size of a turtle, tried to back out of the canal and became stuck. Its difficulty at freeing itself prompted a frantic scurrying and scrambling for foothold and extrication, and after an interminable period of agony for me, the insect freed itself and left. I was exhausted again.

Vaguely, I heard artillery shells in the far distance, and I sorrowed at coming to this ignominious end. Finally, there was only silence. I could hear only my own thoughts. I recited to myself:

> He that dwelleth
> in the secret place
> of the most high,
> shall abide under
> the shadow of the Almighty.
> I will say of the Lord,
> "He is my refuge and my fortress,
> my God, in Him will I trust."

Laboriously, I completed the entire ninety-first Psalm.

> . . . Thou shalt not be afraid
> for the terror by night;

nor for the arrow
that flieth by day;
nor for the pestilence
that walketh in darkness;
nor for the destruction
that wasteth at noonday. . . .
With long life
will I satisfy Him,
and show Him my salvation.

I was strengthened. Suddenly, I knew that this was only an interlude—a brief pause in the progression of my fate. I felt certain that my entombment was not final. As bleak and desperate as this situation was, I felt that my salvation was somehow imminent.

I turned my mind to prayer again. I remembered the teachings of my parents, and I believed again in the Fatherhood of God. Fervently I prayed and remembered the biblical stories of deliverance, even from conditions and situations more helpless than mine.

Never in life had I been so thirsty, and I was hours overdue for urination. This was a problem of some gravity. If I let go, the urine would saturate my trousers. My mind turned back more than twenty-five years, into my infancy, and I recalled the embarrassment and physical discomfort from wetting my pants. In a slight way it was amusing, but only slightly. I considered it an inevitability, but opted to abstain as long as humanly possible.

I forced my mind to deal with things other than myself. I had made up my mind that I was not going to die here and at this time. I believed that, and I knew that I had to continue believing that. I continued with the Ninety-first Psalm.

. . . There shall no evil befall thee,
neither shall any plague
come nigh thy dwelling. . . .

I thought about that old saying, "being between a rock and a hard place," and that is where I was. In my mind I could see the beautiful blue sky, the kelly-green rice paddies, and the bold barren mountains that loomed behind them. I remembered bird songs and raging streams. I was a boy again. I lapsed into a stupor and dreamed of home, and there was Momma waiting for me.

Gradually, the soil became warmer with the rising of the sun. I passed out again.

I returned to consciousness again with pain in every joint and sinew. I didn't really know the extent of my injuries or even if some bones were broken. I couldn't flex or bend any members, and tears welled up in my eyes. Time had lost its meaning. Day, night, and hour were all the same in my reckoning.

I yearned for home and my family, and they were so very, very far from me. With thoughts of family, my faith returned. I had to believe. I had to be freed. Hunger cramped my belly, and thirst was demanding. I started to worry over the condition and location of my troops.

It was difficult to imagine the company without me at its head, making hundreds of decisions day and night. Hell, if I'd gotten out of the schoolyard rather than pushing out all the troops first, I'd be safe and free instead of buried like a corpse. However, that is the way I saw myself, my job, my duty, my life. I felt about my troops as I felt about my own flesh—my children. Cock-eyed, perhaps, but that is the way of soldiers.

The quiet was deafening. It was vacuous and punishing. All I had was hope and faith, and I was concerned, deeply concerned about the limit of my faith. Under better circumstances I'd always felt it to be boundless, but never before in life had I been put to such a severe and absolute test. I ached in every fiber and capillary of my existence, barely on the edge of consciousness. I prayed fervently—not for deliverance, not for freedom, but a prayer of gratitude for guidance and protection throughout a lifetime of vigorous activity. I gave thanks for my beautiful children, my loving wife. Then, nothing.

When next I became consciously aware, my sphincter had failed, and a new dimension of misery had imposed itself upon me. My left thigh, hand, and arm were wet, and tens of thousands of ants were crawling in the wet areas. Or, I thought they were

ants, and I remembered the term *piss ants*. I could do nothing
about it. I wondered how long I could live under these conditions;
no food, no water, exposure, pain, and depression.

Somehow, I could not arrive at a time frame. I knew that I
could survive for many days, but time was not well defined from
my position. I had no way of reckoning or recording time periods
except by the temperature of the overburden upon me, and that
was purely speculative. Perhaps now, because it was very warm,
it was afternoon.

The Twenty-third Psalm came to my mind: "The Lord is my
shepherd; I shall not want. . . ."

I reflected upon the life that I'd lived. The murder done in
the role of a soldier disturbed me deeply. The Ten Commandments made no allowance for my profession, which in stark truth
was killing enemies of the republic. In this I had not only participated, but I had actively trained and forced other men to participate as well. I lived and trained for action on the killing floor in
Europe and now Korea.

In fact or fantasy I was closer to God than ever before. There
was a communication, not by voice but by perception. Despite
all my puny transgressions, I felt absolution—except for the ob-
scure area of having given less than my best effort at improving
my soul, the wherewithal from which temptations would be
quenched. I felt the chill of mortal embarrassment. I stood naked
before God, and I was wanting.

I prayed. I prayed for forgiveness, and forgiveness then was
more vital than survival. I dredged up all those items in my life
that were callous, mean, and inconsiderate. They seemed small,
infinitesimal, almost totally inconsequential. I regretted not taking
the time to improve my soul during the years when I'd had the
opportunity. It had nothing to do with church attendance. It
was involved with the communication, which only today in my
stark misery I had attemped for the first time—real communication
with God, the reality of God. Not the prattling and recitation of
words, but actual communication.

The ants were still biting. I was powerless even to scratch. The
urine stung, and cramps roped up and down the long bones of

my legs. My twisted spine and neck muscles cried for relief, which was not forthcoming. I was ashamed, because in all the days of my life—in my freedom—I'd given very little thought to my soul's salvation, when now, in desperation, I whined and begged for forgiveness, for atonement, for salvation.

I was not only worthy but entitled to divine intervention. After all, I had been a practicing (sometime) Christian all of my life, and I had recently prayed fervently. Deliverance was my entitlement. Why was it I who was trapped, humiliated, injured? "Why me, Lord?" It should really not be me in this prison suffering these pains. It could (should) be someone else, anyone else. Someone not as worthy as I of divine protection, an officer not involved with the command of troops—an enlisted man. Someone without the intellect, the responsibility, the abilities. Anyone else. "Why me, Lord?"

My mental processes slipped from impatience to be delivered to questioning the Deity for having allowed me to be trapped in this ignominious position. Had I looked to my own safety instead of having ensured that my men were safe and clear before fleeing the school area, I'd have no problem at the moment. This was a worthy action for a troop commander, and punishment was not proper. I was a man to be rewarded, not punished. The pains in my neck, spine, and right hip were periodically washing out my consciousness. I'd probably been in a state of shock for many hours. The question crept into my mind, Would a benevolent God inflict this punishment upon his loving and worthy son? "Why me, Lord?"

Answers were inappropriate. Deliverance was the bottom line. Why was my faith not rewarded? Is my God treating me with justice. "Why me, Lord?"

Perhaps I'd become ill. My reckoning of time was nonexistent. The urine on my arm and legs had long since dried, and that must have taken a couple of hours. At least I thought it had dried. The ants no longer bothered me. The porcupine no longer inhabited my ear. But I was hungry and thirsty.

I began to doubt that I would receive answers. No one knew of my whereabouts. I could not cry out. Someone could walk

within three feet of me without being aware of my existence beneath the heap of stone and rubble. Perhaps I'd begun to die.
All my past paraded before me. I brought it all up. I needed to
convince myself of my righteousness.

With great personal bias and self-rationalization, I relived the
moments of my life. Some of them in memory and some in halluci-
nation. I was a child, a laborer, a student, a parent, a fighter
pilot, a soldier. Always the question of survival. Nothing for
hereafter, only survival—life. Now, however, survival was sorely
threatened. It was not a matter of a gunshot death or the flaming
crash of an aircraft. These were deaths that soldiers understood.
It was slow death in a rubble pile. God could surely devise a
more noble demise. But why demise at all? There was much more
living to do: siring of children and their rearing; winning a few
more medals for deeds not yet consummated; hunting in wood
and field; long draughts of cold water.

Reality slapped me hard in the face. None of the foregoing
mattered. Face it! No outs. No fast talking. No tricks. I was weak,
and I'd demonstrated to myself hours before that there was no
escape. With all my recurring energy, I'd come back to struggle
and fail against the weight of the soil and stone. The earth I
loved so totally had claimed me. God had allowed it to be. Unfair.
Unjust. Unreal. How could He do this to me? "Why me, Lord?
Are you real? Where is your tender mercy? Where is your Fatherhood? Where are you? Are you?"

My attitude changed from doubt to pity. I began to be sorry
that I would not be able to view the hills of home, savor the
warm smell of fresh baked bread or the pungent smell of the
newly mown hay, or to soothe the startled cry of my infant child,
or to respond to the kiss of my wife and lover. To leave all that
I knew and loved was too much, I refused to accept it, and tears
came to my eyes—not in response to my physical pain, but to
my mental anguish. I loved the paths of life, and it was impossible
to consider the alternative of the hereafter. The growing certainty
of the end of life was oppressive. I attempted prayers, but they
were prayers without substance. In abject pity I lost my ability
to communicate with Him. I was begging, and, like a beggar, I

surrendered the dignity that men must possess to stand in judgment before God. "Why me, Lord?"

I wallowed in a mire of self-pity. I did not want to die. I felt neglected and cast out. If God will neglect me in my time of need and not answer my most fervent prayers, I had no need of God. If I had no need, I would express myself accordingly. So I declared myself independent of God, and I uttered numerous blasphemies. (Perhaps these might command attention of the Almighty and provide a basis for repentance in exchange for deliverance.) Childish. Desperate. Alone. Suffering in bone, sinew, intellect, and soul. My rejection became complete. My life was at its lowest ebb. I was lost—body and soul.

I entered a state that I'd never known. I discovered a revulsion of the Almighty, and there is no greater degradation, no more inferior condition. I was approaching the gates of hell with no conscious concern. It was over.

Then I recovered. I was the finest and most upright citizen since Noah. I was devout, upstanding, and worthy of all of God's bounties, particularly rescue from the trap in which I found myself. It seemed only right and proper that God would effect a timely deliverance after all. I challenged God to lift the stone and rubble from me. I promised to be more devout, more loving, "Just get me out of this, and all these things I will do unto thee." Nothing. I wheedled through more prayers. Nothing. More. "Why me, Lord?"

And then, like a fire ax between the shoulder blades, I was stricken with sounds; a voice and towering vibrations chilled me.

Why *not* you? Why not *you?* A petty liar. A petty thief. A man who loved his neighbors only slightly, who rarely has exerted or extended himself in anyone's behalf other than his own. A termite who renounced his faith at the first severe challenge in and to his life. A man who prays solely for his own aggrandizement, and in your own jargon—phony. Yes, why not you? You are well above mediocrity, but in no area have you ever striven for excellence. You have not sought the Fatherhood of God. You have only talked of love, then only because you have had no other belief upon which to grasp. At this time you challenge the authority of the Almighty. Why *you* indeed?

You who are unworthy. There is much else for you to accomplish. There is much yet for you to do. There is labor here for you. There is time for you to consider these words and in time become free.

Then it became calm and still, and I trembled in all my soul. I reflected upon my recent, profound experience. I was weak, exhausted, awed, subdued. I fainted again. During the early afternoon I hallucinated in a sea of pain. I was once again a child at home. Finally I reflected again upon my life. My sins.

I felt deep remorse and dire need for repentance for the killing I'd done in two wars and indeed for the petty sins I'd committed. The more I thought about it the more lowly I became. It was difficult not to consider the situation hopeless, but through it all I felt hope and survival to be synonymous. I had to live! Time became motionless. Finally the waves of dreaming became welcome, because they fogged out the pain.

Eventually the turmoil left my mind. I could hear guns in the far distance. I could feel the breach explosions through the ground that encompassed me. The sounds became stronger, and eventually I heard small-arms and automatic-weapons fire, which came steadily closer. I heard voices impregnated with the feverish high pitch that comes with mortal excitement, as in battle. Then the voices faded, but the gunfire became more intense and closer. More voices sounded with the anxiety of the killing floor, and they were all around me, but I couldn't understand the words through the rubble of my tomb.

Then I heard somebody say, "Mothuhfucka," and I knew that those were my people. In my elation, I mustered all my reserve to yell, not in words, but in sound to let the passersby know that there was a human under the rubble pile who needed release. There were soldiers nearby—perhaps an arm's length away. I yelled again and tried to move.

A soldier said, "You hear something?"

I responded with the total of my being, "Help!"

A solder said, "Sounded like a man in that pile of crap."

Another one said, "May be enemy. You dig a little. If it's enemy, I shoot 'im."

"Okay."

He began to remove the rubble. I felt his hand scratch my helmet, and I heard, "It's a GI's hat."

He continued digging. "It's a captain!"

Both men began to dig earnestly, and I felt the weight being relieved from my neck, my shoulder, and my right thigh.

I thanked God with the intensity of my whole being. No man, no man was ever more grateful for deliverance. Few men have come back from their tombs. In my gratitude, I cried like a newborn, and they stretched me out on the grass nearby, and called, "Medic!"

My tears cleansed my eyes, and I felt blood coursing freely through my sore, stiff limbs. I was safe, even on the killing floor, and I gave unlimited thanks to the God of my recent discovery and communication. By sunset I was clean, sore, and aching, but I was ready for duty.

There was work to be done and living to be done. Tears flooded my eyes. My faith was restored, and I had a reunion with God.

Jimmie Hicks

22–28 August 1950,
Haman, Korea

I saw him climb out of a weapons carrier with his duffel and gear. He wore a hodgepodge of GI clothing, including the soft wool cap normally worn in winter under a helmet liner. I heard him ask for "Landscape Six," which was me, and I wondered what he wanted. He half dragged and half carried his belongings and made his way to my office in the schoolhouse. His soldier-guide said, "Sir, this man's looking for you."

A slender black man wearing metal-rimmed glasses and dressed in a correspondent's unmarked uniform extended a hand and said, "I'm Jim Hicks, correspondent from the *Baltimore Afro American*. I'd like to talk to you about Yechon. What went on there? I got a good story on it at regiment, but since it was about you mostly, I'd like to write about Yechon and you. Also, I'd like to know what happened about Gilchrist at Sangju. In the past twenty-four hours I've heard so much about you and your men that I'd like to stay a few days and do some stories on you for publication in the States. With your permission, I'd like to ride around with you and talk to the troops, and just get a firsthand view of everything you do."

I shook his hand and welcomed him aboard. I had known some other correspondents from Hicks's paper during World War II, and they told our side of the story. Almost instantly we were friends. Hicks had the run of our bivouac and did stories on the men in addition to taking hundreds of pictures. He lived in officer country about half the time. He made an arrangement with my jeep driver to be notified of my travels. Frequently, Hicks was in the jeep when I got there. I gave Hicks answers to all his questions. Sometimes he'd be gone for a couple of days while visiting other units. He was busy. He was energetic and genuinely liked.

We reorganized as infantry one night, and Hicks spent a dangerous night on the hills with us. He really had no business there, but that's where he chose to be. He stayed and learned. We only had some probes during the night, but no concerted attack, so we just talked. About 0230 we were sitting in a double foxhole, and Hicks put a question to me: "Bussey, tell me about the mass grave at Yechon. You've never mentioned that, but a couple of the men told me something about it."

I thought back. "Well, Jimmie, I came back from Yechon after it got dark and the shooting had stopped. It was dark as hell, and I didn't want to risk my life trying to walk on the rim of the levee to get to the village, so I left there and drove back to Kumchon. I still had the mail pouch. One of the reasons I went to Yechon was to deliver that mail. The next day was busy, so I didn't get back up there. The following day, Lion Five called and directed me to send the dozer over to report to the CO, 35th Infantry Regiment no later than 1500 hours. It was to be used to clear an area for the Marines to land in or something. I noticed that the road went close to Yechon, so I loaded up the mailbag, and with my new jeep driver leading a maintenance truck and the lowboy carrying the dozer, we were on our way. My 3d Platoon hadn't returned, so I was anxious to get back to Yechon. Regiment didn't have much of a handle on what was happening at Yechon, partly because the 3d Battalion was attached to the 35th Infantry Regiment.

"When I got to Yechon, I noticed people removing bodies from the rice paddies where I'd been firing two days before. Another group was digging individual graves. I broke out the machine guns, mine from the hood of the jeep and the motor pool's gun from the maintenance truck. When the guns were in place, we unloaded the dozer and groused out a mass grave long enough to accommodate all of the 250 or so bodies. It was a tough job. Two days dead at the ambient temperature and serious deterioration had begun. The graves people there didn't know I was responsible for the carnage they were burying. I was glad they didn't. I still hadn't made peace with myself about duty and mass killing. Maybe I'll never be able to. I didn't feel guilty; I just didn't know how to feel. I knew that it was contrary to the Commandments, for sure.

"I packed up our guns, and moved on to our destination. I smelled those bodies for a long time. That's about it, Jimmie. We've got some pictures of it if you want some."

"Thanks."

We sat silently for a few moments. Then Jimmie said, "You're a different type of man than I've ever known. Tell me about yourself—whatever you can remember."

I started talking and told him the story of my life as I remembered it. I told him how I came to be in Korea, and I told him about Yechon. He wrote up the story of Yechon for his paper. A lot of people didn't believe the story, but Jimmie Hicks told it the way it was. Hicks's reporting of Negro participation in the war helped balance the biased reporting of most of the press. I give Hicks credit for helping to influence the NAACP to send Thurgood Marshall to Korea to review the misapplication of military justice to black soldiers. Hicks helped improve the morale of Negro soldiers by bringing the real story of their accomplishments to their folks back home.

The Chinese Moon, 23 August 1950, Haman, Korea

When the chips were really down, when the enemy was obviously winning, and when the infantry couldn't hack it alone, the engineers reorganized and were committed as infantry. I loved the versatility, and I particularly enjoyed succeeding where the infantry guys failed. Most occasions requiring reorganization were defensive in nature.

Such was the case I'm about to tell of here.

There were some bad things about this particular mission to reorganize as infantry. For starters, my company was turned over to our parent engineer battalion, which was always oriented around division headquarters some eighteen to twenty miles or more to the rear of the action.

The commanding officer of the 65th Engineer Battalion was Lieutenant Colonel Rivers. He spent his time in the security of the rear echelon. After all, he was the division engineer! He didn't climb the hills he assigned me to. He knew the theories expounded at the engineer school, but he had no knowledge whatsoever of what the infantry units did or how they did it—except at a conversational level.

Lieutenant Colonel Rivers came to my CP, gave me some storybook directions, pointed at his map, and then pointed at the hills. In his broadest southern accent, he assigned me twin missions: "Occupy those hills yondah. Hold 'em 'til ah releeves ya, puhsun'ly! Second, pratec' them ah-till-ry battalions. We caint affohd to lose no guns."

"Good, sir. Is there any intelligence info? What is the enemy strength? Where are they located?" I asked.

"Wal, ah ain't sho' 'bout that, but ah'll let ya know, laytuh."

Then Lieutenant Colonel Rivers advised me that all fire missions would be okayed by him and only by him. He grunted to his jeep driver and got the hell out of there.

It was 1330 hours when Rivers drove away. It was hot, and there was a lot to be done before sundown. Back at the CP, I called a meeting, briefed my people, organized the transportation and other equipment, sent out my liaison people, and moved to a new forward CP location in the area where the two artillery battalions had their headquarters.

I made a call on the artillery battalion commanders. They knew their missions, possible enemy locations, and all the other information that they, and I, needed. I learned that about six hundred enemy soldiers had broken through the lines the previous night and were thought to be close by. Major Watson, executive officer of the black 159th Field Artillery Battalion, apologized for having his hands tied with respect to providing fire support for my company. His orders were that he could only fire for us upon request by Lieutenant Colonel Rivers from his engineer battalion command post near division headquarters. We both knew that arrangement to be somewhere between awkward and stupid and close to asinine.

When we fought as infantry, working for an infantry commander, we worked as one of his units. Infantry commanders knew their business; we knew ours, and the missions worked out well. The infantry commanders studied the terrain, heeded their intelligence, and understood their support elements. In short, they knew their jobs. Under an infantry commander I could have called for fire of any type on my own initiative and could have received that fire in my own foxhole, if that was where I wanted it. There were times when that was exactly where I needed it.

My company of engineers was committed to defend a range of hills 4,100 yards long and about 400 meters high. Even a reinforced infantry battalion with three rifle companies could not defend that much real estate adequately. We had radio contact only with an engineer lieutenant colonel who had neither the knowledge nor the ability to organize and defend a position against a live enemy.

I assembled the troops and briefed the officers. Then we climbed those hills in heat well over 100°F. Lieutenant Peoples recruited about forty Korean men from Haman, and they backpacked ammo, water, and other necessities to our new positions. This was done in exchange for several hundred pounds of rice we had captured earlier. The native bearers loaded up a herd of cattle with our supplies and impedimenta. Two A-frames were yoked over the backs of the cattle; they were a fine substitute for pack mules.

It was difficult reaching our hilltops. At some locations it was literally hand over hand. The basic load for an M-1 rifle was eighty-six rounds, far too few rounds for a night of fighting. Between the nine-pound rifle, the basic load, a one-quart canteen weighing two pounds, and other equipment, the weight was impossible for climbing hills at 110°F with unbelievably high humidity. Such was the fate of the American fighting man.

We dug in along the crest of 4,100 yards of hills. Our unit strength was about 200 men. I realized that wasn't enough to defend that much real estate against a determined enemy, but we had to do it. That was the way it was. I cut up the ridge with my lieutenants. We planned our barbed-wire patterns, complete with land mines and bouncing betty antipersonnel mines. We developed a communications plan. I briefed the troops on everything I knew. We wired in and got ready for the night.

From the conditions of the previous day, I knew that this night there would be a Chinese moon—a full moon, bright, cooling, and filled with murder. I was right. It was another time of desperation. A time of ineptitude. A time of incompetency, and a time of death—wanton, needless, brutal death.

The Chinese Moon, 23 August 1950, Haman, Korea

From my position on the ridge I could see some casual movement among the trees in the valley below. I noticed the smoke of cooking fires and decided to stir the pot a little to see what we really had. I could identify the white muslin garb of the North Korean soldiers. With the binoculars I counted about three hundred fifty men.

We opened fire on the enemy camp site with our .50 caliber machine guns. We were really out of range but near enough to awaken the camp and disrupt the rice issue constituting their evening meal. I watched them rally and assessed their return fire, and I knew that I had the six hundred enemy soldiers by the tail.

I called Lieutenant Colonel Rivers on the land line and requested artillery fire. From his secure location eighteen miles to the rear, he determined that the enemy position was too close to mine and denied my fire request.

His arbitrary and incompetent decision cost many men their lives that night. I felt that if I requested a fire mission on my own foxhole, I was entitled to it, and no one—no one!—eighteen miles away could deny me that.

(From the perspective of forty years later, I am still bitter about this arbitrary and inane judgment from a man completely out of touch with the tactical situation. Good men died because of his ineptness.)

About a half hour before sunset, a nice-looking young man came up to my command post. Private Crosley explained that he was a chaplain's assistant and that he had been misassigned. He had been attending classes in the School of Divinity at the University of Kansas until six days ago, and as a member of the reserve, he'd been hustled off to Korea. He was a noncombatant and had no knowledge, inclination, or previous training involving rifles and bayonets.

He was sincere, and I believed him, but night was falling, and I had my hands full. I had the mission and two hundred other men about whom I was also concerned. I sent the young man down the ridge to join Sergeant Knight with instructions to tell Knight exactly what he had just told me. I asked Sergeant Knight to give Private Crosley some instruction on firing the M-1 rifle at close range and some basic bayonet instruction.

I further counseled Private Crosley that below us in the groves were approximately six hundred North Korean soldiers who had broken through the 24th Infantry Regiment the night before. I told him that I had stirred them up, but the range was too great for our fire to be effective. With our lack of artillery to really shake them up, they would pay us a visit soon. I told him that his life depended upon his ability to learn to shoot that weapon and to implant that bayonet in some enemy brisket. I pointed out the imposing need of enemy soldiers for size 6 shoes, such as he was wearing. I assured Crosley that come morning, "I'll get you transported back to division for reassignment," but that for the moment and for the long, chilling, and bloody hours before sunrise, "you, too, have to be a soldier." It meant survival. It meant fighting and bleeding, subject to the gross incompetence of my senior officer. I had grave doubts about Crosley's survival as he proceeded down the ridge to Sergeant Knight's position.

On that 4,100-yard-long row of hills on a night sky lighted by a Chinese moon, I came eyeball-to-eyeball with death and destruction once again.

Now, Sergeant Walker was neither a fighting man nor much of any kind of a soldier really. He was a man who loved life. He joked and laughed, and he did his level best. At least he tried. He was a barber who'd found it difficult to make a living in civilian life. So he'd enlisted in the Army, which eventually assigned him to my company. He was on that hill because fate had placed him there.

Yet, Walker's fate, Crosley's fate, and mine were dependent on the whim of Colonel Rivers, who'd set up his chessboard and then moved eighteen miles away to play a game against an enemy he couldn't see or comprehend. No, Colonel Rivers wasn't close to beating an enemy; he wasn't even close to one. He was in the rear, directing our impending fight by radio.

Sergeant Walker, Private Crosley, and eighteen other men died that night, a long way from home but close to God. I always felt guilty afterward because my best, under those conditions, was not nearly good enough to protect my men. I was good enough to protect them from the competent enemy before me but not from the incompetence of the battalion commander behind me.

During my time in Korea, I felt fortunate to have been trained originally as a fighter pilot. It's a very special training for a very special kind of people. It teaches awareness, quickness, animal-like perceptiveness, hypersensitivity, and reaction geared directly to action. Applying my pilot's training, skills, and characteristics; converting the feinting, parrying, and thrusting involved in fire dancing, whether at ground zero or coming out of the sun; and being always at "green and go" made things relatively simple and manageable for ground combat on the killing floor that was Korean infantry action. Although I participated in ground combat because duty demanded it, I actually enjoyed the heightened thrills, the gross apprehension of uncertainty, and the adrenaline-inducing drunkenness that mortal combat produced.

Darkness came swiftly and brought the rise of a gigantic, red-gold moon, which provided good light for the killing floor. The carnage began. We fired from our foxholes and littered the hillside with white-clad bodies. The enemy mortars found range and pinned us down tightly, while the hostile infantry crowded up on us. Wave after wave of the enemy rose and fell amid the screams and blood on a ridge ten thousand miles from home. Men I'd never seen before, men whose destinies were as futile as my own.

There were periods when I hadn't time to reload my weapon. It was up out of the foxhole, which can rapidly become a grave. It was light enough to tell the enemy by the color of clothing. In the murderous frenzy I became a fiend. Perhaps in an ashamed way I secretly enjoyed the bloodletting. At least it satisfied my desire to survive.

Then the enemy reached the hilltops, and it turned into hand-to-hand combat. The adrenaline-drenched blood flowed within me like tapwater. I was no longer fighting other human beings. I was hearing the devil's hornpipe and drums over the Styx with their message of doom and foreboding. THRUMP-A-THRUMP-A-THRUMP-A-THRUMP. DUTT-A-DUTT-DUTT, DUTT-A-DUTT-DUTT, DUTT-A-DUTT-DUTT-DUTT. WHAM! WHOOSH! I was striking my own blow after blow after blow for me and my men, for God and country, in that weird half-light just before dawn.

While Lieutenant Colonel Rivers slept, we fought for someone's freedom. I felt my bayonet go in an enemy soldier, cutting through meat and gristle and slicing through rib bones, and I kicked the dying man in the belly to facilitate withdrawal of my blade. I slung and jabbed the knife into the lumbar of a tiny, grunting madman who had been spraying the night with his .28 caliber machine pistol, grunting, "Uohy! Uohy!" all the while. I killed him in the midst of a grunt. His garlicky visceral fluids squirted out beyond the bayonet guard before I could extract the blade from his guts.

On and on it went until that wave of enemy, momentum spent and madness converted to some semblance of reason, withdrew. I didn't feel that I was killing men, or at least not other human beings. The adrenaline produced a weird high unlike anything else in life; it was more absorbing (but more dangerous and less pleasurable) than sexual release.

Finally it became quiet. The extreme demand of repeatedly

wielding that nine-pound rifle and bayonet with its lethal cutting tip had exhausted me completely. I slumped to the parapet of a foxhole. Private Hargrove, its occupant, was beyond caring about yet another intrusion. I got up abruptly, energy recharged, and started softly calling the names of men who I remembered should still occupy those foxholes close to Hargrove's.

I called for Walker. He was bent at the waist, half in and half out of his foxhole. In the faintly dawning half-light he rolled his eyes a little and, through a deep gurgle of blood clotting in his throat, tried to respond, "Thanks, Cap'n." He lifted his hand feebly a slight inch or two; then it slumped to the ground. I lost a fine barber and a friend. I never knew what it was he was thanking me for.

Simultaneously the mortar shells began to crack overhead once more. They sounded like a gigantic dog's bark, and steel shards of death rained down among those of us who still lived and wanted to live. I knew this renewed firing to be a prelude to yet another attack by another mass of seemingly crazed and very skillful enemy.

Under the barrage the enemy had moved close. We were driven back into the partial protection of our foxholes by the rain of incoming steel. We were precluded from taking the enemy at long or medium range, but the moment those mortars stopped exploding, we were up out of our holes and going at our work hand-to-hand.

Garlic, gunpowder, and death. An ugly diet.

I heard a man scream in the dusky light, and once again I was doing a dance of death on the killing floor to a demoniacal tune. Feint, parry, thrust, retrieve, pivot, thrust, retrieve, butt stroke, swing, thrust . . . poverty, bigotry, hatred, Ku Klux Klan, stealth, fire, hunger, the pipes, and death. Blow after blow for freedom. Thrust after thrust for justice. Rip after rip for equality.

Suddenly, clubbed from behind, my head exploded. I felt like all the bubbles in a bottle of champagne from which the cork had just been released. Desperately I rolled over, and frantically I scuttled sideways. My rifle was gone! Groping toward a sitting position, trying to clear away the cobwebs, seeking to focus, I dragged my hand across an entrenching tool. One learns to survive, if one is reared in a ghetto, with the weapons at hand. So it was. A little man was stalking me, approaching with a long knife-like weapon something like a modified scythe blade. I swung the entrenching tool in its hoe mode and performed a perfect combat lobotomy. Dumping his brains and blood onto my chest, the little ex-man fell forward.

I was already going into action somewhere else, swinging that little hoe. It was effective and deadly. The dance was nearly the same, but I was sticky and wet and sick. The smell of human blood is nausea-inducing. I knew that when that human wave was repulsed, I was going to give up the hill.

The night wore on, and the men who carried our wounded down the hill were failing to return either through fear or exhaustion, or both. During one of the lulls, about 0200, I called each of the platoons for a casualty report, and the word was that we had ninety-eight men for duty. I decided that our efficiency was way down and that we would be most effective from positions in the valley below in front of the artillery battalions. I sent the automatic weapons down the hill and silently withdrew our force right at the crack of dawn. It had been a bad night.

I was not willing to sacrifice any more of my men to the aggrandizement of an absent field grade officer's career. I sensed that our efforts to maintain our position had been commendable and would duly be noted by those with an expert knowledge of infantry tactics. I felt that I could survive any vituperation or any contumacious expression forthcoming from Lieutenant Colonel Rivers, engineer combat battalion commander. I figured it was about time for this so-called commanding officer to awaken, take a shower, shave, dress in starched fatigues, have coffee, and eat breakfast.

Our dying was now and immediate, and it could have been prevented had Lieutenant Colonel Rivers allowed me to communicate my own fire requirements to a nearby artillery battalion. Instead, eighteen miles to the rear, he'd responded to only one of my radio calls that previous night, and in that call he'd denied my request for a fire mission on a large body of easily observed enemy: "Naw, that's too close to youah owen position, Cap'n!"

We repelled the next wave. I got on the phone to the platoons. "Bring your wounded, evacuate to the artillery positions in the valley below and behind us. Acknowledge in order of platoons."

I moved over to talk to Sergeant Knight, and I found Private Crosley. He had a trowel handle protruding from his throat. His chin rested on the end of the handle. His eyes had a terrified look, or maybe it was surprise. He'd lost his shoes. It was for sure, death. It is an ugly transition from divinity school to the killing floor. I hadn't time to pray for him. I still had ninety-eight men to get into new positions in front of the artillery battalions. My night and my mission were far from over.

An instant before the mortars started their next rain of destruction, we all evacuated the ridge line. It was time to disengage while their own mortars kept the enemy at a distance from our defensive positions.

It's a sorry duty giving up positions your own men have expended their lives to keep. We'd held off human wave after human wave, all without the benefit of supporting artillery fire, which was readily available. We'd expended nearly all of our remaining ammo during the sixth, and last, attack. After this, it would have to be some small arms and mostly hand-to-hand combat. There were 500 or so of the enemy against exactly 189 of us scattered over 4,100 yards of ridgeline.

I sent two platoons to join each of the two artillery battalions. We'd reinforce their own organic security, which included their very effective but vulnerable automatic weapons. As dawn advanced, a cloud layer formed about two hundred feet up the mountain we'd just evacuated. The fog masked the enemy's approach until he was quite low on the hill above and in front of the artillery.

We tightened up the perimeter around the artillery battalions and drank the coffee they offered us. The battalion commanders both apologized for not having been authorized to give us fire support. Artillerymen love to send out accurate fire.

I called Lieutenant Colonel Rivers, but he was in the sack with instructions not to be disturbed. I left a message advising him of the time and circumstances incident to abandoning my hill positions and about our support of the artillery battalions. I estimated that we had killed about two hundred of the enemy, but the odds had become suicidal, particularly with the devastating enemy mortar fire.

We were waiting, all conjoined. The enemy mortars could not effectively adjust fire onto our new, combined positions, screened as we were by the low-lying cloud cover. The hill rose rapidly from our position in front of the artillery so that the point at which the cloud touched the hill was less than one hundred yards from the gun positions. As groups of North Koreans came down from the cloud cover, an artilleryman jerked a lanyard, a howitzer belched, a shell slapped the hill, and bodies flew apart—arms, legs, and heads going everywhere. Howitzers became rifles. We engineers had replenished our ammo, so those enemy soldiers who survived the artillery fire were chewed up by our combined automatic-weapons and small-arms fire.

Eventually, as more and more clumps of enemy began filtering through the fog, their rate of advance made it impossible to keep firing while maintaining our positions. Morning came more brightly amid cordite fumes.

It was time to leave. One by one, reducing fire gradually and progressively, the artillery pieces closed trails; prime movers hooked up to guns; and men evacuated firing positions. Still fighting as infantry, my men and I covered the artillery's withdrawal, steadily inflicting casualties upon the enemy and denying him access to our positions. Then, abruptly, we withdrew. We joined the last of the artillery convoy vehicles and drove with them the five or six miles to the rear area.

Safely disengaged and security deployed, we could now relax somewhat. We prepared our dead for removal and our seriously wounded for evacuation. We cared for those less seriously wounded and fed and watered the able-bodied.

At sunrise we were at the large schoolyard that had been designated the rear area for our mess and trains and for the artillery units. As always, Sergeant Lamont had breakfast ready. I found a shirt to replace the one I wore, which was blood spattered and blotched with some gelatinous body fluid, probably brains. The early morning flies were all over me, as was the carnage of the night just ended.

Breakfast over, I started the massive cleanup of bodies, weapons, and gear. An ugly time. I watched Private First Class Napoleon remove a bullet from Private First Class Lundy's tongue. Napoleon bandaged a lot of wounds that morning.

There is a camaraderie among fighting men that is neither shared with nor understood by the uninitiated. Lieutenant Colonel Rivers was one of the uninitiated. True to form, he showed up in our schoolyard shortly following breakfast. I watched him approach my CP. Sure enough, he was immaculate—freshly shaven, uniformed, and starched. His face was livid, and he drawled through gritted teeth: "By God, ah tol' ya not to give up those hills. Ah tol' ya to retain that position until ah puhsonally releeved ya!"

The more he talked the more livid he got. "Ah'm goin' to releeve ya of command, but fust ah want ya to get yoah men togethuh an' go back an' take that hill. Move out in ten minutes!"

I responded, "Colonel, I'll move out, but the chances of our successfully taking that hill are absolutely nil. If we'd had artillery support yesterday and through the night, we'd have been able to attack and destroy the entire force of enemy."

"Goddamit, don' ya sass me. Move out!"

"No sass, Colonel, but if I call for a fire mission in my foxhole, that's where it's needed. No one who is not in that same foxhole or close to it has a right to deny me, the local commander, of the fire I order. I didn't lose that hill. You lost it from division headquarters!"

At that moment a stray small-arms round from a nearby hill came in the doorway and dug a furrow in the pine floor right between Rivers's feet, and he lost his cool. Hell, he lost his mind. He ran headlong through the shanty we were standing in, out the back door, and through the yard. He trampled Private First Class Lundy, lying wounded on a stretcher. He ran clear through the schoolyard to the utter amazement of the thousand or so men standing, sitting, or otherwise lounging around. Rivers ran as though the devil himself was after him, and, by golly, he should have been.

Behind the school was a ditch that curved around and eventually intersected the MSR. The school sewage facility, no more than a pond about thigh deep, was near the ditch. In his headlong flight, Rivers waded, staggering, through the sewage pond and got saturated up to his belt. Then he hit the ditch in a big splash, further wetting himself with fecal matter up to his shoulders.

He followed the ditch around to the spot where it intersected the MSR. Exhausted, he climbed up onto the road. He was a splattered, stinking spectacle. He arrived just in time to meet General Wilson coming up the road in a jeep. Both officers were startled.

The general recovered first. "What in the hell are you doing in that ditch, Rivers?"

"Well, sir," the engineer lieutenant colonel panted, "we're under attack!"

The general looked down into the schoolyard. He observed nearly one thousand men eating, relaxing, and caring for themselves and their equipment unconcernedly.

"Meet me in the yard, Rivers!"

The general motioned his driver to pull away from the stinking colonel.

I went out to meet the general.

"Congratulations," he told me, "for the tough fighting last night. And for hanging on as long as you did. And, further, for bringing the artillery battalions out with you intact."

"Thanks, sir."

By this time Lieutenant Colonel Rivers arrived, preceded by a pungent aroma.

"Rivers, where's the attack you mentioned?"

"Well, General, ah, ah, ah . . ."

"Forget it, Colonel. You are a stinking disgrace. Get back to division. Pack your stuff. You're relieved of command as of this moment. I'll arrange for a transfer out of my division today. Go!"

With a hangdog expression, Lieutenant Colonel Rivers headed toward his own jeep. His was a good riddance.

Ingenuity, 24 August 1950, Haman, Korea

It was a crazy war. During the hot, muggy, mosquito-filled days, the enemy wore white muslin breeches and short-sleeved white jackets. He worked in the kelly-green rice paddies. At night, many of these same men doffed their white muslin and became hard, tough soldiers. Damned tough, damned hard.

One outstanding characteristic of Koreans—both North and South—was their ingenuity. They could make more out of less than I'd ever seen before.

A particular skill that stood out above all others was their heavy, or antitank, mine adaptations. Many of the mines they placed behind us in roadways at night were originally our own mines, which we'd placed earlier in their roads to stop their tanks.

They opened our mines after digging them up, then applied just enough heat to make the TNT slightly plastic, and molded the TNT into cigar boxes. They shaped a small well at the top of the cigar box and fitted a pressure fuse into place. Then they had a mine, weighing five to seven pounds, that was capable of destroying wheeled vehicles and disabling tanks. The cigar-box lid was propped open slightly so as not to activate the fuse. The unarmed mine was easy to carry and to emplace. With a pressure of one to three pounds, the closed mine became lethal. However, it was extremely difficult to detect with conventional metal detection devices. All in all, it was a big problem.

A standing mission for my unit was to sweep seven or eight miles of the main supply route for mines every morning. The enemy dug holes in soil and gravel roads, placed some mines, and covered them over with a thin layer of camouflage. They were virtually impossible to spot. Another problem!

The unit had another standing daily mission: to sweep the countryside of stray cattle that refugees had left behind. These strays tended to set off our antitank (AT) mines as they roamed through a defensive sector. Somehow, they seldom sustained real injury when an AT mine exploded, but it was really no problem when a cow actually was badly injured. The injured cow simply became lunch or dinner.

Instead of laboriously sweeping the road with mine detector crews, I'd drive a herd of cattle down the road. Their sharp hooves were extremely effective in detonating mines placed in the roads by the enemy at night. This way we'd detonate numerous mines without ever missing a single one. And we'd wind up with fresh beef. Our mess hall butchered the injured and dead animals to enhance and supplement our combat rations. Not only did the use of animals save valuable time, but more important it saved the lives of many engineer soldiers who had the very hazardous duty of removing mines from the roads manually. The SPCA could have complained, but you never find the SPCA where only people are getting killed.

The Korean people also provided significant labor for us. We'd contact the local mayor or police chief, explain the urgency of our situation or the importance of our mission, and exchange a significant amount of rice for the required number of broad backs and strong legs. Townspeople under local leadership were highly effective in rendering combat support. They moved a lot of supplies such as ammo, mortar rounds, and other materiel for us and perhaps for the enemy as well.

On one occasion division assigned us responsibility for building a five thousand-foot runway seventy-five feet wide. We had a single piece of mechanized equipment—a D-7 bulldozer. The runway was mandated for completion in seven days. So we had local townspeople contribute their labor in support of our operation. In seven days we managed to grade the runway site-to-be, open an abandoned quarry, improvise a haul road, and transport three- to six-inch stones along the designated runway centerline. Then the townspeople emplaced the stones by hand, tamped them down into a densely compacted interlocking grid, and thus built a highly serviceable, weather-resistant runway for P-51 fighter aircraft. I'd flown this type of airplane during the Big War, and I knew a suitable runway when I saw one from ground level.

From time to time I'd witness yet another example of the Koreans' unique ability to improvise. I was called back from Haman to Masan to attend a conference on barrier planning. It happened that my trip began in conjunction with my development of cattle-mobile minesweeping technology.

When I had safely negotiated my road sector I came across a Dodge two and one-half–ton truck tilted on its side—apparently a casualty of conventional minesweeping techniques. In the bowels of the truck a young Korean man was working busily to remove the engine. There was no one else around and I wondered how one man could conceive of handling such a chore by himself. When I stopped my vehicle to watch his legerdemain, he ceased working. But when it became obvious to him that I meant him no harm, he went back to his imaginative task.

The man had one adjustable-jawed wrench, a screwdriver, and a pouch of small tools. In about twenty minutes the truck engine was free from its mounting, the radiator, and the transmission, and was ready for removal.

(Standard hauling equipment for males in rural Korea was the double A-frame. As for women, carrying was usually accomplished by balancing the load atop the head on a small cloth pad.)

The man took a stout tree limb and rolled the engine over once onto his A-frame on the ground. I was astounded. Then the man took a length of tangled rice-straw rope and began to secure the engine to the A-frame. Placing his tree limb at something like arm's reach, he went into a deep crouch while setting his shoulders into the A-frame harness. Rocking back and forth and adjusting for exactly the right location and position, he reached for the limb and placed all seven feet of it between his feet at precisely the right point for maximum leverage. Slowly and carefully, he leaned forward while simultaneously letting the engine, securely fastened to the A-frame, roll onto his back. Meanwhile, he manipulated his arms and hands to climb the limb increasingly inclined to his front. In a minute or two he was perfectly upright, engine mounted high astride his shoulders on the A-frame, and securely balanced.

He took a few trial steps and then began making his way slowly, ponderously, but somewhat majestically up the embankment to the roadway.

I could hardly believe what my eyes told he had actually happened. I didn't accurately know the weight of a six- or eight-cylinder Dodge engine for a 2½-ton truck, but I could estimate it to be something like 350 pounds, give or take 25. What would have been an impossible feat for a robust, well-nourished, and perfectly conditioned 200-pound soldier had just been accomplished by a slightly built Korean weighing no more than 145 pounds!

The man chugged steadily away from me, feet slapping rhythmically and the stout stick thrusting vigorously ahead. He, too, seemed headed for Masan. I passed him in my jeep, glancing briefly sideways to catch a brief wink as both of us went about our business.

Twenty miles later I pulled into Masan. Some eight hours later, the conference on barrier planning concluded, I was headed back to camp. Reaching the outskirts of Masan, I put my foot down to pick up some speed. Suddenly, I slowed down and began to drift toward the ditch. Some yards ahead, plodding steadily ahead, came the somewhat familiar figure. As I passed and broke into a broad smile I noticed, again, a brief wink. Glancing carefully at my dash odometer, I noted the indicated mileage. I checked the reading again as I drew abreast of the damaged vehicle: precisely 20.1 miles.

Never before had I seen such a demonstration of strength, skill, stamina, and human motivation, not to mention innovation. Never again, probably, will I see such.

On 29 August we were joined by two new lieutenants fresh from West Point: David K. Carlisle and Robert W. Green. Both of these men had graduated with the class of 1950 and had been sent directly to Korea.

Both Green and Carlisle brought a lot of strength and a rare quality of class to our company. They could do it all. They were dedicated to duty, methodical, and professional. Both were fine marksmen and athletes. The officers and men of the company were proud of "their" West Pointers. They both performed in an outstanding manner for me. West Point never produced better men.

In a way, though, I felt bad exposing Carlisle and Green to

the killing floor, jeopardizing their tremendous intellect and persons to the nothingness of war. They both had the potential for contributing significantly to the improvement of the total environment in which mankind toiled and despoiled. They were first-class human beings, and they also were first-class fighting men, and they demonstrated it at every opportunity.

Dave Carlisle and I were particularly close. We had grown up together in southern California. I remembered Dave from Sunday school. It was Dave's older brother, Jim, who beat me at the drill competition back at CMTC. Dave was a complete officer and a lot smarter than soldiers need to be. We are close friends and colleagues still.

Absent Without Leave, 31 August 1950, Haman, Korea

It was still hot, and the mosquitoes were voracious as always. The enemy had been active, violent, consistent. Life had become routine, to the extent that a shooting war ever becomes routine. When I wakened on an otherwise very beautiful morning in mid-August, I had a sharp, razor-like pain in my lower left spine. My back was killing me.

At first I thought it was related to my having slept on the hood of my jeep, but that was routine. We had no cots or beds. We slept on soft spots on the floor or wherever we chose. That is, except for the security people, who slept in their foxholes. But misery can become a habit, fortunately. The only caution was that we wanted a lot of dispersion so if attacked, or if an artillery round came in, our casualties would be limited. We had the luxury of mosquito netting, but if a soldier turned over at night and an elbow, shoulder, or any other body part came into contact with the netting, he had an instant mosquito bite.

The back pain disturbed me, and when I began to urinate, it worried me a helluva lot more, because the urine looked like black coffee. I knew at that moment that I didn't just have a back pain. I had a kidney stone. I'd had one before. Not only was there a pain in my back, but it traveled forward and downward into my left testicle. Wow!

I had to go see the medics. I didn't want to be evacuated, but the regimental surgeon was a no-nonsense guy, and the moment he heard about the kidney stone, I'd be long gone. I didn't want to leave the company.

On some crazy schedule of their own, kidney stones move until finally they reach the bladder where they languish and finally lodge for a miserable stay, with spikes poking the sphincter. Bad news! But that only sets up the victim for the painful inevitability. At some point in time that stone has to travel the length of the penis, cutting and plowing all the way until it's free. Excruciating all the way. But this was still not the time for me to be sitting in a hospital in Japan, and I knew that Captain Hedgepath would prescribe an evacuation for me.

I had some friends in the doctor's camp. I wanted some codeine pills to stop the pain. I needed to stop that razor blade in my kidney from inflicting more pain than I could stand. A small handful of pills would suffice. And so it was that I saw the lieutenant, who owed me a small favor.

After a greeting of sorts, I said, "Look, Hoss, I've got a kidney stone working, an' it's killin' me. I need some help. I don't want to be evacuated. It might take a week or so to get rid of the damned thing. I had some experience with them. No sweat, but I need some help. The pain's a bitch."

The lieutenant took a long look at me and said, "Well I think it's a lousy idea. You should be getting the hell out of here. Kidney stones are no joke. But I owe you a couple, and I'll do it for you just this once. I'll write it up as a couple of dozen pills to be taken two at a time as needed for pain. But ten days from now if you haven't gotten rid of that 'staghorn,' I'm going to tell the doctor, minus this little transaction we're negotiating right now. The doctor would have me tried if he knew I was practicing medicine. Ten days. Friendship be damned."

I agreed. "Thanks, old man." And I went about my main concern, and the pills did their job—temporarily.

At the end of ten days, I was still toting that stone, and the pills had made me flaky and insecure. The stone hadn't moved much, if at all. I found myself needing more pills and getting less and less relief. Common sense was dictating that I do as the doctor ordered without subterfuge. Pride be damned. I still had a lot of guilt about laying up in a hospital trying to hatch a kidney stone alongside of all those kids who were in there for gunshot wounds, all broken up and patched together.

I talked to the doctor about the stone, and he looked me over. He asked, "How long have you been bothered by this stone?"

I responded, "About ten days or so."

The doc asked, "What have you been doing for the pain?"

I said, "Oh, I just grin and bear it, doc."

The doctor replied, "You are good at a lot of things, Captain, but lying isn't one of them. Come back at 1300 hours. Meanwhile I'll take a look at that coffee you left as a urine sample. You have an infection and some fever. We may have to send you back to Japan. We'll see."

I resigned myself to what I saw as inevitable and briefed my executive officer on all of our projects and problems. I let Lieutenant Colonel Roberts know where I stood with the medics and assured him that I'd be back as soon as my physical condition would allow. At about 1400 hours I was on my way to Tokyo. I felt bad about leaving the company. I felt that no one else could do the job properly.

I wound up in Tokyo in a military hospital. After a thorough examination, I lay in that fine, white, clean bed and luxuriated for a few moments. Then I fell off a cliff which was sleep, and I slept for fourteen hours—deep restful sleep. It was clean, cool, quiet sleep—the like of which I had needed for a long time. There were forms, questions, X-rays, and medications. I was set up for a retrograde, which was described to me as a process where the doctor would insert a tube through the penis, up the urethra into the bladder, and with the help of a light remove the stone with some tweezer-like tools. I was feeling so badly by then that it didn't really matter what they did or when. I was completely resigned to my fate.

It happened the following morning. I was completely prepared, and the medications took care of any apprehension. I didn't come out of the anesthesia completely until late that afternoon. The doctor visited me, and he announced that the process didn't remove the stone and that he'd try again in a few days. My morale went to hell, and the pains were coming back.

I lay there in intensive care, very unhappy, until the duty nurse, a good-looking lieutenant, came over and started massaging my hands. She told me her name was Ruby, and it fit her well. At first I thought I was feeling the way I was because I hadn't been around women for so damned long. This girl had a voice that did good things for me, and I forgot about the retrograde failure. The attention and conversation made me feel that she really cared. It was a good feeling. I could forget that I was married, and I did. From time to time she had to do other things than care for me, and I got a chance to look her over well. She had hips like a government mule and D-cups that held divine promises. She was slim at the waist, built for speed and endurance. I had a head full of her, and she was hungry. I wasn't able to do a thing physically. The catheter I was carrying took care of that, even if my senses didn't. We talked about the fantastic things we could do to and for each other after the catheter was removed. I was out of my head, and the promise was sublime. That evening an intern removed the catheter. I began to feel better.

The next day I was back in my room, and during the long day I yearned for that woman. She was my reward for all the hardships of combat—all the hardships of life, including wounds. I lay there with an erection all day. I fantasized loving that beautiful hunk of woman. I nibbled her gumdrop-size nipples, and we both loved it. I played with those fabulous mammaries. I had to control myself to keep from having a wet dream. I was very much awake. I'd never in my life wanted a woman so much. I'd never had fantasies so vivid. Her belly intrigued me, and I loved the feel of her magnificent thighs. The only thing better would be the actual sex act. In my mind I was nearly there. Close. And, of course, this woman was giving me the treatment. I lived with the fantasies of this woman all day.

Ruby came by to visit about 2000 hours and told me she would be off at 2300 hours. We could spend as much time as we wanted in her quarters. She asked me what I'd like to drink. I told her, "J. Daniels, black."

She said, "I've got plenty of it. In fact, I've got everything you need."

I believed she did! I was out of my mind with anticipation. As she readied to leave, she went to the locker where my clothes were secured and brought them to me, so I could leave the building inconspicuously. We planned to meet outside a rear door. It was all set. We had a brief manual going over, then she wisely backed off. On her way out she asked, "Have you heard the news?"

And I had to ask her, "What news?"

She told me about the Inchon landing and the allied breakout from the Pusan perimeter. Instantly my fantasies were dead. I belonged back there. Whatever was happening I should have been a part of it even if I was still carrying the stone, which had moved damned little, if at all.

I told Ruby that I'd see her later as we'd planned. Then I put on my combat clothes and left the hospital. I caught a taxi for Tackikawa Air Force Base and hitched a ride back to Korea. It was easy to hitch a ride over to Korea but very difficult to hitch a ride back to Japan. Once in Korea, it wasn't difficult to hitch another flight forward to the 25th Infantry Division area. We landed on the road a couple of times and asked for the 77th Engineer Combat Company, and I finally found them at Pyong-taek. I assumed command. I was home again, sorry to have missed the first big victory the allies enjoyed.

It was back to work. I made a practice of urinating through some gauze so that I could see when the stone passed. In due time I voided the small, painful stone and proudly took the bloody thing to the regimental surgeon. I never saw Ruby again. I did write to her once, and I told her that she was magnificent and that I'd like to see her again. It didn't happen, but I remember her still. I had been mighty close to adultery, and perhaps I'll always be a little sorry that I chose not to indulge, but that is the way with the male of the genus *Homo*.

That was also the first and only time I ever went AWOL— absent without leave.

Almost Victory

18 September–25 November 1950

reassumed command of the 77th Engineer Combat Company on 18 September 1950 at Pyongtaek, near Seoul. It was good to get back. In my absence, the company had done a lot of work and a lot of fighting supporting the 24th Infantry Regiment on the breakout from the Pusan perimeter and the advance northward. Now it was a time for some relaxation and for keeping busy. The war was over as far as shooting and killing was concerned. At least, we thought so at the time.

General MacArthur's brilliant amphibious assault deep in the enemy rear at Inchon on 15 September 1950 changed the war dramatically. The giant outflanking maneuver was successful, and the North Korean Army began to pull back. On 16 September 1950, the UN forces inside the perimeter attacked and, after serious fighting, broke through the North Korean lines. Many North Korean soldiers, now desperately seeking to escape, were captured. The North Korean Army disintegrated.

The 25th Infantry Division, along with the 2d Infantry Division, spent several days clearing NKPA units in the southwestern part of Korea. Early in October the 25th Infantry Division moved north along the west coast of Korea to Seoul, and then continued past the 38th Parallel, which separated South and North Korea.

The mission of the 25th Infantry Division was to form a general United Nations line as part of the IX Corps of the Eighth Army.

The North Koreans appeared to be beaten. The victorious UN forces moved northward, crossed the 38th Parallel, and moved into North Korea. The fighting was over. The troops expected to be home for Christmas.

Then the fighting started up again as Chinese forces began to be encountered in North Korea. Soon after, it became apparent that the Chinese had intervened massively in the war. We would not be home for Christmas, and there was no telling what would happen. It had almost been a victory.

There had been a change in the regimental commander while I was gone. While on a visit to Capt. Roger Walden's F Company area on 6 September 1950, Colonel Champeny was wounded slightly by a sniper and evacuated to Japan. I was sorry he was wounded, but I was not sorry to see him leave; Colonel Champeny and I had never gotten along. Ultimately this officer became a brigadier general on another assignment.[*]

The new commander of the 24th Infantry Regiment was John T. Corley, who at thirty-six became the youngest regimental commander in Korea. Colonel Corley was a graduate of the U.S. Military Academy, class of 1938. He was good. He had fought well as a battalion commander in World War II in North Africa and Europe, and he was one of the most highly decorated officers in the U.S. Army. Colonel Corley had taken over the 3d Battalion of the 24th Infantry Regiment after Sam Pierce was wounded, and he had done a good job with the battalion. Colonel Corley was the outstanding leader that the regiment needed.

A major factor in the performance of our 24th Infantry Regiment in the early days of the Korean War was the turnover of the senior officers in the regiment. The following table shows the officers—all white—assigned to top leadership positions in the 24th Infantry Regiment in those early days of the Korean War.

---

[*] Blair, *Forgotten War*, 244. A revealing account of how Colonel Champeny got his wound and another appraisal of Champeny's overall performance.

Senior Commanders in the 24th Infantry Regiment
Korean War: July–September 1950

Regimental Commander	White; Champeny*; Corley
Regimental Executive Officer	Bennet; Roberts
Commander, 1st Battalion	Calhoun; Carson; Miller
Commander, 2d Battalion	Roberts; Cole; Baxter; Donaho*; Clayton
Commander, 3d Battalion	Walton; Tunsall; Cook; Baxter; Cook; Pierce*; Corley; Blair

* Combat casualty

There were three changes of the regimental commander, two in the regimental executive officer, and sixteen changes of battalion commanders during the first ninety days of combat. On the average, a battalion commander in this regiment stayed on the job only twenty-one days. Only two of the thirteen battalion commanders who left were combat casualties, and two more moved up to higher positions. Most of the battalion commanders left because they were relieved or wanted to find other, less demanding duties. This turnover was hardly conducive to stability among the troops.

Dummy, 19 September 1950, Pyongtaek, Korea

The company had been fighting and working steadily for two months. Now there was some time to relax a bit and take care of some of the less important problems, which had been too low in priority while the action was hot. One of those minor problems involved getting some help with the housekeeping chores.

It was extremely difficult for senior NCOs and officers to keep up with their duffel and gear because, as leaders, they also had to plan, prepare, and supervise the men. It was hard for them to do it all. It made sense to have some help for the leaders, but having enlisted men serve the leaders was not an economical use of manpower, and it was not good for morale either.

The issue of officer orderlies—or body servants—had been considered by the Gray Committee, which reviewed all GI gripes at the end of World War II. It was decreed that all enlisted people and all officers below the grade of brigadier general would wear the same clothes, eat the same food, and take care of themselves in personal matters.

It sounded good, but we had a real need for a little help. Someone was needed to roll up and store sleeping bags, fetch water, run down mail, and, when necessary, to move and set up at a new location.

We had stumbled along with the problem for weeks. One of the officers was always grumbling about the loss or misplacement of his gear. Ours was a busy life. It is said that necessity is the mother of invention, and that is sometimes true.

I was called to attend a supply meeting back at division headquarters, but I begged off because we were winding up some bridge construction. I sent Lieutenant Carlisle in my stead. That was a good move all around. He attended the meeting and set about solving the body servant problems.

Lieutenant Carlisle showed up in a cloud of dust about an hour before sunset. In the back seat of the jeep sat a young and proud-looking Korean man with a huge scar on his throat. Dave got out of the jeep and "signed" for his passenger to dismount from the jeep. He brought the young Korean up to where I was standing. Dave accomplished an introduction verbally and in signs, explaining that he had engaged the man, whose name was Beck en Kee, but who preferred to be called Dan, from a Catholic orphanage in Pusan. The supervising priest felt that Dan could do a servant's job for all eight of our assigned officers. If not, Dave was at liberty to return him. Dave explained that Dan was a deaf-mute, but that he was adept at lipreading simple English. Dave added that Dan was also an accomplished welterweight boxer. That piqued my interest.

Well, Dave took Dan through the bivouac area, signing extensively. By the time rounds were made, Dan had acquired a new nickname, "Dummy." I resented the put-down, but I guess it was only to be expected. Dan seemed to have no objection.

I felt strongly that Dan would prove unable to care for all of his newfound charges. But the following morning Dan was up early. By the time we were up, he'd delivered jerry cans of water, one hot and one cold. The bedclothes of Lieutenant Carlisle and another officer were airing in the windows of our quarters. Maybe Dan was going to work out; we'd just have to see.

When Dan had completed all his chores, he reported to the mess sergeant. Sergeant Lamont sent him out into the countryside, into the yards and gardens that had been abandoned by Korean refugees fleeing the war. It was to be Dan's job to bring to the mess crew abandoned fowl, onions, garlic, peppers, and other condiments that would improve our normal quartermaster fare. Again, Dan did a superb job.

He became admired and respected by everyone. But his nickname, Dummy, hung on. While many of us resented it, the name stuck to him like glue.

During the first full day Dummy was with us, he did some basic carpentry. He constructed two washstands to hold our inverted steel helmets, making our morning ablutions easier and more pleasant. There seemed to be no end to his innovation and all-around abilities. Before long, we couldn't imagine how we'd gotten along without him.

It was a good time, a great time. We'd accomplished some fine bridge construction. The roads were in good shape. The North Korean People's Army had been essentially defeated. The war was virtually forgotten, and rumors of going home began to circulate. I decided to declare a holiday. We'd set aside a day for speeches, footraces, all types of athletic competition, special foods, and relaxation.

We had a grand time. We'd invited guests from other units. Naturally, General Wilson came by for a couple of hours.

Boxing was always our last and most important event. Some of the bouts were used to settle old grudges, but most were demonstrations between accomplished pugilists. The agitators were active before the event. Based on the rumor that Dummy could mix things up, he was matched against Specialist 4th Class Wiley. I thought it was a poor idea, because Wiley was welterweight champion of the division.

Never having seen Dummy fight, I assumed he'd prove to be

no match for a man of Wiley's experience and skills. Dummy expressed no concern; he even manifested a certain air of nonchalance as one of the men helped him don his gloves.

Once his gloves were on, Dummy began to shadowbox. It was immediately apparent that he knew how to handle himself in theory. Of course, going up against Wiley in earnest was going to be something else. Wiley was rangy, strong, tough, and smart.

Well, by the time the boxers were both warmed up, the tension had mounted along with considerable apprehension. The bell rang, and the match was on!

Wiley knew that he was supposed to put on a show. So he dug in. He fired a hard straight jab at Dummy's head, but the head was no longer in line with Wiley's punch. Dummy countered with nearly incredible speed. He threw a right cross, which landed flush on Wiley's chin. Wiley staggered imperceptibly, and Dummy caught him with a hard left jab. Then he followed the punishing straight blow with a thudding right that dug into Wiley's solar plexus. The champion buckled forward. Dummy chopped him down like a tall tree with an overhand left.

Belatedly, the referee started the count. Eventually, Wiley managed to regain his feet. Dummy went into a dance routine. He put on a show of fancy footwork, while giving Wiley a lot of time to recuperate. Finally, the bout resumed with Dummy teaching a lesson, and Wiley covering to keep from being decked again. Somehow Wiley hung on and managed to survive the first round.

It seemed to me that a long count occurred between Round 1 and Round 2. During the second round, Wiley exercised a good deal of caution. Dummy taunted him, sticking and moving, in and out, around and around. It was an interesting, but not particularly exciting, round, and it ended the match.

As Wiley's handlers were removing his gloves, he declared: "Ah'm outa shape, the war an' all. Figger it's best to call it a draw an' let it got at that. Y'all understand?"

We all did. When Dummy saw Wiley agreeing to come out of his gloves, he knew that the champion wanted no more of him. Actually, he'd known at the knockdown and subsequent long count that he was the better boxer. Being literally speechless, Dummy shrugged his shoulders and stared at Wiley's corner with no emotion whatsoever.

The troops developed a profound appreciation for Dummy's skills. They didn't change his nickname, but they certainly changed its connotation. Dummy had earned their respect. If cornered, more than a few of the men were prepared to put a "Mister" in front of his name.

In early October, Lt. Arthur B. Cummings joined us. "Pat" Cummings was a rugged basketball player with a master's degree in mathematics from the University of Chicago. He had a couple of years of enlisted service during World War II. He was a tall man. His presence was good for us, all the way. He would eventually take over command of the 77th ECC.

When Pat arrived, however, we had a full house of officers, and they were all good. Even with the potential Pat brought to us, it seems that there wasn't an appropriate job for him. I knew that attrition would eventually fold him into the unit, so I sent Lieutenant Cummings to regimental headquarters as our liaison officer where he played a most important role. He kept us completely aware of the big picture, which became particularly important later on when the Chinese Third Army was chewing up the U.S. Eighth Army by the battalion, and our units were being cut off and destroyed. Pat brought a cool, mathematicians's perception to regiment. He kept them aware of our capability for stream crossing, mine warfare, and other support, which eliminated a lot of panic. Simultaneously, he kept us aware of the frenzied U.S. moves and countermoves along the Chongchon River and the gigantic bug out south to the Imjin River.

Railroad Bridge, 10–25 October 1950, Pyongtaek, Korea

We were housed in an inoperative elementary school complex, which served as a headquarters, barracks, maintenance facility, and home. In spare moments I watched the harvest of rice and the collection of faggots to be used for winter heating and cooking. Universally, harvest is a beautiful time. I felt good about it all. I allowed myself to think of returning to the United States, to my family.

For us it was a time of "make-work." It was a time for repair, a time to be busy. There was work in abundance. We built two Class 60, timber-trestle bridges on the main supply route. I drove in the near countryside and found additional projects—culverts, fords, and minor pioneer work.

I also devoted some time daily to close-order drill, and the troops hated it. There were many areas of training where we were lacking, so we held classes, as we had in garrison, on mine warfare, demolitions, map reading, small-arms orientation and maintenance, night fighting, and most important, safety. We had become lax.

Our major project was to build a railroad bridge on the MSR just north of Pyongtaek. Lt. Carroll LeTellier designed and supervised the railroad bridge construction, which is best described as unconventional. With native help we filled rice bags with local soil and interlocked them in stacks, which formed huge piers to support a stringer system consisting of lengths of 120-pound railroad rails. Irrespective of design, it carried many trains loaded to the maximum. Army supplies and construction materials, if they were even available in the country, were not available to us.

To complete the bridge we needed heavy timber—12-by-12-inch and 12-by-18-inch—and heavy decking—3-inch oak planks. We didn't have a prayer. I brought the matter up at the staff meeting.

The First Sergeant offered some ancient wisdom. "There's a timber hoard in every town. Some place there's bound to be a collection of abandoned vehicles, scrap, impedimenta, lumber, and whatnot. Little boys climb fences; they know where all the bodies are buried. I'll have the interpreter work on it."

I was less than optimistic, but, why not?

About 1430 hours, the First Sergeant told me, "Sir, the boys found that lumber hoard. With a few pieces of candy as reward, they located enough timber to build or rebuild every bridge and culvert from here to Seoul. Drift pins, nails, and hardware, too. U.S. government issue."

I was amazed and said, "Let's have a look."

The report was true. The mayor and the chief of police owned a tremendous hoard of engineer equipment, and each plank and timber had "UNRRA, 1948" burned into both ends. This timber was donated by the American taxpayer, ostensibly to provide new opportunity for the Koreans. There before us was at least one-half million dollars worth of taxes, gone to the very private ownership of a group of local Korean politicians.

I confiscated and removed all the material we could use and notified battalion headquarters of our find. They weren't interested except to caution me about private property rights. I made out a blood chit and signed it, covering all the material we removed. In the name of the United States Army, I confiscated that private property for military use and obligated my government to pay for that material at fair market value. The local politicians were less than happy. So was I, but the main supply route was greatly improved. The American taxpayer paid for the material at least twice. It was a phony expenditure.

We decked over Lieutenant LeTellier's bridge. It wasn't the most beautiful bridge in the world, but it was practical. The transportation people used it excessively. LeTellier was proud of it. We were all proud of it; we were proud of LeTellier, too.

I kept the men busy, exhausted, too tired to spend energy to go looking for trouble or entertainment. We built a community warehouse and added another wing to the school. After the rice harvest we trucked the crop forty miles to the market for the benefit of the local farmers. It was probably not strictly legal, but it was good public relations.

I watched summer ease into Indian summer and fade into early autumn. An impatience overcame us. Young, vital men require change, movement, action. Make-work and close-order drill became boring, even more so the calisthenics.

Rumors slowly permeated our ranks—rumors about a strike to the north to subdue completely whatever was left of the NKPA. We were to destroy its ability to make war against South Korea ever again. The army had to be humiliated internationally. We would move and destroy all the way to the Yalu River. Stamp out communism! Strike another blow for freedom! The first units to the Yalu River would be the first units to return home. Home by Christmas! That fired everyone up and snapped us out of our lethargy. Action!

Moving North, 1 November 1950, Kaesong, Korea

The orders came to move up. The move was welcome. We'd sat on the side of the road too long. I was tired of creating work situations and doing nonmilitary jobs just for the sake of busyness. We were ordered north on the main supply route, up to Kaesong, then east into the Iron Triangle area to destroy approximately one hundred artillery pieces. This was an area just north of the 38th Parallel. It was from here that the North Koreans had jumped off on their southward attack the previous June. Here were the Russian-built guns that the Russians considered in excess of their needs. Here also were tens of thousands of artillery rounds to fit the guns. We blew them up, destroyed every one.

The river there was fast and deep, and it accommodated hundreds of tons of ammunition. We placed artillery rounds into gun muzzles and into the breech blocks. We fired the guns with a long, long lanyard and split the tubes. Even if it were possible to retrieve the guns from that voracious river, the guns were totally unserviceable.

As the job wound down, I looked around and summer was gone; Indian summer was gone. It was brisk autumn. There was a bite in the air. It was football weather somewhere. The trees were turning, and the sky was patterned with the birds of passage. Momentarily, I was homesick.

I sent a message to regiment, which had also displaced forward to Seoul. A message came back instructing us to assault a hilltop village, in which a small unit of North Korean soldiers were in residence. "DISLODGE ENEMY AND OCCUPY UNTIL FURTHER NOTICE."

All we needed was some more killing. We moved back to the town and started up the hill. We drew a little fire, but we went up, up to the top, and the handful of enemy soldiers folded and fled before we were ten yards from the road and our vehicles.

We secured the town, brought up the vehicles, and emplaced a lot of barbed wire, mines, and trip flares and dug foxholes.

The kids in the town were out of their minds with joy at our arrival. They gave us the same welcome that kids had extended to others who had occupied towns in centuries before us. The feeling it gave me was great. Hannibal in Iberia, Napoleon at Austerlitz, now Bussey at Hinwan. I sent my interpreter to the mayor with the expectation of being entertained with a party, food, booze, and dancing girls. It happened. The mayor produced it all, and it was fabulous in a primitive way. I enjoyed it immensely.

About midway through the meat course, we heard a mine explode. The party was over! We mustered rapidly on our preestablished positions, fully expecting an enemy attack. Along the side of the road leading to the village, a farmer returning late with his cows, one of which had kicked a trip wire, and a bouncing betty had gone off at eye level. This type of mine is designed to kill personnel, but it had only scratched the farmer slightly. He picked up the smoking base plate and brought it into the village for our inspection, wonder, disbelief, and amazement; but that's what it was. He apologized for inconveniencing us by dislodging our mine.

Back to the party. It picked up speed. As it became late, perhaps 9:30 P.M. or 10:00 P.M., my interpreter eased over to me and advised me that it was expected that I should spend the night with the mayor's second wife, as custom demanded. I considered this situation awkward in the extreme. Not that the woman was unattractive—on the contrary—I'd just never had an offer of a wife before, particularly from a husband. The gathered officers considered it a great and humorous deal, especially in light of my obvious consternation. I went way back in my memory. My father taught me that when a guest in a man's home, I should participate in everything that was not contrary to my morals. (He didn't say anything about common sense.) And, I'd been totally without for five months.

I excused myself and departed through the door being held open by Second Wife. There was no need for conversation. She knew no English, and I knew no more than six words of the

Korean language, none of which were appropriate to the prevailing circumstances.

I went to work on foreplay, which was at least physically, if not verbally, universal. The action was fantastic! I don't remember whether it was so because of my long period of abstinence or because Second Wife knew and enjoyed what she was about. Either way, I approved of the custom and indulged in it throughout the night. Hail, the conqueror!

In the last moments of darkness I began to wonder about the possibility of imposing upon the hospitality of the mayor on subsequent occasions. This problem resolved itself, simply, negatively, and eternally.

A radio message came in from regiment. "JOIN REGIMENT AT KAESONG, MSR, 1000 HOURS. ACKNOWLEDGE."

We were on the move again. I was grateful for, and will long remember, the mayor's hospitality and Second Wife's prowess. Her need? She was about twenty-four years old; the mayor, fifty-five. At that time, and in that environment, he was aged. Bless him.

We were on the road again.

Anatomy of a Bigot, 9 November 1950, Kaesong, Korea

I had gotten along well with Col. John T. Corley since his first day in the regiment. When he commanded the 3d Battalion, I gave him and the other infantry battalion commanders far better support than the book called for. My platoons were always an integral part of the total combat operation. I earnestly and conscientiously supported the infantry battalions and assigned my lieutenants to match the personalities of the battalion commanders. It was good for all parties concerned.

Corley led the regiment through cold, hard intimidation, but he led it better than his predecessors. He was also an opportunist. He was highly decorated, and he knew how to exploit the awards and decorations system. He'd sacrificed a lot of men. In fairness, I have to add that he also jeopardized himself.

I served Colonel Corley well, and he appreciated it. In a sense, we were friends. Having been a fighter pilot during the Big War, I could match his war stories. Our relationship was always candid. We both enjoyed it. We shared each other's whiskey, and whiskey was scarce—hard to come by, but possible. I had a connection back in Gifu. Every month, I received a case or so of Suntory— a Japanese whiskey very much in demand among the troops. I also had a relationship with a British unit that traded rum for food. A bargain for us all.

We joined the regiment on the MSR at Kaesong, and I looked up Colonel Corley. I reported on everything except my activities with Second Wife; that was extra-military. The long convoy, three to four miles long, stood at the roadside. It waited all day through noon, through sunset, and into evening.

Colonel Corley asked me to come up and share a drink with him come sundown. Sundown, so as to be out of view of the troops. We had four or five long pulls, which really diminished his fifth of Harper. The whiskey loosened our tongues and we talked of many things.

Eventually, we got down to affairs of the regiment. Racial affairs. He explained the reason he couldn't give a battalion to Major Williams, a black officer, despite the fact that he was far more able than two of the three lieutenant colonels then in command. I pointed out that his attitude was cowardly and that his prejudices and those of his superiors decreased the effectiveness of the regiment, the effectiveness of the division, and of the Army as a whole. He agreed, but he cited Army policy. Company-level command for blacks, okay. Battalion-level command, maybe in six to eight years.

We talked on. He cited our personal relationship as a mark of progress. Then he told me, "I only recommended you for the Silver Star for the job you did at Yechon, and I only recommended a Bronze Star for your rescue of Lieutenant Lenon and his people. The Distinguished Service Cross was appropriate for the Lenon rescue and well deserved. So was the Congressional Medal for Yechon. If you were white, you'd have gotten them both. You'd be a hero in song and fable, because a nation, a people, are only as strong as its heroes. You will note that there are no black heroes, except maybe Jackie Robinson in baseball. Small matter.

"You see, you are young, vital, and articulate. You'd be a profound role model for young Negroes. The Negro newspapers would lionize you. Hicks is trying to do it now. But, you see, we can't allow it. It was always meant to be a white man's world, and I, like all others of my station in life, am obligated to maintain the control of Negroes in my sphere of activity. I cannot allow you to become a hero, no matter how worthy. I reduced the size of the battalion that you saved to a group, and I reduced the number of men you killed so that finally the job was only worth the Silver Star. As it was, you killed more of the enemy than Audie Murphy, Sergeant York, and John Wayne combined. You are my kind of soldier, my kind of man. But with the CMH— you'd flaunt it. You'd be an inspiration to every young Negro in the country. Through men like you, Negroes would effectively rise above their current state in our socio-politico-economic society.

"Please understand. Please understand me. . . ."

He passed the bottle, and I had another long one. I understood him well—too well. I told him that I considered him a bigot, which is comparable to being a bastard. I'd been had miserably, totally. As I walked away, he stated, "At least I'm honest enough to tell you how it is. Others won't tell you; and, besides, you're a slave to duty anyway."

That was the end of our drinking. I only drank with friends, and Colonel Corley was an enemy now. He didn't hate me personally, but he hated what I was, and that is bigotry at its meanest and most sinful. I am answerable for my deeds, but not for the accident of birth—neither mine nor his. My consolation lay in the fact that I was a better man than he, and we both knew it.

Best of all, I knew myself. I could thrive even in the bigoted environment in which I found myself. It was not new to me. I was bred and born in it, as were my father, my grandfather, and his father as well. We'd come to the American continent enslaved. Only the very strong survived the generations of suffering, privation, and starvation and the mind-diminishing humiliation, rape, and murder of enslavement. We are, and have always been, survivors. Hardship—physical, mental, and emotional—was the crucible in which I'd been tempered. Minor setbacks are of little moment. We are here forever.

It was an ugly, emotional encounter, but I was prepared to face a lifetime of abuse at the hands of Corley's ilk. I could handle it. I could thrive on it. Medals are of extremely short life, like their recipients.

Almost Disaster

15 November–31 December 1950, North Korea

The word came down sounding more like fact than rumor: "The first troops to the Yalu River will be the first troops sent home," and "Home by Christimas!" The word was not in the form of an order, nor was it signed, but General MacArthur was credited with the remark, and sanity was largely lost. There came a period of meandering by divisions, regiments, and miscellaneous Army units, scattered from Pyongyang northward and eastward toward Kunu-ri and beyond to Yongbyon, Ilsong, to Unhung. Largely lost, out of control, totally devoid of command, control, and intelligence, and ignorant of the enemy's presence, whereabouts, or tactics. The Eighth Army was a mass of blundering fools hell-bent for the Yalu River. Home by Christmas. We were acting like it was a victory.

It was not to be a victory. The Chinese, fearful of the advance of the U.S. and ROK armies, intervened massively. There were indications of Chinese entry into the war during October 1950, but these signs were ignored by the U.S. Army. After drawing back from their initial intervention, the Chinese Army launched a major offensive on 25 November 1950.

Taken by surprise, the U.S. and ROK armies staggered and went into retreat. North Korea was lost by the UN forces. The

IX Corps, which had a separate base on the east coast, was withdrawn intact by ships. The forces in the central and western parts of Korea fell back under heavy attack, and the losses were staggering.

The 25th Infantry Division had been part of the general defensive line of the Eighth Army, which withdrew rapidly from advanced positions in North Korea, back through Pyongyang, then back through Seoul. The retreat was disorderly, and much equipment was lost. Finally, the Eighth Army managed to form and hold a defensive position south of Seoul in late December 1950.

The rout of UN forces and their uncontrolled flight from Kunu-ri, North Korea, down to the Imjin River was ignominious. It can be stated truthfully that the Eighth Army lost all of North Korea to the Chinese Army and the local gentry because of reckless disorganization. Had the Yalu River been the objective of a systematic and well-organized military operation, complete with logistical support north of Pyongyang and with well-coordinated air support, intelligence, communications, and artillery, then the debacle might have been avoided and success achieved. There were probably as many casualties from frostbite and lack of medical care as there were from gunshot wounds. Not the Chinese Army, but our own arrogance, absence of planning and logistics, and failure of command defeated UN and U.S. forces. It was willy-nilly, and when the reckoning came it was catastrophic.

The inadequate road system was choked with retreating men, vehicles, weapons, and impedimenta. Men with their beards and nostrils filled with ice—cold, hungry, frostbitten, forsaken—were heading helplessly toward Pusan, Japan, home. Officers were ineffective, separated from their troops. Ambulances were unable to move along the roads, which were choked with immobile vehicles. Wounded men were all over the place. The Chinese soldiers established and manned roadblocks on the road west from Kunu-ri. The killing floor was never more violent. No one knew the locations of the Chinese Army; no one knew the enemy strength. We were aware only of his omnipresence. Nothing terrifies like deep wounds. Nothing frightens like frostbite, and nothing—absolutely nothing—generates the moral anxiety of imminent death, so painful, so futile, so final.

And thus we died, so many of us. Many of us had never had cold weather indoctrination, and very few of us had been trained in night fighting, the strong point of the North Korean soldier. Why had we not spent those months, after the landing at Inchon and before the move north to the Yalu, on training? We had two full months to prepare ourselves for serious combat. Time was wasted instead. Lives were wasted, too.

Our equipment and uniforms were inadequate, our gas-operated weapons, with their heavy ammunition, served us poorly. We were wearing leather shoes when the temperature dropped to 9°F on 28 November 1950. Many troops were unable to flee from the enemy. Food became inadequate, and freezing conditions worsened the situation.

With the Chinese soldier, the case was entirely different. He enjoyed the fruits of victory. He had a crude automatic blowback weapon, which was not hampered by freezing weather. He wore a uniform appropriate to his habits and to his habitat. His ammunition was light in weight, and he carried a lot of it. His food was primarily millet or rice, which he carried over his shoulder in a tubular sack. His protein came from chickens, pigs, or other livestock that he confiscated as he passed through the countryside. He traveled lightly, secretly, rapidly, motivated, and trained for killing.

The flight southward through North Korea in late 1950 was probably the most shameful display of military ineptitude in U.S. history. For some reason, however, the Army's military historians have not dealt with the rout from North Korea. The U.S. Army's official history of the first part of the war, from 25 June to November 1950, was published in 1961[*] as the first of a three-volume history of the Korean War. The third volume, covering the small-unit engagements and truce negotiations along a stalemated front from July 1951 to July 1953, was published in 1966.[**] The second volume, which will cover the Chinese intervention and the rout of the UN forces, has only recently been finished and is scheduled

---

[*] Appleman, *South to the Naktong*, 1961.

[**] Walter G. Hermes, *Truce Tent and Fighting Front* (Washington, D.C.: Office of the Chief of Military History, 1966).

for publication at the end of 1990. Why has it taken the U.S. Army almost forty years just to print a book about its great defeat?

The U.S.-ROK-UN line south of Seoul stiffened and held despite a massive Chinese offensive in January 1951. Then, during the first four months of 1951, a UN forces counteroffensive regained the lost South Korean territory and formed the basis for the eventual cease-fire line between North and South Korea agreed to in 1953.

The 77th Engineer Combat Company fought steadily during the retreat. We and the 24th RCT as a whole maintained unit cohesion during the retreat and managed to bring most of our equipment out of North Korea. This was not the case for many other Army units, and there were numerous instances of units bugging out and leaving equipment. It was a defeat, and it was almost a disaster. Thank God for Gen. Matthew Ridgway; his leadership salvaged the UN effort.

Chilly Mother, 15 November 1950, North Korea

My thermometer stood at −29°F, and that is too cold for fighting. It was bitter. In spite of all the clothes I wore, I was uncomfortable. We were doing some fortifications work on the south bank of a small river, and the work was going well. Poker was good at night. I'd won over a thousand dollars the night before and had mailed it home earlier that morning. There was no imminent pressure from the Chinese Army. The weather was all I had to worry about, and worry I did.

It was 1130 hours, and a call came for me on the radio advising me of a 1200 staff meeting lunch at regiment. It was at least a fifteen-minute drive, so I saddled up. We drove down the road, and with all my clothes and the jeep heater going full blast, I still wasn't warm. Damn!

Peering through the icy windshield I noticed a Korean woman laboring under one of those three-foot diameter bundles they often carried. The bundle contained all her worldly goods: food, utensils, clothing, bedding, lanterns—everything. The woman waved to us. There was no possibility of an ambush at that spot, but against better judgment I had Pinkney stop the vehicle.

I was surprised that the woman had waved. Koreans were totally independent of us. They generally let us fight our stupid war and left us alone. I sensed that this lady needed help desperately. We stopped alongside her, and she beckoned me over. I had no ability to converse with her, but Pinkney knew a few words of Korean. He said she wanted our help getting the bundle down from her head, and with a helluva strain the two of us lifted it and set it on the frozen roadside.

She reached into the layers of her clothing and produced an unhappy three year old who was on a sling over her right shoulder, riding on her left hip. The bitter cold sent him into an instant crying fit. Pinkney put him into the jeep. She started digging into her clothing on the other side and produced a wee one, not more than a yearling. He went into an instant bawling fit, too, when that cold air hit him.

At that moment she groaned a little, and she was standing in a puddle of rapidly freezing fluid. I didn't know whether she'd lost control of her bladder or not, but that's what I suspected. She started digging frantically in her bundle and produced several yards of white rags.

I took the wee one to Pinkney in the jeep. We were both a little embarrassed for this poor woman, alone and friendless in a God-forsaken countryside, with all her worldly goods in a bundle on the side of the road, and two squalling, cold, young-uns in the vehicle of a strange soldier. I looked over to that little woman, wondering what would happen next.

She beckoned to me again and indicated that she wanted me to help her down into the ditch alongside the road. Then she separated all of those garments and went into a deep squat. She motioned me away, and I was glad to back off because I'd completely misinterpreted all that I'd seen.

She was in the ditch for some few minutes, and I could hear her softly groaning or chanting. I stayed at the jeep and Pinkney looked at me as if to say, How did she take care of her elimination in previous times? Certainly not with the hand-holding of two soldiers.

Silently I agreed with him. I was due at regiment, and I was getting antsy. And I was cold.

Then I heard a thin cough, a whine, and then a distinct cry. A baby had been born. I went over to the ditch in time to watch her cover the babe in one of the rags. She lifted it to her mouth and chewed the umbilical cord in two. Then she handed me the bundle. I took the baby back to Pinkney, who was stupefied by the events of the past fifteen or twenty minutes. He was a fightin' man, and he was uncomfortable with his new chores.

I walked back to the ditch, and from the same deep squat the woman was kneading her belly deeply, still chanting an unrecognizable series of music-like groans. In due time she produced a placenta and whatever else afterbirth consists of. She extended a hand for me to help her up from the ditch. She beckoned for help in loading up her belongings and kids.

I didn't have the heart to start her back down the road in her condition, but she was on her feet and insistent. I took her by the arm and almost forced her into the jeep. With a lot of effort, we loaded her bundle onto the hood of the jeep, mostly on my side. Then we drove off to regiment.

Colonel Corley was livid. He was not used to captains showing up late for his meetings. And he was noted for chewing captains publicly.

"Where'n hell you been, Bussey? We been waitin' a half hour for you. Who'n hell you think you are? You damned engineers think you kin get away with murder."

About that time a medic showed up in the doorway and beckoned for Captain Carlson, the regimental surgeon. Carlson nodded to the colonel and hurried out.

"You want to tell me why you're late, Bussey?"

"Yes, sir." I told him in detail why I was late.

" N' you brought the woman here, with three babies?"

"Yes, sir."

"What you think we ought to do with 'em?"

"Well, the doctor can look the lady over. We can feed them, give her some blankets, a little rest, and transport down the road."

"By God, Bussey, that's a side of you I never saw before. Help yourself to lunch, the meeting will start in a few minutes."

The colonel looked over at me as I crammed down the beef and grease that was our noontime fare, and he actually smiled.

Carlson came back, and the colonel asked him how the woman was doing. The doctor said, "Fine. She's anxious to move along tho'."

Colonel Corley looked at the doctor incredulously.

"Did she actually have the baby a half hour ago?"

"Yessir, a beautiful little girl; we're cleaning her up now."

"Well, if she insists on leaving, maybe it's best, but put her in an ambulance and take her back a ways. Maybe her people are set up to care for her."

"Say, don't do us any more favors, Bussey."

After the meeting, I went over to the aid station. The medics were getting ready to move the Korean woman out. As she walked by me carrying her earthly goods and young-uns, she gave me a helluva smile, perhaps conspiratorial. I felt honored because smiles were damned scarce in Korea. I felt good for my small chores that day.

She walked right past the ambulance out onto the badly rutted dirt road. Her back was straight. Her head proudly erect. She held her three youngsters tucked in tightly in the many folds of her clothing, and with her slew-footed walk she padded down the road under that heavy bundle of household goods. She had added another child to her load, but she spurned the warm ambulance ride. She'd accepted all the charity that her pride would allow during one day's span. In her survivor's code it was, Do it yourself. Today!

I turned my mind to the reality of that day. I wondered fondly about my own young-uns and their mother, who fared so much better. I offered a short prayer for them and the little buck-toothed Korean woman I'd just met on the outer rim of existence.

PFC Abernathy, 16 November 1950, near Kunu-ri, North Korea

If your name is Abernathy, there's a good possibility that you will be called "Abnasty." It's a natural. If you are small, sour, and homely, it's a guarantee. Well, Abnasty was one of the dope-heads who joined us at the port after they had opened the Eighth

Army stockade and sent all noncapital offenders to Korea. All of the blacks in the engineers were assigned to my company. Abernathy wasn't a bad man, just a misfit and a nonachiever. He was the butt of a lot of jokes, and he resented it. Most of all he resented his nickname, but being a small man there was little he could do about it.

When the Chinese armies engaged us on the southeast bank of the Chongchon River, we were largely committed as infantry. We were 300 rifles by night and 300 shovels by day. The cold took all the zest out of fighting.

The 4th Platoon was out front that night, and they were well dug in. I used to crawl along from one foxhole to another. In the big ones, I'd get in, get comfortable, and shoot the breeze with the occupants. It was good for them, and I got a chance to know them better. They had a lot of confidence in me, and they were more comfortable knowing I was close by. For months, they'd been referring to me behind my back as Captain Combat, or sometimes Ol' Combat. I kinda liked that privately, and one must support his reputation.

The Chinese armies had been hitting us with a terrible impact. Their force of numbers overwhelmed us. They also fought at night, which we weren't trained for. Our night training was cursory, to be generous. Our troops were edgy. Hell, they were scared.

Around midnight I got into the foxhole with Abnasty. For some reason he was alone, which he shouldn't have been. Before I got all the way into the hole, a bugler from the Chinese forces a hundred yards or so to our front tooted some kind of signal. I could feel Abnasty shaking. He was scared shitless. So I talked to him to settle him down.

I said, "That's just a signal for some movement or other. Don't sweat it. You'll hear the bush rattling when they actually come for us. And you know we've got mines, bouncin' betties, and a lot of barbed wire with trip flares out in front of us. When they move in close, it will look like the Fourth of July. They can't surprise us; we'll know they're coming. Take it easy."

He said, "I ain't scared, sir."

"I know it," I said. But I didn't know it. He was tweaking.

I asked him, "Where do you think that bugle is located? How far out? Put your rifle up on the parapet and point it right where you think you last heard the bugle."

In the darkness I could feel him look at me with puzzlement and disbelief—total incomprehension. But he placed the rifle on the parapet and leaned into it.

I said, "When that bugle goes off again, make a slight adjustment, lay right on that bugle's sound, and touch off a round. You'll be surprised."

Sure enough. Moments later, when that eerie sound in the death-filled night began again, Abnasty moved slightly and squeezed off a point three-oh. With an ear-shattering blast a microsecond later, we heard the bullet smash that trumpet in the near distance. Then dead silence, and I do mean dead. Abnasty grew about three feet taller.

I stayed there for an hour, then I moved on to another foxhole. It had been a long, long night followed by a long, long day, in a very long succession of the same. Finally, dawn came, and the enemy packed up and silently receded into the gloom. After daylight we walked over to their vacated positions, and we found the bugler with his battered horn and his disintegrated face.

Abernathy became a legend. He was an instant hero. He became a tall man—composed, confident, and contained. Whenever I saw him after that we exchanged smiles. We both knew where he came from. We both knew where he was. He was Private First Class Abernathy now, and everyone knew him as such. He was no longer a misfit; he was a fighting man.

Another Road, 20 November 1950, Kunu-ri, North Korea

Whenever we moved and I got things organized to my satisfaction, I went on a reconnaissance. I looked for roads to support the regimental combat team. I looked for bridges, culverts, cuts, fills, and widening requirements. I looked for anything to improve the tactical environment and my discipline environment as well.

Upon arrival at Pyongyang, our lowboy, which transported our

D-7 bulldozer, gave out on us. I didn't know exactly what the long road trip would do to the dozer, but I had two of the troops walk it up the road to Kunu-ri.

I left Sergeant Munro with the dozer operator, Sergeant Spencer, who was an extremely good man. It was a trip in excess of one hundred miles; a hard, tough trip for walking a dozer. Both men knew how vital the dozer was to our support mission. Despite the cold, they crawled up the MSR hour after hour after hour. We left them with a quarter-ton trailer, which they towed behind the dozer. The trailer carried two hundred gallons of diesel fuel, some tools, and necessary impedimenta.

Some time during the trip, the fatigue and the long hours in the cold overcame the dozer crew. Sergeant Munro was the operator, and Sergeant Spencer was sitting on the right arm rest when he fell asleep momentarily, lost his balance, and fell onto the track. The track swiftly carried Spencer's body forward and partially under the advancing track before Munro could stop. In the microseconds of falling, Spencer reacted to the situation and rolled off the track—almost. Instead, the track ran over Spencer's forearm. A disaster! Munro backed the dozer off the injured arm, covered Spencer, and flagged down a vehicle. It raced forward to overtake an ambulance in the same north-moving convoy, but Spencer, unfortunately, lost his arm, and he was lost to us.

Spencer came from Red House, Virginia. I stayed in touch with him, as I tried to do with all my men. Back home, he recuperated well and became an expert in the use of prosthetic devices, traveling to many hospitals to demonstrate the use of his device to other amputees. His presentation was a fine morale and motivation booster. He was a champion. He remained an exceptional rifle marksman despite his handicap.

When the dozer arrived two days behind us, it had thrown at least a dozen tracks. It looked like a snaggle-toothed mule, but it arrived, and we needed it.

The Korean countryside was developed only to meet the infrastructure requirement of a manual labor–intensive agrarian economy. Roads were constructed only to accommodate horse- or cow-drawn carts. In size and numbers, our modern military vehicles were light-years ahead in terms of their requirements for good roads. The roads that existed in Korea were inadequate. Thus, in most tactical situations, movement of troops by vehicles was difficult, if not impossible.

In the Kunu-ri area of North Korea, road conditions were very poor—even worse than usual for Korea. This part of North Korea was almost completely undeveloped; some areas had neither been surveyed nor mapped. Certainly, the roads were inadequate to support a significant military operation.

It was obvious to me that one of my first responsibilities in any new location was to improve or establish a road network to provide ingress and egress to tactical positions. Our equipment and material sources were sorely limited, but we did our best. When tactical conditions dictate retrograde movements (a retreat) on an emergency basis, a one-lane road in lieu of, or in addition to, the main supply route can be a blessing. On a few occasions our best was enough to preclude disasters. Our previous Engineer Road at Haman had been a real lifesaver; it had allowed the regiment to avoid becoming trapped by the 6th North Korean Division, and it had allowed the regiment to return to retake Battle Mountain.

I had noticed that there were no alternate routes off the MSR running south from Kunu-ri. If the existing supply routes were interdicted at any point, it would be necessary to fight our way out. I found a goat track that ran off perpendicular to the MSR about three miles west of the RTO at Kunu-ri. The trail paralleled the road to Pyongyang. Eight or ten miles south, the trail joined a fairly good road, which went west to join the Pyongyang road. This goat track was not going to get us to the Yalu River, which is what this junket was all about. Nevertheless, I had the dozer and a platoon that was not otherwise committed, so we went to work on it. The original goat track was only eight to ten feet wide, but with the dozer and some labor we turned it into a road at least fourteen to sixteen feet wide. The improved goat track would provide an alternate route out of Kunu-ri.

The war went poorly for the UN forces north of Kunu-ri. The Chinese intervention was largely unexpected at troop level. The weight of their numbers, their night tactics, the extreme cold, and our lack of cold-weather clothing or training were devastating. The discipline of the Chinese soldiers worked against us. One example is the Chinese use of bugle calls. The bugle was used to issue commands to the Chinese troops, to which they responded vigorously. We didn't know whether a particular call meant charge, retreat, or whatever. U.S. troops found it all difficult to cope with. We were defeated summarily, totally, ignominiously.

In the hurly-burly of retreat, the goat track at Kunu-ri proved to be a real lifesaver. Tens of thousands of American troops fleeing the Kunu-ri area came out on that road. They were able to bypass the murderous ambushes set up by the Chinese along the MSR. Our foresight and hard work had paid off. That was our business, and we did it well.

Tales of a Winter Night, 29 November 1950, Yongbyon, Korea

Lord, it was cold. Bitter! But more significant was the fatigue. So frequently the circumstances of war abuse the soldiers. One defeat after another, one mission after another, without time between to allow a little rest. I'd been up and hustling for two days without sleep. In spite of my youth and good physical condition, I felt near the end of my tolerance. More than at any time in my life I was looking forward to flopping out.

I enjoyed a good meal and started to the tent. Before I got rid of my headgear, the phone rang, and long before I answered it, I knew there'd be no sleep. I knew there was another assignment. Something else had to be done. I also knew my men were exhausted. They needed rest, but I answered, "Landscape Six here."

The clerk on the other end said, "The Colonel requests that you come to the command post right away. Important."

"Roger." I'd been had again—me and the troops.

Colonel Corley was waiting for me, and he laid out several missions that would take us all night and into the following day. I was unhappy, and I was contumacious in advising him of it.

First, we were engineers and should not be expended on infantry missions. Second, we had been without rest for two days. Third, the colonel had a service company, a headquarters company, and an I&R platoon available to him for these dirty little killing jobs. He heard me out, turned, and beckoned me to the situation map, completely ignoring my protestations.

"There are four elements to the mission," he said.

"One, dissolve the first ambush site at this location; kill the enemy functioning as a roadblock. Leave a small force, concealed, to prevent the roadblock from growing up again.

"Two, repeat this action at the second ambush site, which is located here.

"Three, go to the 25th Division Clearing Station, which has been overrun by a force in excess of twenty-five Chinese soldiers. Kill all the Chinese you can find. Reorganize the station. Try to lure station personnel back into action, and take care of the remaining live patients.

"Four, return to the site where your vehicles will be pooled. There you might be able to rest a couple hours. Come sunup, I'll send you a platoon of tanks if you're still alive. Ride them up to Yongbyon. Open the road and clear the town. Call me. I'll give you my SCR 193 radio in a weapons carrier. Let me know of your success at each stop. Go!"

I responded, "I'd like your sacred tanks to go with me. We'll ride them. Whatever happens to them happens to us."

"No way, no tanks at night. Call me at sunrise. I'll give you tanks. Good luck. What platoons you going to take?"

"Carlisle's and Green's."

"Good."

I saluted and dragged my tired bones out into the dangerous darkness. I assembled the men, and I could hear them grumbling about being called out to give more with their tired bodies.

We drove with blackout lights down a road built of molybdenum ore, which glowed dully to the light of a weak moon. It was cold. We drove about seventeen miles to a wide spot in the road where we dismounted, left a guard, and put our feet on the road.

We walked two and one-half or three miles more, and we came

upon the first ambush site. We were in loose columns on each side of the road, and the inevitable came—a shower of .28 caliber bullets striking the faintly glowing road. We deployed rapidly according to plan, outflanked the ambush site, and did the necessary killing. The site was manned by five men, one of whom was exceptionally big for an Oriental—perhaps six feet six inches tall with the biggest feet I'd ever seen.

I left six men at the site and moved on into the night. By then, I began to doubt my ability to continue. I'd never been so tired in my life. My legs and feet kept crying, No! No más! Nein! No! I wondered, but was afraid to ask, how the men felt.

We trudged on in the blackness, listening hard for clues to the location of the next ambush site. This was dangerous work. At ambushes, people die. Cautious ambushers have a decided advantage, the greatest of which is the element of surprise. I couldn't see my map, but I called a halt, borrowed Lieutenant Carlisle's greatcoat, formed a tent over my head with the coat, fired my flashlight, and found the ambush site about a half mile ahead.

Well before we arrived at the location, I could see evidence of a bonfire around a bend in the road. I could faintly hear excited conversation.

A surprising break for us. I sent a platoon up on the hillcrest, which would bring them directly above the ambush site. They were instructed to fire on the ambushers only after I opened fire. I wanted to be sure that they were, in fact, the enemy. We proceeded in silence and found the ambushers in a jovial mood, eating combat rations they'd found in one of the vehicles. One of the quilted uniformed soldiers was dancing around the fire. How dumb! The ambushers' lack of security accrued to their detriment and led to their death. I fired on the dancer, and my people from the hill made short work of the other six ambushers.

The platoon on the hill remained in place. We were not going to make any mistakes. When the shooting was all over, we moved into the firelight. We found an ambulance overturned, four GIs dead, and a weapons carrier driven into the side of the hill. We righted the ambulance and placed the GIs in it. We moved the enemy bodies off the road. As the work neared completion I heard a voice call for help in English. With a stretcher and two of my men, I climbed down the embankment and found the voice.

I talked to the victim, "What's your name?"

"First Lt. Claude Paige, Heavy Mortar Company, 24th Infantry Regiment."

I got a real jolt. I recognized the voice. "Are you Claude Paige, exec of the 1401st Engineer Battalion, California National Guard?"

"Yes, dammit, and I recognize your voice. You're Charlie Bussey. I heard you were out here, but I've only been here two days and haven't had time to look you up."

"Look, Claude, we'll get you out of here. What happened anyway?"

The troops had carefully placed Lieutenant Paige on the stretcher, and we got more help and carried him up the embankment to the road. The ambulance couldn't run, but the weapons carrier was operative, so we placed Claude in the back. I talked to him further, "Tell me what happened to you."

He told me that he'd just gotten to Korea and had been sent to find a site for Heavy Mortar Company to set up. They needed an area for bivouac, CP, and tube emplacement, and had run into the ambush just as they passed the overturned ambulance. They had slowed way down, and the enemy had shot and killed the driver and the gunner.

"I bailed out under fire from their AK-47s," he said. "I was firing my carbine, and somehow I didn't get hit." As he had passed the rear of the weapons carrier, a hand grenade had exploded in the ration boxes and knocked him flat on his back in line with the rear wheels. Then the weapons carrier had rolled slowly backward down the road and over him.

He continued, "My legs weren't moving so I crawled over the shoulder of the road, down to the creek, and up under the roots of a tree. I hid there while they searched for me. One of them stepped within an inch of my hand. I stayed there until I heard your voice."

I asked him how he felt, and he replied, "My back and my legs are numb, and my ribs kill me whenever I breathe."

I formed up our unit, left a security element, and set off on foot with the weapons carriers in the rear, one of them bearing the injured Paige to the 25th Division Clearing Station. I had many, many thoughts. I was exhilarated at the realization that we had not only saved a life, but the life of an old friend. I was proud of my unit. I called back to Lion Six and gave him a rundown of the night's activities.

As we neared the medical facility, I went into a state of deep fatigue, and my legs threatened to quit responding to my numbed brain. I kept on somehow and turned my thoughts to the tactics of taking over the clearing station, which is a hospital designed to pass the seriously wounded or long-term patients on to permanent facilities. I was worried about the intimidation of patients that inevitably occurred from enemy action and which was sure to be heightened by the shooting about to take place again. Then, of course, I had never been to the clearing station. I didn't know whether it was in a permanent building or a series of tents. I'd have to get there and base my decision on what my eyeballs told me. What had the enemy done to the buildings, and more significant, what had they done to the patients? What was such a sensitive facility doing out in left field like this without a security force? What? Why? How?

It was too dark to assess the situation well, but even in the darkness, I could hear the cries of patients, injured soldiers, wounded and dying. The station had been attacked hours before, and I realized that we should have been sent here first due to the far greater magnitude of misery.

I called a meeting with my lieutenants. Lieutenant Carlisle was responsible for surrounding the installation completely. His people were to be instructed to shoot only persons dressed in quilted uniforms or who were speaking Chinese. This was important, because I thought that the staff and attendants probably had fled into the security of the darkness of night. I was right about that. Lieutenant Green's platoon entered the buildings and tents to make things right. I felt that the marauders would have departed after having disordered or destroyed the personnel, the hospital, and its property. Again my assessment was correct.

The marauders had shot many patients and staff members.

They had turned over beds on top of badly injured soldiers. One soldier in particular, who was in traction, had been turned over and mauled and was in excruciating pain. He was bleeding from all quarters and was in stark hysteria. The place looked like a slaughterhouse. There was blood and bodies everywhere, some alive and some not. The furniture was overturned, windows broken to admit the frigid air. There was a fire smoldering in one of the outbuildings. Lighting had been destroyed, and heating was ineffective. The sobbing and wailing of the injured was heartbreaking, but the care of the injured was beyond our ken.

I began to yell into the night advising the staff that the installation was back in U.S. Army hands.

"U.S. Army personnel, return to your station. The station is under control of the 77th Engineers. Come back! Come back and attend the injured. Come back. It is safe. We need your help."

My troops took up the call. Gradually, slowly, personnel crept timidly out of the dark, traumatized, shaken, shivering, and teary. They crept and staggered back into the hospital. We got some fires going in the mess, fired up the heaters, and reinstalled the lighting. The hospital personnel eventually took over, and we became the helpers. We brought order out of the bloody chaos. Soon it was time to start moving back to the vehicles. Day was breaking.

I was no longer tired, just numb. Dead. We were two miles or more from the vehicles. I talked to the physician who examined Lieutenant Paige, and he advised me, "Lieutenant Paige has a broken back and some badly crushed ribs, L-1, L-2, L-3."

"What is L-1, L-2, and L-3?"

He responded, "*L* is for lumbar, about here," pointing to my left mid-section.

I looked over at Claude and said, "Looks like million-dollar wounds. A trip home. Good luck. Gotta go."

There's something about daybreak. There's something new and exhilarating about walking into a sunrise. There's a renewal of life and hope and an elevation above fatigue. A little bit. It was fortunate, because otherwise I wouldn't have been able to go any farther.

We trudged back to our temporary motor pool where, true to form, the mess sergeant had coffee and sandwiches. Nothing could be more welcome. We inhaled the food, and the troops flopped for the few moments before sunrise. At sunrise I had to call Colonel Corley and arrange for Nordstrom's tanks. With the tanks we'd open the road to Yongbyon. Lord, it was bitter cold.

There was no sleep for me. I used the time to check on the condition of my troops, status of ammunition, and planning for the road acquisition. I arranged for a noon meal, stretchers, ammo for the several types of weapons, a powwow with my platoon leaders—millions of details and considerations. I remembered a sign I once saw in an operations office, "There will be no vast operations with half-vast planning."

The temperature was 9°F, and we were still wearing leather shoes, but fortunately we had no frostbite.

The tank platoon came, and we saddled up. The colonel's weapons carrier transported the SCR 193 radio. We had little more than a platoon left after having dropped off a security force at each of the three sites we had worked the night before. Riding atop the tanks was a lot better than trudging up the roads. There had been significant enemy activity on the road to, and in the walled city of, Yongbyon, but on this bitter wintry morning there was no activity at all.

There were many knocked-out tanks on the roadside; intelligence credited the U.S. Air Force with having destroyed them. Our tanks fired a round or two into each of the damaged tanks to make sure the occupants, if any, were dead.

We went right up the road into the town and up and down the main and side streets. There was the usual small-town activity but no evidence of soldiers. We searched approximately half of the residences but found no soldiers or weapons.

When I was completely satisfied, I called Lion Six. He was happy to hear from us. He could now report success on our four mission segments. He directed that we remain in the town for one hour. We stayed in Yongbyon for the hour—on cautious alert. It was an uneventful period. After the hour we trekked back to our temporary trains area (storage for vehicles and support for kitchens, weapons, and logistics) and then to our CP. At the CP I dismissed the tanks and sent the troops off for some well-deserved rest.

Colonel Corley listened to my account of the activities of the night before, and he said, "Well done."

There was no rest for me, however. We were operating a ferry across the Chongchon River, and the landing sites needed work. So did the ferry. There were ice floes forming, and I anticipated that the ferry was going to be difficult to operate because the ice was going to seize and bind the ferry long before the need for it was over.

Lt. Col. Clayton, 27 November 1950, Chongchon River

I had just dozed off. We'd been in Korea for five months, and they had just that day issued us cots. I had every intention of really enjoying mine, particularly since I'd had no sleep at all the three nights before, when Colonel Corley had sent me with two platoons to open the road to Yongbyon. But let's talk about Lt. Col. George A. Clayton, who commanded the 2d Battalion. A nice enough bigot he was. Privately, he credited himself with "knowing how to handle niggers." To our faces, he was always cheerful, with a "cheese-eating" grin.

Just as I was settling into some real sleep, I heard the field phone ring, and I knew that some bastard was going to deny me another night's sleep. I was prophetic. Colonel Corley said, "Come up here right away. I have a tough job for you. You may take two people with you. Be here in ten minutes. Be prepared to walk all night, maybe longer. Automatic carbines, ammo, one ration, one hand grenade. Out."

The job sounded ominous, and I was angry. When I reached him, I told him again, as I had the day before, that he should use his own men. He commanded a regiment with an I&R platoon, a service company, and a headquarters company. Why did he select me to do his dirty work? I was too tired for it. I was only attached, and I told him so.

The colonel said, "I'll let that pass, but I'm giving this one to you because it's tough. It must be done. It's vital and must not fail. I'll show you."

Colonel Corley went to his situation map. He indicated the location of his command post and pointed to a trail that led a few miles northeast then disappeared into an unsurveyed and unmapped area, which was identified by a large patch of white on the map.

"Somewhere in this area is the 2d Battalion, and I've lost contact with them. They're in a blocking position to keep us from being outflanked by the Chinese Third Army. Intelligence has indicated a massive push by the Chinese on the west bank of the Chongchon River. If they break through, this battalion will be isolated and lost with no way out. With no communication, I can't advise them, so I want you to find them. Tell Clayton he has to be here by sunset tomorrow. We'll take positions west of the Chongchon River near Kunu-ri, but the bridge he went in on has been blown. Wherever you travel to find him, he'll have to reverse and follow you out. You heard of the 'message to Garcia?' "

"Yessir."

"Move out."

And we did.

When I got the colonel's initial message, I picked two people that I could rely on totally. There were plenty, but two especially: Lt. David Carlisle and Sergeant Woods. We were on the same wavelength. Presented with a situation, we'd react in a similar manner, eliminating the need for a lot of talk, doubt, and indecision. We could make it happen, and if one or two of us was lost, the third might accomplish the mission.

We moved out into a bitter cold night, and I considered the distinct possibility of never having the opportunity to savor another night like this, nor another sunrise, nor even another hour. There was work to do, so I concentrated on the task at hand.

I didn't have a clear handle on the task, though. Where was the battalion? How far? Where was the enemy? How many? What was the terrain? It didn't show on the map. The route the battalion had used to enter the area was no longer available; a big bridge behind them had been destroyed. I figured to follow the trail to its end and follow recognizable terrain features, looking for tire

tracks, impedimenta, voices, gunfire, garbage, spent shells—anything to indicate the presence of troops.

The roads in that area were filled with ore, which was slightly
luminous in the pale light of a cold and lonesome quarter moon.
Lord, was I ever tired. When we had been on the trail about
two hours, we heard the terrified scream of a woman pierce the
night, and I anticipated enemy trouble. Through the night I
vaguely made out a farmhouse, and as we moved closer, I saw
that a mud fence surrounded it. I hand signaled for Carlisle and
Woods to go around to the far side of the fence, wait for about
twenty seconds of listening watch, then go over the fence, and
do a little killing once inside. I expected Chinese soldiers molesting
a native woman, and I was partly correct, but only partly.

We eased over the fence silently. I could hear the woman sobbing, and I moved closer. I heard, "Hit that muthafucka ag'in,"
and I knew I wasn't hearing a Chinese.

I could see two black American soldiers. I jumped into the
room with my carbine ready to fire. "Hold it! Don't breathe or
move."

One of the soldiers, whom I recognized as Sergeant Hawkins
of the Heavy Mortar Company of the 24th Infantry Regiment,
let go of a Korean teenage boy, who fell limp at his feet. A trembling
ancient man and woman stood in front of a third person, whom
they were shielding.

I asked the second soldier, a master sergeant I didn't recognize,
"What the hell are the two of you doing out here?"

Sergeant Hawkins responded, "Well, sir, we're just out here
to have a little fun. You know how it is. We ain't had no women
since July. That's a long time. We weren't going to hurt the
girl. Just a little sex. Sure surprised to see you out here,
Captain."

"I'm going to advise Captain Keiler of your actions. What you've
done here is a court martial offense."

"Well, sir, Captain Keiler understands us, and besides, thanks
to you, we didn't really do anything but intimidate the girl. When
I moved on her, she jumped into that vat of shit. You saw her.
The kid was her husband. I just hit him out of frustration. It
ain't no real crime." Hawkins continued, "We're damned good

soldiers. Captain Keiler might chew on us a little, but he understands the way it is with soldiers. We took this country with the blood of good men. In war, the victors take the spoils. That woman is spoils."

I looked at the girl. She was covered up to her armpits in semiliquid fecal matter. She was trembling. (The fecal matter was stored in a well behind the house. It was used as fertilizer.)

I answered, "I agree with your choice of words. She's spoiled all right. You must be eight or nine miles from camp. The Chinese Third Army is on the move. You better get back to the river; there's big trouble coming. Have you seen or heard anything of the 2d Battalion, 24th Infantry Regiment?"

"No, sir, this is as far as we've been."

"Give it up, sergeant. This ain't your night."

"Okay, sir."

We split up, and I continued with my mission. Carlisle and Woods chuckled off and on all night.

The cold became bitter, and I was so tired that my hip sockets felt hot as we walked into the winter night. Exhaustion is synonymous with soldiering. This was my third day and night without sleep. We followed a gradually narrowing trail during the night trek. We trudged uphill and down, always on alert for Chinese soldiers. They, too, were somewhere in this uncharted country.

We'd brought along a ration each, and we ate as we moved into the night that was suddenly darkening—that peculiar darkening that occurs just before dawn. Dawn came, first tremulous, then halting, and finally bold. I thought of home and the warmth of my wife and our bed, but the thought passed as I felt the chill that comes with dawn. I was a long way from home, from love, from tenderness. For a moment I was lonely.

In the near distance I saw a hut with smoke coming out of it. Again the three of us separated and silently surrounded the crude dwelling. I forced the door with my foot and entered behind my carbine. The smell of rotting flesh assaulted my nose and choked off my breath. Gangrene—once smelled—is unforgettable.

Again there was an ancient couple, too old and infirm to flee from the path of the invading Chinese Army. They were prisoners of old age, but the smell came from a badly wounded and dying Chinese soldier. His legs were abnormally swollen; each the size of his torso. The weeping holes in those elephantine legs indicated that he'd been shot five or six times in each. Woods came in, retched, and backed out.

The soldier was beckoning for me to shoot him. He used explicit sign language indicating putting the carbine against his head. I looked at those legs, with their greenish bloat. His eyes were wild, and his gesticulations became wild. He wanted badly to escape the sickened misery his life had become.

I left the hut and talked to Carlisle and Woods about it. They agreed that it was the thing to do. We couldn't go off and leave the poor gangrenous bastard to die ever slowly. He was probably far beyond medical help, which wasn't available anyway. No soldier should have to suffer that way. Being wounded is punishment enough, but the slow poison on top of it is worse. He'd obviously been left a few days before, when his comrades tired of carrying him and left him in the shelter in the care of those ancients. The decent thing to do was shoot and bury him.

Firing a shot in this country, however, would probably jeopardize my mission. This was a serious consideration. But it was the humane thing to do, so I risked exposing our presence.

We moved the Chinese soldier on his stretcher out into the yard next to a pile of earthen bricks. I fired through a pillow, and it was over. We buried him under the bricks. I couldn't leave a soldier in that misery.

We moved off eastward. The trail had long disappeared behind us. We were traveling on hope and instinct.

I was becoming discouraged. We'd walked nearly nine hours now, with no sign, no indication of the presence of the battalion. Someone had wounded the Chinese soldier, but I estimated that his wounds were seven to ten days old. I wished I could have communicated with him verbally, but alive or dead we had no way to ask or answer questions.

We were out nearly thirty miles, I estimated, and still somewhere in the white area of the map. I considered discussing our situation with Carlisle and Woods because their lot was the same as mine.

But I decided to wait to have a powwow until we made a ridgeline about a half mile ahead.

We were still headed eastward, when a soldier popped up out of a foxhole that I hadn't seen. "Halt, password."

I spread-eagled, extending my arms outward, and stated, "Don't know the password, son, but I'm Captain Bussey, 77th Engineers. Who are you?"

"You're supposed to have the password, sir."

"Yes, I know. Yesterday it was 'Golden Gate,' but I don't know what it is today."

"It's okay, sir. I know you anyway. You're a friend of Captain Walden's. I'm in an observation post (OP) for Fox Company."

"Great. Where's Captain Walden?"

"Straight ahead in the middle of that ridge, sir."

"Call him on the radio. Tell him Landscape Six is coming up."

"Got no radio, sir. Battalion collected all radios a couple of days ago, but I can get him on a land line."

He raised Roger Walden, and I talked to him on the phone and then moved up the ridge to his CP. It was good to see Walden; he needed a shave. Captain Walden was one of the best black officers in the 24th Infantry Regiment, and he was an experienced rifle company commander. We talked as old friends do. I explained our mission and talked of the events of the night before. I asked where his radios were. He explained that Lieutenant Colonel Clayton had collected all the battalion's radios.

I asked, "Why?"

"Damned if we know."

Walden continued, "Chinese could be all around us, and we can't communicate except by telephone, but we haven't had any action yet."

"I'll see you later. I've got to give the word to Colonel Clayton. You folks have to get out of here now. The Chinese have been eating battalions wholesale."

We went to a large hut in a little draw, and there was Lt. Col. George A. Clayton, commanding officer, 2d Battalion, 24th Infantry Regiment, U.S. Army. He was well-pressed and shaven.

Colonel Clayton asked, "What you doing here, Bussey? How'd

you get in? We're surrounded. There's Chinamen all around us. We been fightin' for three days and nights. I personally killed over a hundred of them. It is murder. If it wasn't for my courage and skill, this battalion would be lost."

I explained my mission. I'd seen no Chinese except the one poor soldier found in the hut. I came in over Fox Company, and they said they'd not fired a round. He reddened and repeated his original statements. I repeated mine. Then I noticed a mountain of radios in the hut, all from his companies and platoons. I asked him, "Why did you collect all of these radios?"

He rolled his eyes, and said, "We'll talk about that later."

I explained the route we'd traveled from regiment to this CP. I told him that I'd pull his vehicles up the escarpment near regimental headquarters using my dozers, which were at our end of the trail.

I explained again the urgency of my mission and the hard requirement for him to leave these positions immediately. I referred to the handwritten message from Colonel Corley, and I turned to leave.

He screamed, "You can't leave here! We're surrounded. Can't go no place, Halt! You can't leave!"

I walked toward the door behind Carlisle and Woods, and I heard him rack the bolt of his carbine back and chamber a round.

Again, he screamed, "Can't leave! Surrounded!"

I was scared as hell, dealing with a maniac, but I continued deliberately to and through the door out into the yard. I expected to see my brains blown out through my headgear at any second or at least to feel my spine shattered. But nothing.

The colonel continued to scream. I didn't look back. We went up the draw and back to Fox Company. I explained it all briefly to Captain Roger Walden, and we moved back in the direction of regimental headquarters, hoping that Clayton would follow us.

We topped some high ground and stopped to rest our aching feet and eat the last of our rations. Through Carlisle's glasses, I could see the battalion column about ten miles behind us, following the route I had described to Lieutenant Colonel Clayton. Thank

God for that! I knew they wouldn't get to the escarpment before the early winter sunset, but we'd done our job. With some luck I knew we could winch the battalion's vehicles up to the MSR. I felt good inside; one always does when a job is well done. We had far to go, so we were off again. It was much easier traveling by daylight, and it is always easier to retrace one's steps.

Finally, finally, we were back at regimental headquarters. I asked for Colonel Corley, who'd been up all night and day. It was 1500 hours, and I had his striker awaken him. I, too, needed sleep. I'd been up three days and three nights at this time.

The Old Man came into operations, rubbing the red out of his eyes, "Well, it took you long enough. Where's my 2d Battalion?"

"They're back about ten miles. I told Colonel Clayton how critical it was to be back before sunset, but he took a couple of hours to get started."

"Why? Did you give him my message?"

"Yes, sir. We found them about thirty miles away, in this area." I indicated it on the situation map. "Colonel Clayton had collected all the battalion's radios, which were piled up at battalion headquarters."

"Why?"

"Don't really know, sir. When I talked to him, he claimed that he was surrounded by Chinese, but I saw none, and his people I talked to claimed they hadn't heard a shot. He's playing some kind of game." I explained the details of my departure from 2d Battalion Headquarters.

"I'll court martial the bastard. Are you sure you're givin' me all the details?"

"Yes, sir." Carlisle and Woods nodded their assent. The Old Man stood there in incredulous stupor, and he demanded a reiteration, which I gave him from start to finish.

I didn't tell Colonel Corley about the actions of Sergeant Hawkins and his companion. I glossed over the attempted rape episode because no matter how much I abhorred rape, I couldn't condone the Army's goody-goody attitude about it, which would send a guilty man to Leavenworth for fifty years. I felt a limited agreement with Hawkins's attitude about the victor and spoils. There was a time when a soldier's pay consisted solely of spoils—booty, women, booze. We are at least as bestial as our counterparts of old. I don't know what the punishment should be for rape but for sure not 50 years.

I told the colonel the details of the mercy killing of the wounded Chinese soldier. He had no comment.

When I finished, Colonel Corley took a long look at me and paid me a supreme compliment, which almost compensated for the abuse he'd subjected me to. "No other man in my total reckoning would have found that battalion under those circumstances, and I'm personally grateful to you. You did take the 'message to Garcia.' That is why I insisted that you do this job. I couldn't depend on anyone else."

"Thank you, sir."

Colonel Corley finished, "Our God is, I'm sure, pleased with your action."

I clasped his extended bony fingers and joined in a rare handshake. He dismissed me, and I left regimental headquarters.

On the way back to my own CP, I stopped off at Heavy Mortar Company to let Capt. Mike Keiler know about the rape attempt by two of his men. Mike said, "You mean to tell me that the two of them were nine or ten miles away and they weren't able to pull off a rape of a teenaged farmgirl? I should try them both for inefficiency."

I replied simply, "It's your problem, Mike."

I went back to my own CP to get a few hours in on my new cot. All was well. I checked with LeTellier and Wilson. They'd put hundreds of refugees across the Chongchon River that day. Lieutenant Cummings was doing a liaison stint with regiment. Later that day, after I had some sleep, we went up to the escarpment to watch our equipment pull the 2d Battalion vehicles to the top and onto the dirt road we called the Main Supply Route.

Lieutenant Colonel Clayton and several others were already on the road, and so was Colonel Corley. He had Clayton off to the side about fifty yards and was eating a ton of him.

I overheard, "I'm going to prefer charges against you. You belong in Leavenworth."

The rebuking went on. Finally, I heard, ". . . back to division."

I know that Colonel Corley accomplished the paperwork necessary to court martial Clayton, but politics being politics, the charges didn't stick.

Rout, 10 December 1950, Kaesong, Korea

I left regimental headquarters in disgust, and I was scared, too. The press of the Chinese armies was devastating. The Chinese had cleaned up several battalions of the 2d Infantry Division. I had some good friends in those outfits. Regiment was sending us out on a salient, at night. No one knew how far south the Chinese had advanced or what their strength was.

It was cold as hell. We'd lost thirty-nine men to frostbite two nights before. Small peat moss fires kept our feet warm enough, but the fumes were so noxious the fires were nearly impossible to use. Peat moss was abundant in the countryside southeast of the Chongchon River. I'd like to farm there someday, but it could never happen.

We saddled up and moved to the positions designated on regiment's operations maps. As always, we had no information on enemy locations. The G-2 people called it intelligence, but it was really the lack of it. After an hour's drive by blackout lights down the makeshift MSR, we turned east onto the goat track and drove about four miles. I could make out a line of low hills. We unsaddled and moved into our positions.

I was worried about the condition and position we were in. The ground was frozen down to about twelve to fifteen inches, but we were still wearing leather shoes. What a sorry logistical system. We'd been fighting since 12 July. You'd think that the Army officers and civilian bureaucrats in the Pentagon would realize that after summer comes autumn, and after that, winter. Above 38° north latitude winter means −28°F to −30°F temperatures. It had happened to Napoleon coming back from Russia, and in our time the same thing happened to the Nazis attempting to retreat from Moscow.

According to my overlay, a mile or so up the goat track there was a communications line we were to tie in to so we could contact the regimental and division headquarters. Without communications, we could easily be left out on this salient, with the division and the regiment bugging out from their own concerns. We'd been left before.

Our liaison officer, Pat Cummings, as reliable as he was, could easily become swallowed up in a maelstrom like this. Even if he got through in time, traffic on the MSR could preclude his getting to us. I sent for Cpl. Sledge, our commo chief. I gave him a copy of the overlay, which he fitted to his map. Hammer was not much of a fighting man, but he did know his job. When he assessed his wiring mission, he looked at me and said, "Chances of gettin' this job done are slim. I could get killed going out there."

I took a long, mean look at him, and said, "If you don't get the hell out of here and get me wired in, you're going to get killed right here."

He got the signal and moved out. Twenty minutes later I got a call from regiment to move back to the MSR and proceed southward for a rendezvous at Pyongyang. Cpl. Sledge sneaked back in sheepishly. We cut the wire and headed south in the bitter cold night.

On the MSR there were thousands of ragtag troops, mostly stragglers, moving headlong down the road, hopefully to Pusan, to Japan, back to the United States. We picked up hundreds of them. Most had thrown away their rifles, canteens, cups, and bandoliers. There were thousands of weapons and impedimenta of all kinds. Anything that impeded their rearward progress was dropped in the road. It was a pitiful sight. I never thought I'd see a day of rout of U.S. forces, but it was there—a shameful spectacle. Thousands of men, mostly leaderless, were trudging back down the road, which took them away from contact with the Chinese army.

I wondered how I could feed all the hungry mouths we now had. The roadside was also choked with vehicles. When they ran out of fuel, the drivers continued on foot. Helter-skelter. Men, equipment, in a headlong rush southward.

We were in good shape for rations for our own strength, but

we had more than twice that number of people now, squeezed into the trucks, standing on running boards and up on the canvas shelters. I didn't like it, but under these circumstances I felt it was the thing to do.

I considered all stragglers to be mine, because I knew there would be, someplace alone the line, a requirement for fortifications, and every pair of hands fit a D-handled shovel. Usually after a day on the shovels, infantry soldiers were anxious to rejoin their units, and I made that possible for them. Stragglers are always a problem. Their units need them and don't know how to report them. The stragglers are usually scared stiff, scared of enemy action, and even more scared of potentially harsh discipline. Their plight was pitiful.

We drove all night in fits and starts. I dozed. I'd had no sleep for three nights and three days. Never, never before in my life had I been so tired, tired to death. In those intervals of sleep, I forgot about the war. I hallucinated. I was home again, in bed, enjoying the warmth of my wife, in peaceful surroundings, without war, without bloodshed, without fear, and without dying. Then we'd hit a bump, and I'd be shocked back into the cold and misery and dying that was Kunu-ri, Yongbyon, Ilsong, Unhung, and the Chongchon River.

We came into Pyongyang by early morning, and true to pattern Sergeant Lamont had coffee and breakfast ready. The meal was prepared on the move. He assured me that he could feed all of our stragglers. He did. He got me off to the side and asked permission to visit a farmhouse about a mile up the road. On the way north, he had made a batch of raisin jack, and he wanted to pick it up. I thought it was a good idea. That was the only bright spot of the morning.

We were off the main road because we couldn't feed all the GIs coming down the road—leaderless hordes hell-bent for Pusan. The officers were concerned with their own problems. NCOs ignored it all, and the troops just trudged along, headin' south. Identification lost. Friends lost. Leaders lost. Weapons lost. Tired, cold, footsore, lost. I was reminded of pictures of the German Army returning home in the Russian winter. Rout. Southward.

The rout continued down to the vicinity of Kaesong, where barriers were established and the direct influence of the commanding general of Eighth Army came to bear. Troops were assembled, units were identified and reorganized, and we became an Army again. Then we moved down toward Seoul and out on the Imjin Peninsula where we awaited the second Chinese onslaught.

One thing I did find out during the rout was that whites could run fast, some of them faster than blacks.

Recovery

January 1951, Korea

It was colder than a whore's heart.

The Chinese Army had stomped the hell out of us. They did it not by dint of fighting ability but by overwhelming numbers, durability, and certainty of purpose. They'd eaten us up in battalion-size bites. We'd been humiliated, debased, overwhelmed—routed.

The proud folks at home wouldn't know about that. The news writers would slant it all to sound like a minor setback. Take it from me, however, it was carnage. Intelligence said they hit us with one-third of a million men. I believe it. They turned our Army into a leaderless horde, running headlong for Pusan. Our soldiers had lost every bit of confidence in all of their leaders, from the commander in chief down to platoon leaders.

It was still bitterly cold, and we were still poorly clad and ill equipped and supplied. Food was barely adequate. I had no idea where we were going, or if we'd get there. Nor did I know where the ignominious defeat would stop.

We had gone north a proud and seemingly invincible army. We had been well rested after the total defeat we'd imposed upon the North Koreans after the landing at Inchon and the breakout from the Pusan perimeter. The North Korean People's Army had been out of it completely. We had been welcomed sincerely by folks in the North Korean countryside; they were glad to be out from under the heel of Kim Il Sung and his communist regime. Neither they nor we realized that their freedom would be so short-lived. We had been greeted with hysterical cheers by the women and children, who were glad to be "free." Many of their young men had been captured, had surrendered, or had simply disap-peared. Some were imprisoned on Cheju-do Island; those who weren't on Cheju-do were not to be found.

It was sad crossing back through Kaesong and over the 38th Parallel. I was ashamed. All my life I'd been taught that Americans were invincible in battle, in sports, in technology, in everything. In the past seventy-two hours, I'd come to realize that these lifelong convictions were only partly true. In fact, they were untrue. Ameri-cans could be defeated; we *had* been defeated.

We were defeated by the ineptitude of our politicians and gener-als, who gambled with our lives that the Chinese would not enter the war on the side of their communist cousins. From the Chinese side there had been no guarantee that marauding UN forces would stop at the Yalu River. We approached the Yalu in a ragtag fashion, goaded on by the rumor that "The first outfit to the river will be the first outfit home," and "Home by Christmas." We moved up without reconnaissance, plans, or coordination, and we were defeated in the very same manner. The gamble had been idiotic, and our losses were staggering.

The move northward had resembled the great land rush into Oklahoma Territory a century or so earlier. It was a complete debacle. If a gamble is to be taken, then by all means base it upon known odds and sound intelligence. Keep the troops well equipped with weapons, vehicles, and ammo that function in cold weather. Keep them informed of enemy strengths, dispositions, and capabilities. Commit them to a mission clearly understood as compatible with our national purpose. We had not been fur-nished with any of these essentials—not one.

Another oversight was training. The troops weren't trained in basic things like night fighting, guerrilla warfare, arctic combat, and survival techniques. It is extremely difficult to conduct basic training at company level in frontline positions while committed to action.

The 77th ECC was still dressed in summer clothing, wearing leather shoepacks. My God! I had lost the equivalent of a platoon to frostbite in one night despite the officers' and NCOs' best efforts to keep their men awake and blood circulating.

Well, the rout slowed down at Kaesong and stopped on the outskirts of Seoul. Thousands of men and tons of equipment had been lost, but their loss was replaceable. In the Orient, where such a consideration counts, much "face" had been lost, and this loss was irreplaceable.

Seoul was little more than a ghost town. It had been pillaged by soldiers and by civilians. Only the carcass remained of what had once been a mighty city. It showed the scars of war, of vandalism, of looting, and of abandonment. The city itself was as defeated and as bedraggled as the hordes of tired and battle-weary UN soldiers who trooped through its streets. We were like the Grand Army after Waterloo.

For several days the enemy rested. He'd pursued us headlong in our desperate flight. We had not sought to engage him along the way. We had been beaten by an army traveling exclusively on foot. The Chinese supply lines were long and comparatively feeble, and they'd outrun them, which gave us some time to recover.

We turned west across the Imjin River, where we took up positions on the hills along the south bank. Winter's cruel jaws snapped shut. The Imjin was a respectable river, a tidal estuary for much of its length. Before it froze, we burned all the boats on the north shore for miles in both directions. Every night we blew the ice crust away with bangalore torpedoes. In this way we attempted to make night crossings impossible, stalling the Chinese on their side of the river.

Our commanders, however, became careless about keeping the ice broken up regularly in their respective sectors along the Imjin. It was 29 December when, at high noon, their lethargy was broken. The Chinese mounted a bold assault across a sheet of ice that should never have been allowed to provide a ready access route to our side of the river. Every artillery piece in the corps was rapidly brought to bear on the crossing site, but more than fifty thousand Chinese soldiers stormed over the river and into the hills to the south before the artillery exploding on the icy surface could chop the rest of them into bits.

Trained and disciplined, the enemy soldiers knifed through a gap they forced between the two British brigades and our own 25th Infantry Division, charged into our rear, and then fanned out, cutting communication wires and killing rear-echelon paper-shufflers all the while.

Overrun, our strength sorely sapped, we were forced to withdraw, legging it for all we were worth. As we ran, our artillery, mortars, and automatic weapons fired onto the highlevel railroad bridge that spanned the river and afforded an additional means of crossing for refugees and enemy soldiers alike. Hundreds of civilians were slaughtered.

Although it was true that Chinese soldiers disguised as civilians had been infiltrating the UN line, still it was cruel to stop pedestrian traffic across the bridge with concentrated artillery fire. Sure, we had announced in leaflets we had dropped on the far shore that on a particular date at a given time all foot traffic must cease and that artillery fire could be expected to commence. Thus, we had also alerted the enemy to make his surprise assault before the stated deadline.

Had we thought matters through carefully, my engineers could have erected a physical barrier to foot movement across the bridge to be used at a given time. Or, of course, the bridge could have been prepared for demolitions and blown up after suitable on-the-spot warning had been given.

What we did, instead, was brutal—needlessly so. At the same time, it was highly effective. Hundreds of women and kids were certainly blown to bits that noon. Possibly, a significant number of Chinese soldiers likewise became mincemeat.

Bully for our side!

We found it necessary to fight our way to the rear in order to gain the freedom we needed to start running again. Never was there an obstacle course more realistic in its demands upon one's physical fitness. Either you had the breath of life, or you didn't. It was a wild and deadly game, and our losses proved considerable. So, fight and run or run and fight we did, all the way back to Pyongtaek again.

We moved back into the same schoolhouse we'd vacated three months earlier, and we established ourselves and our routine much as it had been. We knew that we could not plan to winter in Pyongtaek because there was absolutely nothing but international law to stop the Chinese. True, we'd destroyed much of the food and other supplies we'd seen along the main route southward. True, the enemy's supply lines were considerably overextended. But we knew that somehow Chinese Army logisticians would scrounge up enough of our own materiel—rice, clothing, ammo— to sustain their riflemen, machine gunners, artillerymen, and mortarmen through the cold winter.

We arrived at Pyongtaek, and I was glad to finally get out of the weather. We badly needed a respite after the debacle we'd experienced and the gauntlet we'd run. We'd lost only one man out of our company and a couple of items of heavy equipment. Since we had an overstrength of officers and other units were short officers, I was advised that the company would have to relinquish two officers. I submitted the names of Carlisle and Green, which would have contributed to integration in other units. However, Wells and LeTellier, both of our white officers, were transferred. We were all black again.

We'd zigged when battalions of the 1st Cavalry Division and of the 2d, 24th, and 25th Infantry divisions had zagged into the enemy's gristmill. The shores of the Chongchon River and the fields around Kunu-ri were littered with the bodies of brave U.S. and other UN soldiers—fighting men no more, who'd fired a last round or two even as they'd fallen. It was a horrible waste of young manpower.

There was little glamour to it, except as it was depicted by military correspondents and other writers. They should have been with us. Had they been, they'd have understood, as had one real soldier a century earlier, "War is Hell!" Then their civilian journals would have described events more accurately, devoid of buzzwords like *gallantry*, the *last full measure of devotion, strategic with-drawal, heroism, disengage from the enemy, attack to the rear*, and all the rest.

Gen. Matt Ridgway became the boss general out there. Some say he spent most of his time in or over Korea. For sure, he stopped the rout. Pyongtaek was a good place to bring this shame-ful episode to a halt. Enemy supply lines were overly long. Fortui-tously, winter finally began to take a heavy toll on the Chinese soldier himself—his physical resistance, his bodily demands for internal energy and fuel, his weapon's demand for ammo and efficient lubrication, and his own morale.

It was damned tough going no matter the perspective. It took a helluva CO or CG to put starch back into the spine of either bedraggled army. On the American side, battalion-size patrols moved forward a half mile, a mile, or more every morning. Then they pulled back behind regimental main lines of resistance at night. On the Chinese side there was little or no activity for days on end. Occasionally, when individual Chinese soldiers or small units were encountered, UN battalion-size patrols chewed them up and spit them out.

Gradually, confidence was renewed. Even though the weather continued to work against us more than the enemy, our rations improved markedly along with the supply situation generally. So did our pride and our esprit de corps.

Digging In, 15 January 1951, Kunsan, Korea

Someone in the planning business determined that auxiliary defen-sive positions should be established substantially in the rear, just in case the UN forces were forced to yield again to the Chinese Army. The new positions were called the "Abraham Lincoln Line." Orders came down for the 77th ECC to build a section of the line near Kunsan, a port on the west coast. We were reinforced with some heavy equipment. It was a good job, and we needed it. Idleness is trouble.

We had a few days to ready for the move, to acquire the demolitions, the timbers, sandbags, barbed wire, and other barrier materials. While checking the loading of some demolitions, I overheard the troops discussing the prospects of women being in Kunsan, including a company of Korean WACs. One miserable cuss went through the procedure for raping a woman and stated his express intention of doing so. This was a problem I did not need, and I set about finding a solution.

I sent Lieutenant Green and a few NCOs to Kunsan with a truckload of rice. The lieutenant contacted the mayor and chief of police and requested the establishment of a relief station, or house of prostitution. The *quid pro quo* (payment) was the truckload of rice, which was to be exchanged for the services of sixteen young professional ladies and a house directly across the street from the schoolhouse we were to occupy. One of our sergeants would be on duty evenings to maintain a semblance of order. Green returned the following day. He had Corporal Napoleon, the medic, shoot the ladies of the evening with gigantic doses of penicillin in beeswax. VD we didn't need. We further ensured against VD by giving each participant a shot, which incidentally was the price of a soldier's admission to the house. We used a lot of penicillin after we occupied our positions at Kunsan. The first night was busy, and so was the second night, but business slacked off a little after that. The house served the greedy more so than the needy.

I was calling reveille at 0430 and work call at 0530. The days were brutally long in that miserable cold, barren land—a winter desert. We did our job installing barriers, gun emplacements, bunkers, foxholes, and all of the landscaping necessary for an infantry and/or artillery organization to move into and fight a defensive action. It was essential that these chores be accomplished by engineers because the ground was frozen. We were trained in the use of demolitions and heavy equipment, which were required for that work. The long hours and the exposure diminished the activity at the relief station. I sent six of the girls back to the mayor. There was insufficient use of their services. I was approached about setting up a private house for officers, but I considered that less than ethical. The officers did without.

The job was done. No women were molested. No VD was reported. We went back to Pyongtaek.

During the two weeks or so of our absence, the infantry guys got some rest and renewed confidence. They were talking about moving up, even attacking. It was good to hear the infantry talk like that, and they did move up. Thanks to Gen. Matt Ridgway, there was never a use for the Abraham Lincoln Line. We moved back up across the Han River, back across the Hantan, and eventually back to where it started at the 38th Parallel. Victory?

I had another kidney stone that was killing me, and the pills I took for the pain were only making me jumpy. I had a couple of small pieces of flak that needed to be removed, so I held still for an evacuation back to a hospital in Osaka, Japan. I left things with Lt. Jim Wilson. I had watched him make notes on things I had been doing for months. I never knew what the comments were, but I was certain that he could make things happen. The thought once crossed my mind that with his notebook and my state of total exhaustion, perhaps he could do the job better. My ego suffered from that possibility, but I was dog tired and needed to leave the killing floor for a while.

Rotation, 25 January 1951, Kunsan, Korea

Theoretically, I was being evacuated back to Japan to a general hospital to have a kidney stone removed. Perhaps I'd be there two weeks, more or less. Two weeks at the outside was as long as I wanted to be away. But I knew that I was used up. The war had been long down there at ground zero. I had been in command of the company for too many days of combat-related activity. I had been too long without a bed to sleep in, too long without my family and love. There had been too many firefights, too many improperly treated wounds and other medical problems, too much tension, too much anxiety. Besides that, I was just plain tired.

It was −28°F the day I was to be evacuated. I had a foreboding of not being able to return, so before I left I called a formation, and when the troops were in place I made a speech.

Men, I'm being evacuated to Japan for some repair and maintenance. I expect to be back shortly, but one never knows about hospital tenure. We've been together, it seems, for a long time, but it has only been eight months. We have worked hard and fought hard during that period. From Gifu to Pyongtaek has been a long trail.

You have been an organization of which I have been proud to have been a member.

I will always be proud to have been one of you. Records show that we are the most decorated company-size unit in the theater. That is no accident. You performed. As I've told you many times previously, you are good.

You were good at Kumchon; damned good at Yechon, Sangju, Haman, and Chindong-ni. We put some fine bridges and culverts in the MSR. Our support of the infantry was always exemplary. In fact, we were finer fighting men than they were. We were more formidable than any of their battalions. Your work was good in the gun destruction in the Iron Triangle. I was particularly proud of you at Kunu-ri, Yongbyon, and Ilsong.

More than any unit in the theater, you came back from Kunu-ri with dignity. You came back intact, with all of your gear, weapons, and equipment. The support we provided on the Imjin River was spectacular. Finally, the barrier construction at Kunsan was exemplary.

There has never been a moment when I was not proud to be a member of this company. If for any reason, I do not return, I will not worry much because I know that you will continue to perform commendably. Lieutenant Wilson will assume command, for which he is well prepared. He is a fine officer and soldier, and he has been taking notes on all my activities for months. My biggest concern is that he will do a better job than I've done. But why not!

No commanding officer ever was closer to his troops than I am to you. No commander ever knew his men better than I know you. As time goes by, you will always be welcome wherever I happen to be. I will always share my lot with you. Never forget that. So long for now, and God Bless You!!!

I was into the jeep and was gone. I never went back to the 77th. In the hospital, I had the kidney stone and some pieces of flak removed. I had been in command of the company for 205 days of almost continual combat in Korea. Those days were the most adventurous, challenging, and demanding of my life. I had used those days well, and those days had well used me. I had a long period of recovery, and then the doctor sent me home.

The 77th Engineer Combat Company continued to fight on after my departure under the command of 1st Lt. James Wilson, 1st Lt. David K. Carlisle, 1st Lt. Arthur B. Cummings, and others. Upon the termination of hostilities in Korea, the 77th Engineer Combat Company was deactivated in 1952. By that time there was no longer a need for a black engineer company for a black infantry regiment. The 24th Infantry Regiment had been integrated in October 1951 and replaced by the 14th Infantry Regiment. The 77th Engineer Company was one of the most highly decorated company-size units in the entire Korean War. It did a good job from beginning to end. I am proud to have been its commander.

Aftermath

31 May 1951–1990

I was glad to be home. My daughter, who had been eight months old when I left, and was almost two years old when I returned, didn't know me. She could not identify me with the picture on the wall. She referred to me as "that man," but time took care of that. My son knew me right away, and we got along famously from the first moment of my return.

My wife and I had some small problems. We didn't see eye-to-eye on too many things. She had become accustomed to making independent decisions; it had become habit. We had domestic personality problems. Most of it was my fault. I went back to flying, which she hated. She went back to teaching. We had two more children. Life went on.

I couldn't sleep well. I awakened at frequent intervals to check security, and I lay there and listened to my heart beat, afraid to venture out. I had terrible dreams upon entering or awakening from sleep. Sometimes I was at Yechon with that murderous gun. Other times, the boulders rained on me on the banks of the Kum River. Frequently, I was buried again at Haman. I perspired by the gallon, and sometimes I screamed.

My wife didn't quite understand it all. Neither did I. At night I went back to the killing floor, and it was ugly, very ugly. It was worse emotionally probably than the original action. The worst episodes happened when I lay on my back, and ten thousand Chinese soldiers trampled over my shallow grave and double-timed over me. Their footprints made my rib cage sore, their feet stuffed sand in my nose, and breathing was difficult. At these times I fought to turn over or to get my hands up to protect my face. I sweated through the bed clothes, and I yelled out. During most nights I slept three to four hours but frequently less. The sleeplessness produced exhaustion during the day.

I was trapped and wished that I could be back on the killing floor. I identified more with being out there, where my problems whatever they were, were mine alone and disturbed no one else. I felt sorry for my wife. She was being punished for offenses not of her making. Further, it was something we couldn't talk about. I was okay on the job, but I had a world of problems on my shoulders. I needed badly to unload it all verbally, but my wife couldn't deal with the blood and gore that haunted me. She wanted to hear nothing of killing, maiming, frostbite, barbed wire, fear, trembling, doubt, arson, exhaustion, death, or blood—none of it. Who could blame her?

I had many discussions with physicians and psychiatrists. They had no idea of appropriate treatment for my problems. So I carried that ugly world of misery in my chest for twelve or fifteen years, while my wife and I grew further and further apart, until we were unable to communicate at all. Finally nothing was left except divorce, which also was no solution.

Time lessened the burden slightly. Slowly, very slowly, the intensity and frequency of the nightmares receded, but the nightly security checks continue. Dumb! When I awaken four or five times a night, I force my mind into blankness, listen to the blood coursing in my arteries, and thank God that it is so.

I stayed on in the Army that I loved so much. Upon recovery and recuperation from my illness and wounds, I was assigned in August 1951 to the Engineer School, Fort Belvoir, Virginia. In 1952 I was put back on flying status, and I logged many hours in helicopters and fixed-wing aircraft. I served in Germany and in many bases in the United States. I enjoyed the work, and I did all right. I received the Silver Star medal for the battle of Yechon and the Bronze Star medal for valor for the rescue mission in the Valley of Death. I also received the Purple Heart for my wounds suffered in Korea. Subsequently, I received the Legion of Merit for meritorious service. I had already received the Air Medal for my combat flying in World War II. I retired in 1966 as a lieutenant colonel with twenty-two years of active duty. Not bad for a black officer in the Jim Crow Army of the 1940s and 1950s.

While I can look back on my life in the military and my successes afterward as a civilian in retirement, this book should signal to you that I have not been totally content. I have been haunted by the generalized and not completely objective portrayals and comparisons of how black soldiers performed in the Korean War. If we were so poor then, why did black soldiers get such high marks in the Vietnam War, only fifteen years after Korea? I have some ideas. When the Army began to respect its black soldiers and give them responsibilities, perhaps the Army in return received respect and responsible soldiers. More important, in both World War II and Korea, black men had formed the mold for the high-quality performance of black soldiers in Vietnam and in today's Army.

You now understand that in my unit I saw all types of soldiers and large amounts of courage, heroism, sacrifice, and leadership. This contrast between what I experienced and what was written has bugged me until today. Writing a book is not an easy thing, and in some respects it has been as hard as anything I have ever undertaken. I have tried to be honest, to be fair, to be just. I have suppressed my rage and kept my story truthful and objective. This difficult book may be the way I finally put the terrible memories of that war behind me. I have now done what I knew I needed to do and have shared my troubles with thousands of you.

In rereading the drafts of this manuscript, I realized that all of you will not love nor respect me. You may be puzzled at some of the actions I took or didn't take. At times, my behavior does not match the values I profess. But, for better or for worse, you are seeing me, my strengths, my flaws, my life.

Through it all, I think I have remained a very religious person. Having been a fighter pilot in the Big War, I learned to pray and communicate with God without the aid of an intermediary who knew less of life and death than I did. I go to church rarely and then mostly to expose my kids. But I don't feel the need for attendance. I pray daily, and I am sustained mightily. Mostly, I am a lover. I love life. I love my fellow man, my wife, my kids, and my kinsmen. I thank God every morning and periodically during the day for another opportunity to labor in the vineyard of life. I am a giver of alms in secret and in silence. I tithe before God, in silence. I never ask God for small favors. All my prayers are utterances of thanks. My only request of God is that He makes me more worthy of His love. I work hard at being a Christian, which is synonymous, in my view, with being a Muslim, Buddhist, or Jew. I am happy to be a child of God and brother of all men.

Despite my grievances, I still deeply love the U.S. Army and the honor it gave me to lead men, sometimes in very trying times. I am proud to be an American. When I hear our national anthem, I can feel the hair rise on my spine, and goose pimples cover my arms. My breath deepens. I am afraid I will someday die still an American soldier—vital, eager, bold, confident, prepared. I can only hope that you will not judge me too harshly and will forgive my transgressions and mistakes. Most of all, I hope that you will now understand the courage and the racism that I experienced in the Korean War.

Appendix: Another Bit of Evidence

A good indication of combat cohesion is the number of artillery pieces lost. Artillery is seldom destroyed by enemy fire; most losses are due to gun positions being overrun or to troops abandoning them. The losses of Eighth Army artillery pieces during 1950 were staggering, shameful, and scandalous. The table below shows these artillery losses.

Eighth Army Artillery Losses, 1950

Division	Period	Pieces Lost
1st Cavalry Division	November 1950	21
2d Infantry Division	November 1950	62
7th Infantry Division	December 1950	12
24th Infantry Division	July 1950	36
25th Infantry Division	August 1950	11
	Total Eighth Army pieces lost	142

Eighth Army lost 1 8-inch howitzer, 27 155mm howitzers, and 114 105mm howitzers. The Republic of Korea Army during the same period (July–December 1950) lost 90 105mm howitzers and 5 75mm howitzers. During all of World War II, the U.S. Army only lost 53 guns from being overrun or having surrendered. So, by the measure of artillery pieces lost, the Eighth Army as a whole did not do a very good job in the early days of Korea.

The facts are as hard and bitter as gall. The much maligned 24th Infantry Regiment was blamed by senior officers and historians for inefficiency and cowardice—all the negatives that could be attributed to soldiers. But the 24th Infantry Regimental Combat Team never lost an artillery piece to the enemy.